The Garland Library of Narratives of North American Indian Captivities

Volume 76

311 titles in 111 volumes
selected and arranged by

Wilcomb E. Washburn
*Director of the Office of American Studies
Smithsonian Institution*

Contents

Brayton, Matthew. *The Indian Captive.*

Page, Larsena A. *The Indian Captives.* From: Oquawka Spectator, Ill., v. 13, no. 16, May 17, 1860.

Kimball, James. *Short Narrative of James Kimball.*

Persinger, Joseph. *The Life of Jacob Persinger.*

Brown, Samuel J. *In Captivity.*

Abenteuer unter den Indianern (Captivity of the Haverland Family).

The Indian Captive
(Matthew Brayton)

Garland Publishing, Inc., New York & London
1977

Copyright © 1977
by Garland Publishing, Inc.
All Rights Reserved

Bibliographical note:

this facsimile has been made from a copy in the
Newberry Library
(Ayer.256.B75.B75.1860)

Library of Congress Cataloging in Publication Data

[Bone, John Herbert A   ]1830-1906.
   The Indian captive (Matthew Brayton).

   (The Garland library of narratives of North
American Indian captivities ; v. 76)
   Reprint of the 1860 ed. published by Fairbanks,
Benedict, Cleveland.
   Issued with the reprint of the 1860 ed. of Page,
L. A. Narrative of Larsena A. Page. New York, 1977,
the reprint of the 1930 ed. of Kimball, J. P. Short
narrative of James Kimball. New York, 1977, the
reprint of the 1961 ed. of Persinger, J. The life
of Jacob Persinger. New York, 1977, the reprint of
the 1896? ed. of Brown, S. J. In captivity. New
York, 1977, and the reprint of the 1863 ed. of
Abenteuer unter den Indianern. New York, 1977.
   1. Brayton, Matthew, 1818-1862. 2. Shoshoni
Indians--Captivities. 3. Indians of North America
--Captivities. 4. United States--Biography.
I. Title. II. Series.
E85.G2   vol. 76 [E99.S4] 973'.04'97s [970'.004'97][B]
ISBN 0-8240-1700-5   76-54518

Printed in the United States of America

ADVENTURES
OF
MATTHEW BRAYTON,
THE
INDIAN CAPTIVE.

THE INDIAN CAPTIVE.

A NARRATIVE

OF THE

ADVENTURES AND SUFFERINGS

OF

MATTHEW BRAYTON,

IN HIS

THIRTY-FOUR YEARS OF CAPTIVITY

AMONG THE

INDIANS OF NORTH-WESTERN AMERICA.

CLEVELAND, O.:
FAIRBANKS, BENEDICT & CO., PRINTERS, HERALD OFFICE,
1860.

Entered according to the Act of Congress in the year 1860, by
DAVID BURNS,
In the Clerk's Office of the District Court of the United States, for the
Northern District of Ohio.

PREFACE.

THE following brief narrative of the unparalleled adventures of MATTHEW BRAYTON is compiled for the satisfaction of those who wished to preserve a memorial of his romantic history.

Extraordinary as the incidents may appear, there is abundant proof of their entire truth. Living witnesses bear testimony to the circumstances of the mysterious loss of the hero, and his identity is established by incontrovertible proofs. Numerous circumstances also confirm the account given by him of his adventures during the thirty-four years spent among the Indians.

THE INDIAN CAPTIVE.

CHAPTER I.

THE LOST CHILD.

That portion of North-western Ohio, situated to the South-east of the Black Swamp, was but sparsely settled at the close of the first quarter of the present century. The hardy pioneers who had left their New England homes to open up the Western wilds, here and there built their modest dwellings and tilled the few acres won from the dense forest and luxuriant prairie. The dusky aborigines, driven from all other parts of Ohio, clung tenaciously to this comparatively neglected spot, and the smoke from the log hut of the settler rose within sight of the Indian wigwam. The two races were at peace with each other, for neither cared to convert a passive neighbor into an active enemy. The Indians had realized their inability to drive back the constantly advancing wave of civilization, and the white settlers had no desire to provoke the savage retaliations of their dusky neighbors unless compelled by necessity to do so.

In the neighborhood of the junction between the Sandusky and Tymochte rivers, in Wyandot county, a remnant of the once powerful Wyandot tribe still remained. One of their villages was at Upper Sandusky, and another at Springville, in Seneca county. A small band of Senecas were also located in the neighborhood, and some scattered Ottawas had their wigwams on Blanchard's Fork, a few miles to the west of the Wyandot settlements. An Indian trail led from Upper Sandusky to Springville, and thence, through the Black Swamp, to Perrysburgh. At the latter place it crossed the Maumee, and reached the shore of the Detroit river opposite Malden, in Canada. Some of the Indians living in the North-west of Ohio had sided with the British in the war of 1812, and these annually crossed over to Malden to receive their presents of guns, ammunition and blankets. The Canadian Indians sometimes visited their dusky brethren in Ohio, and thus the trail was frequently traversed.

Among the settlers who had located themselves in the neighborhood of the Wyandot villages was ELIJAH BRAYTON, a thrifty farmer from New England, who had established himself near the Tymochte river in what is now Crawford township, Wyandot county. In the year 1825, Mr. BRAYTON was thirty-nine years of age, and his family consisted of his wife and their six children. WILLIAM, HARRIET, LUCY, MATTHEW, MARY and PETER. In that year Mr. BRAYTON was busy erecting a mill on the Tymochte, and towards the Fall of the year he went to Chillicothe for the purpose of bringing up the mill-stones. The journey at that time was long and tedious, and the home affairs were entrusted in his absence to Mrs. BRAYTON and the eldest son WILLIAM, then a lad of sixteen.

On the 20th of September, 1825, WILLIAM BRAYTON, with his younger brother MATTHEW, then nearly seven and a half years old, started out to hunt up some stray cattle. They proceeded for two or three miles in the direction of the spot where WILLIAM BRAYTON at present lives, but found no traces of the missing cattle. Here they met a neighbor named HART, who was also looking for stray cattle. MATTHEW had become tired, and declared his inability to proceed any farther. After a short consultation it was agreed that WILLIAM BRAYTON and HART should proceed in search of the cattle, and that MATTHEW should take the path which led to the house of Mr. BAKER, about sixty rods distant, where he could amuse himself with his young playmates until the return of WILLIAM. The two set out on their cattle hunting expedition, leaving little MATTHEW to pursue his way along the narrow and ill-defined path.

At the close of the day's search, WILLIAM BRAYTON called at Mr. BAKER'S house for his little brother. To his astonishment he learned that MATTHEW had not been seen by any of the family. He then turned his steps homeward, thinking that MATTHEW had changed his mind and gone home, but on arriving there no tidings of the missing boy met him. The alarm and apprehension that filled the breast of the mother may be conceived. A thousand fearful thoughts flitted through her mind in rapid succession. But no time was lost in useless grieving. The men and women who braved the dangers of frontier life were quick to think and prompt to act. A little party turned out at once to search for the missing boy and restore him, if possible, to the anxious household. From the spot where the brothers had parted, the path to Mr. BAKER'S house was narrowly searched, and the marks of the child's feet were clearly discernible. At no great distance from the commencement of the path it was intersected by a track made by some logs recently drawn from the woods. At this point the traces showed that MATTHEW had stopped in doubt. They also showed that he had finally taken the log track in mistake for the regular path. Up that track his little footsteps were traced for some distance, but, after awhile, they became fainter, and at last disappeared altogether. The woods on the margin of the track were searched in vain for traces of his feet.

The Indian trail, before spoken of, crossed the log track near where the footsteps became invisible, and it was possible that he had taken that trail; but his footmarks—if he had really followed that path,— had been obliterated by the feet of passing Indians.

The party sorrowfully returned from their unsuccessful search, and met the anxious mother with heavy hearts. The night that followed was one of sleepless agony to Mrs. BRAYTON. To what suffering, or dreadful fate her little boy might be subjected, it was impossible to conjecture, but the dark night and the lonely woods were fraught with dangers to him and with terror to her. The absence of the father at this critical juncture on so long and distant a journey, aggravated the troubles and distress of the time.

Morning broke at last, and never was daylight more eagerly welcomed. With the first dawn of light, messengers set out in all directions for assistance, and soon the woods were astir with searching parties. The Indian villages were examined, but the Wyandots professed entire ignorance as to the movements of the missing boy, and joined with much zeal in the search. The relations between the BRAYTONS and the Wyandots had been of the most friendly character, and there seemed to be no possible reason for their interfering with the peace of that family. They stated, however, that a party of Canadian Indians had passed up the trail on the day that the boy disappeared, but could not say whether he had been carried off by that party or not. Another night came, and again the sorrowful mother met the dejected hunters at her door and received no consolation. At daybreak the parties again set out to search new tracts of country, but all without avail. Mr. Bowe, who yet lives in the neighborhood, acted as storekeeper of the party, and filled the bags of the searchers with meal as they returned from their long expeditions. The settlers for many miles around turned out in the exciting hunt. Days lengthened into weeks, and then it became evident that all farther search was useless. Every foot of territory for miles around had been examined, and no trace of the lost child could be discovered. He could scarcely have wandered off and perished by starvation or wild beasts, for in either case some trace would have been left. The only inference remaining was that he had been snatched up by the party of Canadian Indians and carried off into hopeless slavery, if not to meet a horrible death. Pursuit now was useless, had the boy been thus carried off, and the search was reluctantly abandoned.

Meantime Mr. Brayton had returned from his journey, and the sad affliction that had befallen his house, fell with crushing weight on his heart. For the sake of his wife and remaining children he bore up nobly, but his distress was keen, and every straw of hope that floated by was eagerly clutched at. From time to time came vague rumors of the boy having been seen in different directions, and the faintest hope of success sufficed to send off the bereaved father or some trusty messenger to follow up the clue, but always without success. The last information that assumed the appearance of probability was received in 1829, from a man who had been traveling among the Indian tribes of Illinois, and who asserted that he had seen among the Indians of that country a white child whose age and appearance corresponded generally with that of the missing MATTHEW BRAYTON. Without an hour's delay Mr. BRAYTON wrote to General CASS, then Indian Commissioner, but his answer crushed out the last remnant of hope. The letter bade the anxious father to renounce all hope based on such a rumor, for there was no such white child among the Indians of Illinois. On what authority the General based his assertion, cannot be said, but it is more than probable that in this he was mistaken.

The weary years passed on but brought no comfort to the stricken household. As all strong impressions fade in the course of time, so faded away the memory of the loss from the minds of men. But deep in the hearts of the parents remained the image of the lost boy, and the thrilling scenes and emotions connected with the search of him recurred again and again long after others had nearly forgotten the incidents. The father never forgot him. His "lost MATTHEW" was ever in his heart, and his name was often on his tongue. The eldest brother, WILLIAM, could not forget him, for the mother's reproaches, silent or spoken, for his neglect in sending so young a boy alone on such a path, sank deep into his heart. And could the mother that bore him forget the missing lamb of the fold? The paling cheek, the wasting form, the decaying strength told how deep the love, how bitter the anguish of the mother for her lost son. If she were but sure of his fate,—if but one rag of his clothes, but a particle of his body, had remained to assure her that her darling had perished by wild beasts, or been slain by still wilder men, it would at least have given rest to her weary heart; but this torturing mystery was too great to be borne. So the years dragged slowly onward, and each succeeding anniversary of her boy's loss drove the sharp grief still deeper into her heart, until sixteen years after the loss, she tired of this world, and the peaceful turf closed over her sorrows. In her last thoughts the memory of the lost boy had a place. She died of a broken heart.

MATTHEW BRAYTON was born April 7th, 1818, and was therefore seven years, five months and thirteen days old at the time of his loss.

CHAPTER II.

MATTHEW BRAYTON'S NARRATIVE.

Stolen by Indians and Traded from Tribe to Tribe—Siouxs—Sioux Dog Dance—Sold to the Snakes—Digger Indians—Fight with the Diggers—Utah—Quarrels with the Blackfeet—Flat Heads—Snakes join Utahs, Crees, and Flat Heads—Join with Copper Heads.

The first seven or eight years of my captivity among the Indians were so full of changes that I cannot distinctly remember the events that occurred, and I am compelled to trust to the accounts given me by the members of the various tribes who were cognizant of the circumstances. From their statements I learn that I was taken from Ohio by a party of Canadian Indians, and by them borne to their village in Canada. The only motive alleged to me for the theft was that the party who stole me had a difference with some white families in Ohio, and that I was taken out of revenge. Among these Indians I remained secreted for some time, the tribe fearing to let me be seen by white men lest I should be taken away.

From all that I can learn, I remained some six or seven months with this tribe, and was then sold to a party of Pottawottomies, who took me across to Michigan. The compensation obtained for me by the Canadian tribe, consisted of three and a half gallons of whiskey. With my new owners I remained about half a year, when the Pottawottomies either being afraid to keep me any longer, or having an unappeasable thirst for whiskey, traded me off to the Paw-Paws for five and a half gallons of firewater. I could not say how long I remained in Michigan with this tribe, but I was at length transferred to the Winnebagoes of Illinois, my value having increased with my age to the amount of seven and a half gallons of whiskey. I did not remain long with this tribe, but was sold to the Wisconsin Chippewas for nine and a half gallons of whiskey, and with them remained one year From the Chippewas I passed into the hands of the Sioux in Minnesota, and remained with them nearly three years. During my stay with the Siouxs I visited the site of what now forms the city of St. Paul. In that vicinity there were then seven shanties or huts, made of poles and sticks set up endways. Two or three French and Dutch, with some Indians then occupied the place.

About the ninth year of my captivity among the Indians, the band of Siouxs to which I belonged made an expedition westward. In the course of their hunt they came on a tribe of Snake Indians. The Snakes and Siouxs were generally at war, but there was peace between these two parties. Some differences that had occurred between the bands were settled at the meeting, and the Siouxs celebrated the fact by a great Dog-Dance.

This dance is peculiar to the Siouxs, and I never saw it at any other time. The manner of doing it was this:—A party of warriors squat around in a circle, smoking and talking. A dog is then taken and its legs tied, after which it is thrown into the circle of warriors. One of the "medicine men" kills the animal with his tomahawk, cuts open its side and takes out its liver, which is cut into strips and hung on a pole nearly the height of a man. The warriors spring to their feet and commence dancing around it; all the while smacking their lips and making grimaces as if they were anxious to have a taste of the delicious meat. In a short time one of the dancers makes a grab at the liver and bites off a piece, which he chews and swallows as he dances. Then the others follow his example until all the liver is eaten. If any of the pieces should drop, the "medicine man" picks it up and carries it in the palm of his hand for the dancers to eat, after doing which they lick his hand. As soon as the liver is all eaten, the warriors sit down as before, and wait to see if another dog is thrown in. As long as any one gives a dog, they are compelled to eat its liver raw and warm, and no one is allowed to handle it except the "medicine man." Women are forbidden to join in this dance. The Siouxs think that those who thus eat the liver of the dog will possess that animal's bravery and sagacity.

Before the meeting was over, the Snakes took a great fancy to me, and in order to celebrate their new made truce the Siouxs offered to trade me to the Snakes for eleven gallons of whiskey, which was done, and I was once more transferred to new masters.

My new owners made me change my dress and paint to conform to their style, and I was adopted into the tribe. An Indian who had lost a son in battle took me into his family, and from that time forth I was told to consider him as my father, and his squaw as my mother. But although thus made one of themselves, the Indians did not fail to treat me with considerable harshness, and I was compelled to do some of the severe drudgery usually imposed on the women.

The Snakes at that time hunted in Iowa, but in about a year after my joining them they had repeated quarrels with other tribes, and with the whites. For a few months they remained in Missouri, but eventually packed up and struck the trail for the west side of the Rocky Mountains. Our tribe hunted through Utah for a while, but quarreled with the tribes already in that country, and therefore we once more pushed west, and crossing the mountains that divided us from California, entered that country. Here we lived, for about five years, generally at peace, but having occasional skirmishes with the Digger Indians.

These Indans are a wretched and degenerate race, cowardly, treacherous, filthy and indolent. Instead of living by hunting, as was the case with our tribe and nearly all the others east of the California Mountains, these obtained a scanty subsistence by digging for roots. The women do the digging

whilst the men stay in the lodges or are playing at
some game. I have seen hundreds of the women
at a time out in this employment. They car.y on
their backs heavy baskets of the shape of old fash-
ioned straw beehives, and in their hands long sticks
with which to dig the roots. Early in the morning
they go out and keep at work until evening. when
they return with their baskets full of roots. Sometimes they procure enough not only for their present
eating, but to lay up for winter use.

The men among the Digger Indians wear very
long hair, but that of the women is cut short. Both
are nearly naked, and filthy in the extreme. Most
of them are tatooed, the women especially display-
ing in general a large number of designs on their
person. They do this merely for ornament, and not
for the purpose of showing a difference in rank as is
the case in most tribes where the custom exists.

Their houses or lodges are very simple. In the
summer they put a number of bushes together in
the shape of a cone, and into this they creep for
shelter from the sun by day, and to sleep by night.
These lodges or tents are more designed to keep off
the rays of the sun than for shelter from inclement
weather. For the cold and wet seasons the Diggers in the northern part of California have a different kind of dwelling. They dig a pit several
feet deep, of the size of the proposed lodge. Then
they drive poles into the earth around the edge of
the pit, and bend them over so that they will meet
at the top, where they are fastened together, making
a covering over the pit. They then cover the whole
building with earth to the thickness of several inches,
or even a foot, leaving a small hole at the top to
serve as a chimney. Another hole is made at the
side, large enough to admit the body. When they

wish to sleep they build a fire in the centre of the lodge, then creep in feet foremost and lie in that position to the fire.

The Diggers have a curious way of marrying. When a man takes a fancy to a girl and wants her as his squaw, he speaks to her parents and talks to her a little. Then he lies down with her, and if she lies still they are considered man and wife; but if she gets up and runs away, the courtship is at an end, and the man never tries to get her again. A Digger man can have as many wives as he chooses, but the woman can only have one husband.

When a Digger dies they burn him, with all his implements, and have a great mourning during the ceremony. They believe that when a man dies his spirit goes to the East, and keeps going until it comes to a great water. A large boat is there to to take him over. All the good get safely across and go to a very large house where they eat, drink, and gamble, until they are tired, when they go off among the trees. The bad people who go in the boat reach the middle of the water, when the bottom falls out, and they are lost forever.

Whilst in California we frequently visited what is now San Francisco, but which was then a small village of a dozen houses, known by the Spaniards as "Yerba Buena." A few French and Spanish traders were the only white residents, and to those we carried down bear meat, buffalo robes, and furs of various kinds, together with small bits of gold found in the mountains, receiving in exchange blankets and "snakyeye," or whiskey. These trips were made several times during the year, but were finally terminated by the occurrence that resulted in our leaving that part of the country. A large party of Diggers surprised a small hunting party of Snakes and took from them their ponies. A number of warriors were sent out from our tribe to demand them back, but the Diggers had surrendered the ponies to the Spaniards, and now asked their protection from the vengeance of the Snakes. The Spaniards granted their request, and warned our party off. As soon as the news arrived at the Snake village, there was a general excitement, and all who were able to bear arms at once took the war path. The Diggers fled, but were tracked to the coast, where they were supported by several Spaniards. We attacked their camp at day break, and a desperate fight ensued. The Diggers are generally lazy and cowardly, but their numbers far exceeded ours, and they were assisted by white men. In the end we were victors, and our party mercilessly tomahawked and scalped all within their reach. Nearly a hundred and fifty scalps were borne off in triumph by the Snakes, and among the trophies were the scalps of some white men.

The result of this fight was a general movement of the whites on the one hand and the California tribes on the other, to drive us out of the country. For a time our tribe stood its ground, but at length it became evident that we could not remain peaceably in that region, so we once more turned our faces eastward and re-crossed the mountains to Utah.

During our stay in this Territory, which did not exceed six or seven moons, our principal encampment was on the banks of the Great Salt Lake, near the present site of Salt Lake City. At that time not a white man lived in that vast wilderness, though not many years afterwards a large city sprang up where our wigwams had formerly stood.

Once more our tribe became restless and dissatisfied with their location, and we changed our hunting ground to Oregon, remaining there about two years. Here we came into collision with the Blackfeet Indians, one of the most ferocious and cruel tribes in existence. They are always at war with the tribes around them, and make long journeys for the purpose of attacking some other nation. Several skirmishes took place between our bands and those of the Blackfeet, in which sometimes one and sometimes the other would be successful. In order to defend ourselves from the attacks of the Blackfeet, our tribe made an alliance with the Flat Heads. These are a very singular race, who strap boards on the heads of their children so as to change their shape. There are two kinds of Flat Heads, those who have the head flattened from the forehead back, making the head look like a wedge with the sharp edge in front, whilst the others have the sides flattened so as to have the point of the wedge upwards. The party allied with us were of the former kind. A part of the Utahs also joined us, about this time, as did the Crees.

Our associated tribes kept going farther North, not finding any place to settle, owing to the constant attacks of the Indians through whose territories we passed. With the Bloods and the Blackfeet we had repeated fights until we got above their country, beyond the territory of the United States, and into the country of the Copper Head Indians, who roamed over a vast extent of territory extending to the Esquimaux on the North.

Our associated tribes united in the North with the Copper Heads, and here the whole lived in undisputed possession, from that time to the present.

CHAPTER III.

MATTHEW BRAYTON'S NAARRTIVE CONTINUED.

Government of Snake and Copper-Head Tribes—Women worked hard—Marriage Laws—Children taught the use of weapons early—Funeral Ceremonies of the Copper-Heads—Their Religion.

The Snakes and Copper-Heads are ruled over by one general chief, or *Inkupudia*, who remains in power for life, unless deposed by the vote of all the tribes. Since the union of the tribes there has been but one General Chief, now an old man, eighty years of age, named *O-wash-kah-ke-naw*. He reigns supreme to a certain extent and appoints sub chiefs to govern the different tribes. These sub-chiefs are appointed for a period of time, and not for life. The General Chief makes known his laws or decrees for the government of the tribes in various matters, and it is the duty of the sub-chiefs to communicate these decrees to the tribes under their charge. The laws in relation to stealing are very strict. Any one proved to have stolen from a person belonging to the associated tribes is condemned to death, and is generally burned at the stake. It is looked upon as very disgraceful for an Indian to tell a lie to his fellows.

The men dress with leggings fastened to their moccasins. The leggings extend up to the knees. A tunic of furs is worn about the waist, and the bare place between the tunic and the leggings is daubed with oil and paint. From the waist upwards the body is daubed with oil and paint, and the hair is worn long, extending down over the breast and back The women are dressed in a somewhat similar manner.

The men do nothing but hunt and fight, leaving the women and captives to do the drudgery. The women are very hard worked, having to collect wood for fires, cut up the game, carry the heavy burdens and do the other work which the warrior considers beneath his dignity to perform. They are very hardy and can perform with ease labors which many white men would shrink from.

The marriage laws vary among different tribes. Among the Copper-Heads the marriage is for life. The Utahs marry for twelve moons, and if at the end of that time they separate they cannot re-marry at any subsequent time. If there is a boy born of the marriage, it goes with the father, and if a girl the mother takes it. The Snakes marry for three years, and if after that time they choose to live together they are married for life.

The birth of a child is accomplished without any trouble or assistance from either doctor, midwife or nurse. The mother retires to her lodge, or if on the march, steps aside and spreads her blanket, and in the course of two or three hours she is up and about her accustomed work, or on the march, as if nothing had happened.

The child, when young, is wrapped around with bandages, strapped to a board and carried on the mother's back. When in the lodge, or at any other time that she wishes to take the child down, the board with the infant on it, is set to lean against the wall, or is hung to a peg.

As soon as a boy is able to run about his education for the chase and the war path is commenced. A bow three and a half feet long, strung with the sinews of the deer or elk, is placed in his hand, and a bundle of two feet arrows, with flint heads and feathered shafts, is given him. With these he practices at a mark until he is proficient. A board is then set up, and a circle about six inches in diameter is described on it. The young Indian takes his position at a short distance from the board, and commences throwing his knife at it with the endeavor to strike the centre of the circle. When he succeeds in doing this frequently, he increases his distance from the board, and keeps on retreating until he can strike the circle with unerring aim from as great a distance as his strength will permit.

The tomahawk practice comes next. A mark is described on the bark of a tree, and the young Indian throws his tomahawk at it with great force, endeavoring to make it whirl three times in the air, and then to strike with the sharp pick at the back of the ax-head, so that it shall remain sticking in the mark. As in the knife practice, success at one distance is immediately followed by a retreat of a few paces, until the feat can be accomplished at a considerable distance. The same routine is gone through with the ax part, so that it shall cleave the bark in the very centre of the mark. At about ten years of age, a long bow, with arrows of proportionate length, is put into the hands of the boy, and when he becomes of sufficient age to manage it properly he is instructed in the use of the rifle.

The boys are incited to begin hunting and trapping early, and their first success in trapping a beaver, shooting a martin, or spearing a muskrat is celebrated with as much triumph as is the first scalp taken in battle by a young warrior. When about twelve years old the boys join the hunting parties, and are very expert in the use of the bow. Many widows are supported entirely by their sons who have just passed their twelfth year.

The small children and the very old people are
allowed the use of cooked meat, but all others eat
their food raw. No salt is used, but pepper is frequently obtained from the Russian and Hudson
Bay trading posts, and is eaten with the food as a
great addition. Besides the privilege of eating
cooked meat, the very old people are well cared for
by the tribe, and are allowed to remain in their
lodges without being called out to hunt or work.
Everything is done for them, and they enjoy perfect
rest until their death.

The Copper-Heads do not, in general, bury their
dead in the same manner with many of the tribes
in the United States territory. In some cases,
when a warrior dies, the dead body is placed in a
birch bark canoe, in which are also laid the dead
warrior's rifle, tomahawk, pipe, knife, and all the
other articles belonging to him when alive. Two
blankets, and provisions to last six months are also
placed in the canoe. A poor miserable dog is next
procured and hung up by the hind legs to a tree or
pole stuck in the ground. The throat of the dog is
cut and the animal suffered to bleed to death. The
object of this ceremony is to provide a dog to hunt
with in the spirit land, and the bad blood is let out
so as to fit the animal for its new sphere of existence. A poor dog is as serviceable as a good one
for the happy hunting grounds, if the bad blood is
taken out. Some powdered roots are then sprinkled
over the body, and the canoe with its contents is
launched on the river, if there is one in the neighborhood, and the deceased warrior goes on his way
to the happy hunting grounds. If there is no river
near, the canoe with its contents is placed on the
branches of a tree, or on a temporary scaffold, and
there left. Sometimes in conformity with the wishes

of the deceased, the body is buried under the roots of a tree, or placed in a hollow log, to wait until there is some good company to join in the journey to the happy hunting grounds.

The religion of these tribes is very simple. They worship the Great Spirit by standing and praying, with arms uplifted to the sky. At times when they see a dark storm-cloud rising up the sky they address it, believing the Great Spirit to be hid within it. After a prayer, on some particular occasions, they drink "snakyeye" or whisky, and dance with whooping and yelling. They do not believe in a place of punishment hereafter. Those who have committed crimes in this world will be punished here by their tribe, or else the Great Spirit will visit them with sickness or trouble. After this life is over, the spirits all go to the happy hunting grounds, where there is plenty of game, and where no enemies will come to disturb them.

CHAPTER IV.

MATTHEW BRAYTON'S NARRATIVE CONTINUED.

Climate—Esquimaux—Trading—Mode of Sleeping—Method of Taming Ponies and Elks—Weapons—Making Pipes.

The territory occupied by the Copper-Heads and the associated tribes, lies west of the Rocky Mountains, in the high latitudes, extending so far north as the Russian Possessions. Their hunting grounds cover a space of several hundred miles, and the natural characteristics of the country are much diversified. Barren mountain ranges alternate with wide plains, fruitful valleys and dense forests. We met with but few rivers in our hunt, but from the Esquimaux, and a few stragglers belonging to tribes on the east side of the mountains, we had reports of many rivers and big waters on the other side. Our northern head-quarters was about three weeks' journey from the Arctic Ocean. To the north east of us, about two weeks' journey, was Big Esquimaux village.

The climate in the northern part of our hunting grounds is cold through the greater part of the year, and the ground mostly covered with snow. The trees in this region are of pine, cedar, white hemlock, and some other kinds. During the greater part of the year they remain bare, but as soon as the temperature begins to moderate a little, the leaves come out about the size of a squirrel's ear. They continue out but for a short time, when they drop off, and the tree is once more bare. The elk, reindeer, and the ponies of the Indians all feed on the bark of the trees, and the moss.

Snow falls repeatedly during the year, but no rain. There are numerous storms.

With the Esquimaux, who live on the shores of the Arctic Ocean, our tribes have formerly had skirmishes, but the difficulties have all been settled, and there is now a lasting peace, although but slight intercourse between the races. The Esquimaux are a dirty people, generally short, thick set, with matted hair, and afflicted with the scurvy. They wrap themselves up in furs, and live on any kind of carrion. They will eat worms, bugs or snakes when they cannot get game; but their principal luxury is oil. They make oil from the carcasses of the animals they obtain, and enjoy it as a great luxury. They live in huts made of snow and ice, and when moving from place to place they have tents made of furs and skins. In traveling, they use sleds drawn by reindeer and dogs. The Copper-Heads never have sleds, but use ponies and elk, both for riding and packing game and other burdens

The Copper-Heads principally trade with the Russian posts, and make trips to them several times a year. They also send an expedition twice a year to the Red River settlement, and from there to St. Paul. All the dried meats, furs and other articles are packed on the backs of ponies and elks or carried by women and such captives as are in the keeping of the tribe. The mode of packing on the backs of women is for a belt, three fingers wide, to be passed across the forehead, and lie down the back. The pack is placed so as to rest on the bottom of the belt, and lie on the shoulders and neck. The bearer is obliged to stoop forward in walking, and the back is frequently bent from this cause. Being a captive, I was sometimes compelled to carry a load but about fifteen pounds less than my own weight, and the squaws have to carry within about twenty pounds of their own weight.

From the Russians we obtain blankets, powder, rifles, and other necessary articles, in exchange for furs and dried meats. Among other things purchased of the Russians, the tribe possesses a compass and a watch, enclosed in a copper case. They have learned the use of the compass sufficiently to enable them to travel by its aid.

The lodges are made of poles stuck in the ground and tied together at the top, so as to leave a hole in the centre. Furs and skins are then fastened around and made tight, except at the entrance. A fire is built in the centre of the lodge, and the members of the lodge creep in and sleep with their feet to the fire, and their heads to the side of the lodge.

In traveling, when the snow is on the ground, and the party do not take the lodge fixtures along, the snow is stamped down and the blanket spread on the hardened snow. On this the Indian lies down and rolls himself up in the blanket. With this mode of sleeping there is no danger of taking cold.

When the snow is very deep and light, the hunters wear wide snow shoes to prevent their sinking at every step. The ponies are also shod with wide moccasins stuffed with hair, when the snow is so deep that they cannot travel with ease.

The beasts of burden used by the Indians are ponies, elks and dogs. Both elks and ponies have to be broken into submission to man before they can be used. When the Indians want to break in a pony for riding, one of them mounts a well broke pony and, after riding around for a little while, suddenly dashes up to the untamed pony, and, seizing it by the mane, leaps on its back. The first effort of the surprised animal is to throw the unexpected burden over its head, or failing in this to rise on its hind legs and throw its rider backwards. To prevent either of these purposes being accomplished, the rider clasps his arms around the neck of the pony and crosses his legs under its belly, so that the toes are inserted between the forelegs of the animal. By these means the pony is rendered unable to jerk the rider off in any direction. Foiled in its efforts to dislodge the unusual encumbrance on its back, the pony generally sets off in a wild gallop, in which it is indulged by the rider, and an unexpected difficulty of breathing soon brings the unruly beast to terms. As soon as it gets somewhat tired of its useless excitements, the rider steals his hand down to its nose and there holds some sugar and salt. If the animal prove insensible to the temptation thus held out, the rider gradually works his hand up until he gets some of the mixture into its mouth. The taste of these articles is generally sufficient to subdue the strong will of the pony, and to complete the work the rider puffs tobacco smoke up its nostrils. It is now thoroughly broken in, and will sit easily under a rider or follow its owner like a dog. The Indian never abuses his horse, but always treats it as a friend.

The elk is of great service to the Indians in high latitudes, and shares with the pony the attentions of its owner. The method of catching and taming elk is for one hunter to throw a lasso, or running noose at the end of a long line, on one horn, whilst another hunter does the same to the other horn. The lines are then quickly made fast to two trees, and the hind legs tied to two other trees in a similar manner. Whilst thus fastened in a nearly immovable position the man who is to break in the animal comes up and leaps on his back. The ropes are simultaneously cut by the other Indians, and the elk dashes off with its burden. The rider embraces the horns with his arms and crosses his feet below the belly of the animal, as in breaking ponies. The elk pursues his headlong career for miles, the branching horns preventing his dashing among the trees in such a manner as to hurt the rider. After the elk is thoroughly spent by his long scamper, it is treated in the same manner as in the case of ponies.

The weapons of the Snakes and Copper-Heads consist of rifles, bows and arrows, spears, tomahawks, hunting knives, scalping knives, and war-clubs. The arrow heads are made of flint, and much care is used in digging up, selecting and splitting the proper kind of flint. The pipes are also made of flint, and take a large amount of patience and labor in their manufacture. The pipe I made for myself was first squared out from a flint and then drilled with a steel implement, worked by hand. I worked thirty days to complete the boring process. using bear's oil and water to moisten the stone. After the hole was bored, another steel chisel was taken, and the pipe chipped into proper shape. In doing the chiseling, the pipe was placed between two other stones to act as a vice, and the whole pressed between my knees. Then I chippped away, using my clenched hand as a mallet. After the pipe had been chipped into shape and then ornamented with cut designs, it was first oiled and then dyed a pale red with a pigment extracted from a root. A stem of cherry or other wood inserted in this pipe completes it.

CHAPTER V.

MATTHEW BRAYTON'S NARRATIVE CONTINUED.

Hunting Buffalo—The attack—Cutting up the carcass—Packing to the camp—Drying the meat—Buffalo hunting in winter—Trapping bears and wolves—Spearing muskrats—Dressing skins—Different modes of fishing.

Hunting is the principal occupation of the Indians, and their only means of subsistence. The climate does not admit the raising of crops, even if the Indians were disposed to till the ground, which they are not. During the fall the camps are removed to the lower part of the British territory in order to hunt the buffalo.

To show how the buffalo are killed, I will relate my experience on one of the hunts in which I was engaged.

Our hunting party, with the families of the hunters, traveled for seven days before reaching the traces of any herds. A few stray bulls were killed, and some of their flesh eaten, but it was too hard and tough for good eating. At length we arrived at the place where there were strong hopes of finding buffalo, and our camp was fixed. Early next morning the hunting party rode off, leaving the squaws and children to make arrangements for preparing the meat when it should be brought to the camp.

After riding a short distance, we came on traces of a large herd, and then rode forward in high spirits. We soon came in sight of some bulls feeding quietly, and beyond them could discover a large herd of cows. The difference between the sexes can be seen at a long distance by their mode of herding. The bulls feed singly, and are scattered over the prairies, whilst the cows huddle together as if for protection. The bulls are the most savage, but the cows are the fleetest of foot, and are very difficult to approach. Their flesh is, however, more highly esteemed than that of the bulls, it being more tender and juicy.

On reconnoitering the respective groups it became evident that we could not reach the cows without first breaking through the herd of bulls, and this we prepared to do at once. Riding slowly up so as not to alarm them, we approached within a few hundred yards of them before they took much notice of us. Then they ceased feeding and commenced bellowing furiously.

At this the signal was given, and our fleet ponies were spurred rapidly towards the herd. When close to them, each hunter singled out a buffalo, and dashing impetuously past the animal, discharged an arrow into its neck. Those whose arrows did not fatally wound the beasts were at once exposed to imminent danger, as nothing exceeds a wounded buffalo in ferocity and strength. Rising for a moment on their hind feet, they dash furiously at the hunters, butting at them, and attempting to upset horse and man. Sometimes they suceeed, and then the hunter suffers terrible wounds, if not death, from the horns of the enraged animal.

Five or six bulls were killed in the attack, and the rest scattered wildly over the prairie. The sight of the immense herd of cows in the distance excited the hunters, and prevented them from stopping to make any use of the bulls we had killed. We rode forward at a moderate speed for some distance, reserving the strength of our horses until we should be compelled to use their speed. At length the scouts of the herd saw us advancing, and in two or three seconds the whole herd was in motion. The first movements of the buffalo are slow, increasing in speed as they go. At the first symptoms of alarm our party raised a shout to encourage the horses, and we were suddenly flying along at full speed, the horses as much excited as their riders. The excitement was intense. At last we were close to them, and the arrows flew thick and fast into the herd. In a few moments we were in the midst of the press, firing arrows and using spears among the animals right and left.

The scene was full of wild excitement and not
without danger. Some of our party were thrown
from their horses and suffered severe bruises and
wounds from the feet and horns of the enraged buffaloes. At last the signal of recall was given, and
our party reined up to rest from the chase and dis-
pose of the spoils.

After dismounting and hobbling the ponies, the
hunters rested awhile before proceeding to the work
of cutting up the buffaloes in order to take them
home. When rested, the hunters began the labor
of skinning and cutting up the carcases. The animal was first placed on its knees, and its hind legs
stretched out to their full length, so that the principal weight lay on the belly of the beast. The small
hump of flesh about the neck was first cut out and
carefully placed on one side. The skin was next divided along the back bone, and stripped down on
either side. After this the animal was cut up in various pieces, all the best parts being taken and the
offal left for the wolves. The fat and tallow were
put in the hide, which was then slung around the
necks of the packing ponies. Along each side of
the pony's back was placed a pole, fastened to the
animal's neck. The foot of the buffalo's hind quarter was thrust through the gambril of the fore quarter, and the quarters then slung across the back of
the pony and hanging down on each side. The
poles keep the burden off from the sides of the pony, and prevent its back being broken. The other
portions of the game were carried in a similar manner.

When the meat was brought to the camp, the
women cut it into long strips, about a quarter
of an inch thick. These strips were hung on sticks
to dry, which operation takes several days. When

thoroughly dried, the women bend it up and tie it into bundles, in which shape it is preserved for home consumption or taken to the trading posts, to be bartered for ammunition or other articles wanted by the Indians. Some parts of the buffalo, not fitted for making the dried meat, were dried by a very fierce fire until it became brittle. A buffalo hide was then spread out, with the skin uppermost, and the dried pieces of meat spread on it, and thrashed into small bits by sticks. The tallow of the buffalo was cut up, melted and poured on the powdered meat, which was then worked up until it became well mixed. Whilst still warm, it was pressed into bags made of buffalo skin, which were then sown up. When cold the mixture, known to the whites as *pemican*, becomes as hard as a rock, and makes good eating. The marrow bones were boiled in water for their oil, which, when extracted, was poured into the bladder of the animal. One bladder will hold eleven or twelve pounds of oil.

Buffalo are frequently killed in winter without any of the dangers experienced in the fall hunt. The alternate thawing and freezing forms a thick crust on the surface of the soft snow. The heavy animals break through this thin crust, and plunge cumbrously into the deep snow, whilst the Indian hunter glides easily on his snow shoes close to the side cf the unwieldly monster, and dispatches it at his ease.

Elk. reindeer, grizzly bears, wolves, with some other animals, are killed with rifles, or arrows, frequently with the aid of dogs. The dogs are of a strong, powerful breed, and are trained to catch by the ears or jaw, so that the fur is not injured. The elk and reindeer are very difficult to approach, having a keen scent, and show fight if close pressed.

The attack on a grizzly bear is also dangerous, and the hunter frequently has to fight desperately for his life.

Black bears and wolves are frequently caught by a peculiar trap. A young sapling tree is bent down so that it its top is but a few feet from the earth. A rope, formed of pieces of raw hide firmly twisted together, is fastened to the top of the tree and a strong double hook of iron or steel is attached to the other end of the rope. One arm of the hook is lightly caught in a log or a stake driven in the ground, and on the other arm a piece of meat is firmly attached. The bear or wolf seizes the meat, and in its endavors to carry it off or tear it to pieces, releases the hook from the log. The tree top suddenly flies up, the hook catching the animal in the mouth or lip, and lifting it partially or completely from the ground. In this position it is found and dispatched by the hunter, when he comes to examine his traps.

Beaver are trapped in great numbers, as are martins and other fur-bearing animals. In the depth of winter the muskrat houses are sought out and pierced with strong and sharp spears which transfix the muskrats and bring them out on the points.

The skins of the animals killed are dried and cured by the women. When the hide is taken off and brought home, the women scrape off the flesh with a bone, sharpened at one end. When the skin is thoroughly scraped, small holes are cut all around it, and strings run through it, which are then lashed to the poles of the lodge inside. The fire burning the lodge dries the skin in one night, and in the morning it is taken down and folded so as to be packed. In dressing the skins, the grease is taken off and the skins dipped in water containing the brains of a deer, after which they are boiled and stretched on four square poles tied and pushed into the ground. The skin is then scraped with a bone and kept before a slow fire until perfectly dry. It is then dipped in the brain water and scraped dry again, after which it is dippped in the water a third time, and every time the water wrung out before the skin is stretched. If it remains hairy or stiff after all this working, it is drawn over a cord as thick as a man's finger, as hard as the women can pull, and this softens it greatly. The skin is next smoked. A hole is dug in the ground, about a foot deep, in which is put a little water and some rotten wood. The skin is then sewed in a bag and hung over the smoke for about ten minutes, when is ready for use.

The steams are well stocked with fish, and these are caught in various ways. Sometimes they are speared, and some are shot with arrows, and some caught by stakes arranged across the bed of the stream. When the rivers and small lakes are frozen over in winter, a hole is cut in the ice, and over it a little tent is made with three sticks and a blanket, so as to close out the light. The Indian lies with his face over the hole. He can then see to some depth, and when a fish passes, it is pierced with a short spear, and brought to the surface.

There are various other ways of hunting, trapping and fishing, but these will serve as specimens.

CHAPTER VI.

MATTHEW BRAYTON'S NARRATIVE CONTINUED.

Is recognized as a white man—War dance—Fight with Blackfeet Indians—Tomahawking and burning captives.

Nine years ago the winter in the north was exceedingly severe, and the game was compelled to seek a more southern latitude to get something to eat. We followed them down, but were in great danger of perishing of famine. In this strait our only hope was in obtaining some additional supplies from the trading posts. A large detachment was therefore sent off to the post of the Hudson Bay Company, for the purpose of obtaining supplies. With this band I traveled.

We arrived at the post after a long journey, and were received with kindness. The few furs and skins we were able to gather up we traded for provisions, but we were still in great want. That night we camped near the trading post, and waited to plead our cause with the agent next day.

In the morning whilst the chief of our party and some of the leading warriors were talking to the agent and explaining to him the deplorable condition of the tribe, one of the traders came into our camp. Whilst looking around and talking, he came close to me, and something seemed to attract his attention. Looking me in the eyes he suddenly spoke in French. I did not understand him but he immediately addressed me in Indian language, saying: "You are no Indian." I replied that I was, for I never remembered anything of a life different from the one I was leading. He insisted that I was no Indian, but a pale face, and demanded that I should come before the agent. I was about to do so, when some of the tribe interfered to prevent me. An angry discussion now took place between the trader and the Indians, ending in my being taken before the agent himself.

On my entering the circle where the chiefs and principal warriors were conferring with the agent, I was at once brought before the latter by the trader, and my white birth stated by him. The agent examined my features closely, and endeavored to get from me by conversation whether I was a white or not. I was surprised by these statements, but replied that I always considered myself an Indian. The members of the tribe present in the council were greatly disturbed when I was brought before the agent, and on being appealed to strongly asserted my Indian parentage. I could not fail to remark their alarm lest I should be claimed as a white, and pondered over it for some time.

The agent was quieted for a time, but was not satisfied, and all at the post continued to watch our movements narrowly. Next day whilst getting some provisions from the post, our chief was again asked about me, and was told that no more provisions would be given the party unless I was surrendered to the whites. At this the chief returned to the camp in dismay, and a brief council was held, from which I was excluded. The result was that our camp was suddenly broken up, and the trail immediately struck for the main body of the tribe, leaving the rest of the needed supplies behind us.

On our homeward march we fell in with a party of Blackfeet, who wished to rob us of our ponies and provisions. After a short skirmish the enemy was driven back, but continued to hover on our trail in order to find out our destination.

A busy scene presented itself at the camp on our arrival. Our hunters in their excursions in pursuit of game had come on traces of the Blackfeet Indians, and had followed the trail until they discovered the camp of a large war party which had evidently come out with the intention of meeting and driving us back to the north again. A grand council of the tribe was gathered and the warriors were giving their opinions as to the proper course to be pursued. Two alternatives presented themselves, One was to go back to the snows and starvation of the northern winter, and the other to meet the opposing Blackfeet and endeavor to force our way through them to the hunting grounds farther south. There was a general disposition to take the latter course, and several chiefs made stirring appeals to the pride and vengeance of the warriors. The numerous battles with the Blackfeet in former years were referred to, and the blood of the slain invoked to stir up the hearts of the warriors to revenge. Finally one of the chiefs sprang to his feet and commenced chanting an account of his warlike deeds, and boasted of what he would do in the approaching fight. Whilst he sang he danced around in a circle, stamping fiercely on the ground at every step. Every now and then he stopped to raise his war-cry.

In a few minutes another warrior sprang up and joined the dance and song, to the music of a small drum and rattle. Then another and another leaped up, until all the fighting men of the tribe signified their intention of attacking the enemy. During the dance the utmost excitement existed, and the piercing yells worked the warriors up to mad frenzy. Knives and tomahawks were waved in air, and all the movements of fighting and scalping an enemy gone through with.

Next day a large war party set out in the direction of the Blackfeet camp. I accompanied the party. In a short time we struck the trail of one of their bands, and followed it up till evening, when we discovered ourselves in the vicinity of the enemy's camp. A hurried council was held, and it was decided to conceal ourselves in the woods until morning, and make the attack at sunrise. After placing sentinels to keep watch of the camp, our party lay down among the brush and waited for day.

At the first dawn of day we were all awake and creeping stealthily towards the edge of the wood, beyond which the camp was pitched. As we neared the opening the Blackfeet discovered our approach and raised an alarm. In an instant there was great confusion in the camp, and their warriors were rushing backwards and forwards, snatching up their weapons and attempting to seek a place of shelter from the coming attack.

At this moment our war chief blew a blast on a horn carried by him, and at the signal a volley of shot and arrows was fired into the camp. Several of the Blackfeet were killed and wounded, and the others ran to the woods for protection. Some of our warriors dashed into the opening, cut down the wounded and rapidly scalped them, raising a terrible war whoop as each bloody scalp was snatched from the head of the prostrate foe. As soon as the work was done they again sought the protection of the trees.

The fight was now conducted from behind the trees and every one fought after his own fashion.— Sometimes one side appeared to gain the advantage, and then the fortune would change. Hours passed away, and both parties were very much scattered, but the Blackfeet were generally in retreat. At last they broke up and fled, when our warriors returned, plundered the camp of what little was left in it, and took the trail homewards A number of scalps were borne home in triumph.

Three captives were taken and their arms tied firmly to their sides, after which they were driven before us to the camp On arriving there the party was received with shouts of triumph, and the women and children made a tremendous noise Some of the squaws who had lost husbands in battle came up to the captives and loaded them with insults and abuse, shaking their fists in the faces of the victims and acting like mad women. The captives remained perfectly indifferent to these insults, and made no sign of being aware that the women were in existence.

When the party entered the camp, the prisoners were tied to different posts. The warriors then indulged in a great rejoicing. "Snakyeye" or whisky was brought out and drank. The warriors boasted of their deeds in battle and divided the captives. Then they sprang up in a wild dance, and menaced the captives with their knives and tomahawks. One of the Blackfeet replied in contemptuous words to the taunts of the Copper-Heads, which so exasperated them that several of the latter at once rushed to the posts and tomahawked two of the captives. The third was saved by a chief of our tribe, who proposed that he should be burned instead of tomahawked.

This proposal met with favor, and preparations were at once made for carrying it into execution. Wood was brought and piled up around the victim until it ascended above his knees. He was then tormented by descriptions of the horrible sufferings that he was to endure, but the threats failed to shake his constancy in the least.

As soon as all the preparations were complete, a large number of warriors and squaws encircled the victim and commenced a wild dance. Fire was applied to the pile, and in a few moments the flames ascended around the body of the captive Blackfoot. He commenced chanting a deathsong, and did not stop till life was extinct. The dance was kept up around the stake until the body was consumed, when a yell was given and the assemblage dispersed to their lodges.

Next day another council was held, and it was decided not to go any farther to the south, but to return and get through the winter as well as possible in a territory where we should be out of the Blackfeet range. Accordingly our tents were struck and packed, the ponies loaded, and we once more took the northward trail.

CHAPTER VII.

MATTHEW BRAYTON'S NARRATIVE.

Marries the Chief's Daughter—Tattooing—Packing for the South—Camping Out—Crossing the Mountains—Skirmish with Blackfeet—Wounded—The Red River Settlements.

The fact that the traders at the Hudson Bay Company's post had claimed me to be of white birth, was communicated to the principal chief after the war excitement of the latter was over, and caused considerable anxiety on his part. Nothing was said to me about it, but I could see that the old chief feared my escape, and that the tribe would be made to suffer some punishment at the hands of the whites for my captivity. I had always considered myself as an Indian captured from some other tribe, and could not yet think it possible that I was one of the pale faces.

With the return of Summer the tribe again sought the Northern regions, and I had almost forgotten the affair at the trading post. The old chief, O-wash-kah-ke-naw, appeared to have taken a great liking to me, and in September of that year (1851) he gave me his youngest daughter, Tefronia. (Tame Deer) to be my squaw. She was then nineteen, and a handsome Indian woman. My own name in Copper Head language is Owah-owah-kish-me-wah. By this squaw I have two children, Tefronia, a girl now over five years of age, and Tululee, a boy over two years old.

After marrying his daughter I was kept by the old chief around the village, and was not allowed to join any expeditions in the lower country. Three years passed in this manner, and my girl was born. The tribe once more moved farther south, and the old chief become anxious about my being claimed by the whites. One day he told me that if I went south with the tribe I must be tattooed, so that I could be identified by them in case I should be carried off by the traders under pretence that I was of white parentage. I did not consent to this, but was then told that there was no choice left me, as it was the will of the chief that it should be done.

Next day I was seized by two men of the tribe and made to lie on my back along a log. I was next bound down so that I could neither move my head, body, hands or feet. My breast was bared, and one of the Indians came forward to do the work of tattooing.

First he took a sharp knife and made some light incisions down my breast, so that small strips of skin were cut. These he peeled off and threw on one side. My agony was intense, but I did not wish to be considered a coward, so I held my tongue, though the pain made me bite my lips till the blood came; other similar strips were next taken off at the distance of about an inch, but parallel with the first marks. I now suffered tortures and was racked with an intense thirst. The attendant Indians brought me water and poured it into my mouth and over my head to keep me from fainting.

Parallel strips were now cut at right angles to the first incisions, and then other strips at right angles to the second series of cuts. Some other incisions were also made, but by this time I was almost insensible to pain. During these operations a smooth stone had been remaining in a strong fire, and as the marks were all cut the stone was taken up and applied to my lacerated breast. The pain for the moment was maddening, but the effect was to sear the wounds and stop the bleeding. I was now released from my fastenings, and sought my lodge, with marks on my breast that I still carry, and shall to my dying day.

After this time I was allowed to go with the rest of the tribe in the excursions to the southern part of the territory over which we ranged. About two years since I joined the half yearly train that left for the Selkirk settlement on the Red River and for St. Paul's.

As I stated before, this train starts twice a year,— in the Spring and Fall, laden with furs, and brings back supplies of various kinds. The journey occupies about six "moons" each way, and one "moon" is allowed for stoppage at St. Paul's, so that the trains meet about half way on the journey. A large number of Indians travel in these trains so as to fight their way down in case of resistance by hostile Indians.

Previous to starting on the journey, all the furs, skins, and other articles intended to be taken down, together with dried meats for the journey, were packed in readiness to be carried by ponies and elks, or by the squaws in the manner already described. When everything was ready, a grand Council was held, at which the old men of the tribe sat around the council fire, smoking their pipes in silence. Then the principal chief arose and appointed one of the subordinate chiefs to the command of the party, giving him in a few words some general instructions relative to the policy to be adopted in dealing with the whites, and exhorting the warriors attached to the party to drive from the face of the earth all who should oppose their progress. Particular charge was given that I should be kept away from the whites as much as possible, and watch kept that I might not be stolen from them by the pale faces.

The old chief sat down, and the newly appointed chief of the expedition rose and made a speech, as did some others of the tribe. Then there were some dances, after which the Council broke up and all retired to their lodges.

Early next morning the party set out on their journey. The ponies and elks were loaded with packs, the squaws carried some articles attached to the straps passed across their forehead, and the men rode or walked in single file. The journey was long and tedious, day after day passing with but few incidents to change the monotony of our progress. Hunting parties started off occasionally in pursuit of game for the support of the band, and met at appointed places, but the main body kept advancing steadily in the one direction.

Only four hours was allowed for sleep, when fires were lit and we all lay around in our blankets, with our feet to the fire, and heads outward. There are two reasons for adopting this mode of sleeping: it keeps the feet warm, which is very important, and it allows more people to sleep around one fire than would be possible in any other position. On stopping for sleep the ponies were hobbled in such a manner that they could feed or sleep, but could not run away. Sentinels were posted to prevent the camp being surprised either by wild animals or by hostile Indians.

As soon as the time was up the signal was given and the whole camp was speedily awake and ready for resuming the journey. A hasty meal was despatched, and then, after determining the course to be taken, the band set forward. There were no fixed hours for meals, and no stoppages for that purpose, but each person took a piece of dried meat whenever he become hungry, and gnawed away as he felt disposed.

The country through which we passed changed from dense forests to barren plains, and then again to rolling prairies, high hills, and grassy valleys. When large streams opposed our progress there was a halt on the banks, and preparations were made for swimming across. The packs were disposed of so as not to be wetted, and then each animal, led by an Indian, was brought to the stream and swam across to the other side. When the animals and their burdens had all safely been got over, the remaining men and squaws plunged in and swam over. The very young children were carried on the backs of the swimmers, or floated across on boards, which the mothers pushed before them.

At the North Pass of the Rocky Mountains the band crossed from the west to the east side. The crossing was the work of time and difficulty, both animals and Indians having to creep slowly up the rugged heights of the Pass. Sometimes we were many hours making half a mile progress, and great caution was requisite to prevent serious accidents among the precipices around which we crept. At times we wound our way through a deep gorge, on either side of which the enormous walls of rock towered far over head. Then a toilsome ascent brought us on an elevation from which we looked down on rugged peaks and deep clefts below. At length the difficulties and dangers of the Pass were over, and we emerged on the rolling land to the east of the mountains.

Up to this time we had met with no hostile Indians, or, at least, none that attempted to molest us. We were now in the territory hunted by the Bloods and Blackfeet, and were therefore not without fears of an attack. On the second day after leaving the Pass I joined a hunting party and set out in pursuit of buffalo. The party consisted of thirty hunters, all well armed either for the chase or war. A herd of bulls was discovered at a distance, and we rode quietly towards them.

As we rose on a ridge that commanded a wide view of the country, we became aware of a party of mounted Indians at no great distance from us, in pursuit of the same herd of buffalo. They appeared to have discovered us at the same time, and both parties drew up to reconnoitre. In numbers both were nearly equal, and there appeared to be little doubt that the opposing band were some of our old enemies, the Blackfeet. A short council was held without dismounting, and there was a question as to the policy of fighting them on the spot, or of falling back on the main body and keeping prepared for the larger band of Blackfeet that probably lay in our course towards the Selkirk settlement.

The question was settled, without farther discussion on our part, by the appearance of the Blackfeet galloping towards us. Our party dashed forward to meet them, and as the two bands neared each other, rapid discharges of bullets and arrows were made by both sides I received a rifle ball in my instep, and was thrown from my pony by a Blackfoot that dashed against me.

The fight was desperate, and several scalps were taken on both sides. A Blackfoot warrior singled me out for combat, and for some time we fought hand to hand. Severe blows were given on both sides, and I felt faint from loss of blood, having received a frightful gash in the thigh from a tomahawk, besides an ugly knife wound in one knee and in the calf of one leg. In the end the hostile party was repulsed, though with severe loss on our side, and we retreated to the main body of our party.

Here my wounds were found to be of sufficient importance to require some attention. I was lashed to a log in order to prevent my writhing during the process of dressing the wounds. The gashes were then cleaned out and washed with water. Some kinnikenick bark was chewed up and mixed with tobacco, which was then put into the wound to stop the bleeding. The washing and dressing was repeated until the bleeding had completely stopped. One of the men took a thin buckskin thong and sewed up the wounds by piercing the skin and running the thong through it. Only two stitches were made for each gash. The pain of this operation was intense, and was more difficult to bear than the original wounds. The marks of the stitches are still visible on my person.

Whether the defeat of the smaller party of Blackfeet had discouraged the larger band, or whether there was no large party in the neighborhood at that time, I cannot tell, but it was certain that we were not again troubled with them during our journey. Occasionally a straggling hunter or two would be seen, but they always made off before any of our warriors could reach them.

We had now reached the hunting grounds of the Selkirkers, or colonists of English, Scotch, French and half breeds, who lived on the territory granted to Lord Selkirk for the purpose of establishing a colony there. The land from the Rocky Mountains to the Red River is pleasant to look at, and rich with game of all kinds. Buffalo, deer, and smaller game, range in great numbers over the plains, and the hunters and trappers of the Selkirk colony are scattered in the season, in all directions over this splendid territory. Soon after getting into this country we fell in with some trappers who were returning to the settlements, and they traveled with our train as far as we went in their direction.

In the course of our journey with them, they noticed my appearance and spoke to me of my resemblance to whites, even though disguised with paint as I was. They became interested in me and taught me several words of English, which I learned very rapidly.

On reaching the Selkirk settlements we camped for a few days in order to rest awhile before striking the Red River trail, and to do a little trading with the settlers. Here the traders who had been teaching me English told some of the other whites about me, and I was visited by several Selkirkers. After conversing with me for some time they summoned the chief, and charged the tribe with having stolen me when a child from the whites. He denied it, but the Selkirkers became more determined in their suspicions, and demanded that I should be given up to them, threatening to take me by force if not surrendered peaceably. I was appealed to as to what my wishes were on the subject. So much had been told me by the traders about my having probably been stolen from my white parents, that I had become anxious to know something about the facts, and I frankly said so. On this the Selkirkers became more eager to have me left with them, but our chief dissuaded me from consenting, by representing that I had no clue to my parents, even if it was true that I had been stolen from the whites, but that if I returned to the tribe, I could undoubtedly get part of my history from the old chief, who would also probably give me leave to go, in case I chose to hunt up my family. With this I was content, and the Selkirkers let me go after exacting a solemn promise from the chief and principal warriors that I should be allowed to proceed in search of my parents if I felt disposed to do so.

CHAPTER VIII.

MATTHEW BRAYTON'S NARRATIVE.

Selkirk People—Selkirk Trains—Trading at St. Paul—Return to the North.

With the dawn of day we again set forward on our journey taking the Red River trail towards St. Paul. The trip between the Selkirk settlements and St. Paul occupies from thirty to forty days, and passes through the battle ground of the Siouxs and Chippewas. Several times we came on small parties of the Siouxs, but had no more than short skirmishes with them, our numbers being too formidable for them to attack us. About two days journey from the Selkirk settlements we came to the settlement of Oshawkapee, inhabited by French and half breeds. From this point we passed over a magnificent rolling country interspersed with occasional woods and watered by several streams.

Whilst crossing this country we met the Red River settlement train returning from their trading journey to St. Paul. The train was composed of four or five hundred ox carts in single file, with drivers on foot, or riding on the wagons, hunters and guards mounted on ponies, and women and children riding with camp fixtures in covered wagons.

The Selkirkers' wagons are of a peculiar kind, no iron being used in any part of their construction. There is but one pair of wheels, having felloes about six inches thick. There are about fourteen spokes to a wheel, and these spokes are about three feet long. The linch pins, axles, and in fact everything about the carts, are of wood, very massive and cumbrous. No grease is used on the axles, so that an incessant groaning and creaking is kept up. The body of the cart is nothing but a frame work similar to the woodracks used in the lower country. Sometimes a tilt covering is used for the wagons that carry the women and children. Each cart is drawn by one ox fastened to the shafts by straps of raw hide. One man has charge of five wagons, a strap passing from the tail of one wagon over the horns of the ox drawing the wagon immediately following it. When the driver whips the first ox it starts forward, and the oxen in the squad of carts attached to the moving wagon have to start at the same time.

The drivers of these trains are mixed French Canadians, English, Scotch and half breeds. In most cases the women are Indians, and these travel with the train to do the cooking and general work of the camp. When they camp for the night they bring all the wagons into a close circle with the shafts outwards. Immediately inside of this circle each ox is tied to the cart to which it belongs, and within this inner cicle of cattle the ponies are picketed. The tents are then pitched within the whole, sentinels placed, and the camp composed to sleep.

Salutations were exchanged with the Selkirkers' train as we passed, and our journey was again resumed. At length we arrived at our village a short distance from St. Anthony, and here preparations were made for staying one month, during which the trading was to be done.

In this time our furs and skins were taken down to St. Paul, and, by means of our interpreter were traded for whiskey, powder, rifles, provisions of various kinds, weapons, and such other articles as were needed by us. During these tradings I practiced myself in speaking English, and could soon talk so as to make myself understood. I held some conversations with the settlers, and become more anxious to discover the facts in relation to my supposed parentage. I determined that as soon as I went back I would demand my history from the old chief, and if I could obtain any trace from him, I would then prosecute the search after my parents.

When the trading was over and the supplies brought back to the camp, there was a grand feast given, and the camp became a scene of drunken debauchery for several days. Whiskey was drunk in great quantities, and many quarrels took place between the men. As they had taken the precaution of putting away their weapons before the drinking began, no one was killed in the quarrels.

At length our time was up, the Indians got over their debauch, and everything was made ready for the return trip. We were soon on our way, and marching with our faces to the North.

The journey to our northern headquarters had no particular incident to interest me, my mind being now full of the idea that I had white relatives and friends, and that the savage life I had led for so many years was not the one for which I was born. I longed to reach our village once more, that I might question the old chief as to my history. At last we reached the main body of our tribe. I was rejoiced to meet my Tefronia and the children once more, but at the same time a new feeling had entered my breast. I waited impatiently two or three days until the rejoicings caused by our return should have passed away, and then I sought out the venerable chief, O-wash-kah-ke-naw, now over eighty years old, and begged him to tell me truly the secret of my birth.

For some time the chief bade me go back to my lodge and be content with what I already knew, but, finding that I was resolute in discovering the facts, he told me to await a few days in patience, and then he would give his decision. I returned to my lodge in much agitation, for it was evident that the chief knew something that had hitherto been concealed from me. I had been so long accustomed to savage life that I remembered no other.

A council of the leading chiefs only called on the following day, which I rightly considered was to consult on the course to be pursued in respect to my demand. At last I was summoned before the great chief and a few leading warriors, and was instructed as to the course allotted for me.

I was then informed that when a child I had been stolen from the whites by a band of Canadian Indians who had by this course revenged themselves on the whites for some real or fancied wrongs; that I had passed through the hands of several tribes and had at last, as I already knew, been sold by the Siouxs to the Snakes, and remained with them until their union with the Copper Heads. The decision of the head men of the tribe was that I should join the train about to set out out for the settlements, and should then proceed in company with a few picked warriors, to visit the remnants of the tribes in whose possession I had once been, in order to learn more of my former history. At the same time I was sworn to return to the tribe within a year after I left the train at St. Paul, and to ensure the fulfilment of this condition, my wife and children were to be retained in the old chief's family at the headquarters of the tribe. To these conditions I freely consented, and waited eagerly for the day when I should set out on my journey.

At last the day arrived and I took a farewell of my wife and children. The thought of them checked little a my eagerness to set out, but at length I left them, fully intending to return as soon as I could discover something of my former history.

CHAPTER IX.

MATTHEW BRAYTON'S NARRATIVE.

Return to St. Paul—Sick at Chicago—Sets out in Search of his Parents—Reaches Cleveland—Gets his Story Printed—Visits Warren, O—Attends Camp Meeting—Experiences Religion—Reaches Sugar Grove.

The snows of winter had begun to fall when our party set out on the route I had so recently traveled. The present company was placed under command of a son of the principal chief, he being also the brother of my wife. There is no reason for again describing the route, as we traveled in the same trail that we pursued with the former party, and this time there were no incidents of consequence to diversify the monotony of the progress. About the beginning of April, 1859, we reached our camping ground near St. Anthony, and on the tenth of that month I arrived with a detachment of the tribe at St. Paul. We remained here a few days, making enquiries of the Siouxs and Chippewas that occasionally came in to trade, and from them I obtained a clue to farther discoveries.

On the 16th of April I obtained leave from the chief to set out on investigations, promising faithfully to return to St. Paul in July, when the train would be ready to return.

To aid me in my researches I was accompanied part of the way by the chief himself, and some members

of the tribe, and our party was furnished with three
ponies and five dogs. In pursuance to the information obtained from the Siouxs and Chippewas, we
proceeded in search of a party of Winnebagoes
said to be located in Northern Wisconsin. After
traveling some days days we reached the Wisconsin
river, and following it towards its source came on
the Winnebagoes, who were making sugar in the
woods. From them I obtained the particulars of
my purchase by them from the Paw Paws, and was
directed to a family yet living in Michigan who
could probably give me some further information.

Filled with hope I started, in company with my
brother-in-law and the other Indians, for Chicago.
We traveled through the woods and across the country, I acting as interpreter, being now able to speak
English with tolerable proficiency. Before reaching
that city I was taken sick, and on arriving there I
fell into the hands of some sympathizing persons
who placed me under medical care. My escort,
finding that I had become so sick that I could
neither prosecute my researches for some time, nor
return with them, quitted me and returned to St.
Paul, leaving me only my faithful dog, Nawah.

I was very sick and do not remember much for
two or three weeks, when I found myself in a hospital, with my long hair cut off close to my head,
and the paint scrubbed from my skin. To get it
off they had used hot water, soap and sand, and in
the process had transformed me from an Indian to a
white man. I remained in the hospital for more
than five weeks, and then I was discharged as cured,
though still very weak.

On letting me go they gave me a suit of white
men's clothing instead of my Indian costume, leaving me nothing but my stone pipe and my scalping

knife. Nawah and I at once set out on our adventures, and my steps were directed towards the place where the Paw Paw family was said to reside. I found them after walking for two days, and then was directed to a small village of Pottawottomies in Branch county, Michigan. I walked to the place described, sleeping in the woods at night as had been customary with me, but I soon found that I could no longer do so with safety. With my long hair cut off, and without my blanket and furs, I was unprepared for camping out. The result was that I caught a severe inflammation in my eyes that increased to an extent threatening my sight. I could no longer bear the light, and had to walk with my head down.

On reaching the Pottowottamies I found they consisted of four families and their chief, Mr. MACGWAGOR. They had settled down to civilized life, and were living as farmers. Mr. MACGWAGOR remembered the whole transaction in relation to my purchase from the Canadian Indians, he having been present at the transfer. He said the Canadian Indians had stated at the time that they had taken me from the south side of Lake Erie, and that, from their description, the party had probably brought me from Ohio, as they spoke of having crossed the Sandusky river during the journey on which they fell in with me.

On learning this I set out for Detroit and crossed over into Canada, but without obtaining much farther information among the few semi-civilized Indians and half breeds that I met with there. All I could gather was that I probably been taken from somewhere in the vicinity of Cleveland.

I now retraced my steps to Detroit, and proceeded into Ohio, telling my story as I went, and requesting information. At Fremont I fell in with a man who listened to my story with attention and remarked that he had formerly heard of a family named TODD, who had lost a little boy from the neighborhood of Cleveland a number of years ago. Acting under his suggestions, on the following day, I got on the railroad train and came to Cleveland, where I arrived in the latter part of August.

I was in Cleveland about one day, making enquiries relative to the TODD family, and telling my story, but without getting any information that was of use. The TODD family had removed many years since, and I could not learn their whereabouts. I had begun to despair of ever finding traces of my parents, when a friendly colored man who had met me and learned my story, took me to the office of the *Cleveland Daily Herald*, for the purpose of telling my story to the editors. We succeeded in finding one of them, Mr. J. H. A. BONE, in the office, together with another gentleman. I told my story to them, and was cross-questioned by them very closely. In the end I was directed to an old citizen of the place for the purpose of making inquiries, and was told to call again and tell the result.

The person to whom I was directed was out of town, and I learned nothing farther that night. Several persons took considerable interest in my story, and wished me well in my journeyings. Next morning I was on the street when I saw some furs and other articles of Esquimaux dress at the door of a building, and was told that a Panorama of the Arctic Regions was on exhibition, and that one of the men belonging to it—THOMAS HICKEY—had been in the far North. I went up to see him, and to him and the proprietor, Mr. LA RUE, told my story.

I then accompanied Mr. LA RUE to the office of the *Herald*, and there I again met Mr. BONE. who made me repeat my story and then printed it with a request that any person possessing information of probable use to the "Indian captive," would at once furnish it.

The interest taken in my story by the editors of the *Cleveland Herald* has been the means of my return to my relatives.

I remained in Cleveland several days, and my story excited much interest. Some persons furnished me with portions of clothing of which I stood in need, and I was furnished with food and sleeping room at one of the hotels. The people at the house were surprised at my refusal to sleep in a bed and to eat cooked meat or anything that had salt in it, but I could not endure the method of eating or sleeping used by civilized white people.

In a few days I learned that some persons in Warren, O., could probably give me some information, and thither I went, the Cleveland and Mahoning Railroad Company taking me without my paying fare. On arriving there I found that the people to whom I was directed had gone out of town to attend a Camp Meeting in Mahoning county. Some persons going to the meeting invited me to accompany them, and in their company I arrived at the Camp Meeting.

A short time sufficed to convince me that I had got on the wrong track, and that I was not the missing son of JOSEPH TODD. Great interest was, however, occasioned by my story, and many questions were put to me. I showed the Presiding Elder papers given me in proof of my belonging to the Indian tribe, and related my adventures. Finally I showed them my dog, scalping knife and pipe.

The Presiding Elder, Mr. ANSON BRAZEE, was so much interested in my story that he got me to repeat it to the whole meeting. I remained with these people throughout the meeting, and before it broke up, I became thoroughly convinced of the truth of the christian religion, and joined the Church of the United Brethren. In token that I had forever abandoned the bloody practices of heathenism, I broke my scalping knife in two, giving the handle and part of the blade to Elder BRAZEE, and the other part of the blade to a circuit preacher, the Rev. WILLIAM McINTYRE. When the camp broke up I accompanied the Elder and some of the Ministers to a Conference in Stark county, and from thence went to Williamsfield, Ashtabula, where I stayed with some farmers belonging to the Church of the United Brethren.

After staying with these good people about a fortnight, I went to Monroe, Ashtabula county, in search of some information that I expected to get there, but failed to obtain anything of use, I then accepted the invitation of Elder BRAZEE, and went to his house in Pierpont, Ashtabula county, where I stayed a short time. From there I went to Conneautville, thence to Clark's Corners, and to Connorsville. From that place the minister sent a letter to Cleveland stating that I had gone into Pennsylvania, and giving directions where I probably could be heard of.

I continued to wander from place to place, whereever the faintest hope existed of my getting any information, and in this way I visited Erie, Waterford, Wattsburgh, and finally reached Warren, Pa., where the Rev. WILLIAM McINTYRE was stationed. I remained with him a short time and then retraced my steps to Ashtabula county, after which I again returned to Mr. McIntyre's and from thence went to Columbus, Pa.

My hopes of finding my relatives had now almost died out. Nearly six months had passed, but I seemed no nearer the object of my search than I was when I left St. Paul. Wearied out with fruitless efforts, I had resolved to make one more attempt, and if that failed, to abandon the search for ever and return to my tribe on the approach of Spring. My eyes remained very bad, and I therefore labored under great disadvantages, having to be careful lest the inflammation should increase and destroy my sight. I had gone to school for a few days in Pennsylvania, but the state of my eyes compelled me reluctantly to abandon the idea for the present, at least.

From Columbus I went to Sugar Grove. Warren county, Pa., close to the New York State line. My intention was to remain there a day or two, and then set out for the Cattaraugus Indian Reservation where I intended making my last effort at obtaining information. If I failed there I meant either to return to the Rev. Mr McIntyre's residence and attend school for the Winter, or go into Canada and remain with the Indians until Spring, when it would be time to return to St. Paul. On the 18th of November I was at Sugar Grove when Mr. W. T. Smith, a farmer living in New York State, just across the line, drove up with his wagon early in the morning to take me to his house, where I was to stay a few days previous to leaving for the Cattaraugus Reservation. I little dreamed, when I arrived at the house, that the end of my journeyings was so near, and that the object of the search which I had almost abandoned in despair was already within a few hours of attainment.

CHAPTER X.

FOUND AT LAST.

The narration of the circumstances which led to the discovery of MATTHEW BRAYTON by his relatives requires us to go back a little from the point to which his account has brought the reader.

The intervening years between the loss of MATTHEW BRAYTON by his relatives and the present time have caused many changes in the neighborhood once so excited in concequence of that loss. The red men clung for many years to their last foothold in Ohio. Four years after the loss of the boy, the Delawares left their village below Upper Sandusky, and set out for their new homes farther West. Two years afterwards the Senecas extinguished their council fires and sought a resting place nearer the Rocky Mountains. But the Wyandots held tenaciously to their homes, and eighteen years passed away before they finally consented to abandon Ohio to the exclusive occupation of the white race.

Fine farms now cover the site of the waste land and woods over and through which the weary hunt for the missing boy was conducted day after day. Towns and villages have sprung up where humble log cabins here and there stood in the incipient clearings, and the huts of the red skins have passed away forever.

The sturdy farmer, ELIJAH BRAYTON, who once returned to his cabin from the weary journey to Chillicothe after millstones, and was met by news that made the blood forsake his parental

The Indian Captive.

heart in a sudden rush, had passed by some years the allotted period of man's life, and is fast progressing towards his fourscore years. WILLIAM, the boy of sixteen who had set out with his little brother on that search for stray cattle, but had returned without him, has reached the meridian of life, and sees around him a young family springing up. Long since, the paternal cabin near the Tymochte Creek has disappeared, and two or three miles away from it, somewhere in the direction where the two brothers had separated thirty-four years ago, a fine brick house has become the dwelling of the oldest son of ELIJAH BRAYTON. Up at Springville, some five or six miles farther to the northwest, and at no great distance from the trail on which the young boy was borne off by the thieving Canadian Indians, lives another brother, PETER, and one of the married sisters. Here also lives the patriarch himself. There are other sisters who mourned when their brother was lost, and they too are married. A son and daughter born to the patriarch of the family after the loss of MATTHEW have long since died, and another son, ASA, younger yet, pursues the practice of medicine in the adjoining town of Carey.

The publication of the "Indian Captive's" narrative in the *Cleveland Herald* was the means of creating considerable interest in his fortunes. The story was extensively copied, and several letters were received by the editors of that paper from people in different sections of the country who had lost children many years ago, it was supposed by means of Indians. None of these letters afforded any clue by which the Indian Captive could trace out his family.

A weekly paper containing the story, copied from the *Cleveland Herald*, was sent by a friend to the BRAYTONS, and this first gave them an idea that there might be a possibility of recovering the missing member of the family. On the 26th of September, one month after the first publication of the narrative, Dr. ASA BRAYTON wrote to the editors of the *Herald*, stating the manner in which he had met with the article, and giving some particulars of the method in which his brother MATTHEW had been lost. About a week afterwards a cousin of the Doctor called at the office of that paper, and made enquiries respecting the Indian Captive. He was followed in a few days by Mr. PETER BRAYTON, one of the brothers of the missing MATTHEW, who went to Warren, O., in search of the "Captive," but lost trace of him there and returned discouraged.

The interest in the subject did not abate, and from time to time the *Herald* gave some intelligence regarding the wanderings of the "Indian Captive." The more the BRAYTONS considered the matter the stronger was their desire to satisfy themselves, and on the tenth of November WILLIAM BRAYTON, the eldest brother, who had accompanied MATTHEW on the morning of the day when the latter was lost, set out with the determination of not returning until he could satisfy himself as to whether the "Indian Captive" was identical with his lost brother, or not.

Previous to setting out, WILLIAM was charged by his father to examine the man for two marks by which his identity could probably be established. One was a scar on the top of the head, caused by a razor cut which the father had made in lancing a boil, and the other was a scar on the great toe of the right foot, resulting from the cut of an axe.

WILLIAM BRAYTON came to Cleveland and learned that the person of whom he was in search had been heard of in Northern Pennsylvania, and was directed where to go. At the place pointed out he struck the trail of the "Captive," and traced him to Sugar Grove. Here he learned that the man had crossed the State line into New York. The chase was too near at an end to allow any delay, so Mr. BRAYTON took along a doctor as witness of the interview, and set out for the house of Mr. SMITH, where it was said that the "Captive" had gone.

It was seven o'clock in the evening when the two arrived at the house, and the daylight was fast fading into darkness. They knocked at the door, and, in response to an invitation from within, entered the house. A man, with his boots off, was drying his feet at the fire. Mr. BRAYTON stepped forward eagerly and enquired where the "folks" were, and was told they were out doing some work in the yard. Mr. BRAYTON said he wanted them called in, and wished a light struck at once, following up the request with the question whether the man to whom he spoke was the "Indian Captive." On being told in the affirmative he became greatly agitated and proceeded at once to get a light. The "Captive" hastily drew on his boots, buckled his dog to his belt, and drew back with suspicion from the strangers. As soon as the light was obtained Mr. BRAYTON bade the "Captive" bare his head, and then both he and his companion examined the spot where his father had told them to search for the scar. The emotion of WILLIAM BRAYTON may be imagined when the scar was plainly revealed to his eyes, unmistakeable in its character, and situated precisely where he had been told to look for it. In an agitated voice he bade the man take the boot from his right foot, which was done, and there too was a scar visible, just where it had been described to exist.

The emotions of WILLIAM BRAYTON may be imagined, but cannot be portrayed. The brother for whose loss he had always reproached himself was at length found through his means, and the sorrows of thirty-four years were at an end. For some minutes he paced up and down the room, his whole frame convulsed with agitation. Then he turned to the cause of all this emotion, who sat perfectly astonished at the proceedings, and the "Indian Captive" was declared to be the long lost MATTHEW BRAYTON.

A letter was at once sent home, containing the glad news of the discovery, and, as soon as possible, the re-united brothers set out in the same direction.

At every station on the road home, crowds gathered, and at Carey, where they were expected to stop, hundreds were collected. Old men who had searched for the lost boy—aged mothers who had held him in their arms—young men who had heard the story narrated by their parents. But the couple stopped five miles north of Carey, at Adrian Station, and at once started for WILLIAM BRAYTON's house.

Here the family were gathered. The old man, seventy-three years of age, but still hale and vigorous—the brothers and the sisters. When the oldest brother entered with his charge the intense feeling that prevailed the hearts of all in the room can scarcely be imagined—cannot be described. The aged father arose, placed his trembling hand on the head of the stranger, and searched for the scar, which he could scarcely distinguish through the mist that filled his eyes. Then he knelt to examine the foot. For a moment every breath was hushed, and the hearts of the other relatives almost ceased to beat. Then the old man tottered to his feet, and with a gush of tears—the stream of affection that had been pent up for the third of a century—fell on the neck of his son—MATTHEW BRAYTON! It is useless to atttempt a description of the scene that followed. The father that had so long secretly mourned for his child—the household pet; the brother who never forgot that it was from his company that the little boy had passed away to a mysterious fate; the other brother who had been his playmate; the sisters who had fondled their little brother in infancy—all were gathered to share in that happy meeting. There was one absent whose presence was needed to make the cup of joy full to overflowing, but her motherly heart might perhaps even then be rejoicing in heaven for the happiness on earth.

The news of the return spread like wildfire. The return was on Thursday the 17th of November. For days afterwards the house was besieged by anxious people eager to see the "boy" so long lost, and so strangely found. Old men who had shared with zeal in that weary and hopeless search thirty-four years ago, came up, and all who had known him as a little boy, acknowledged the identity.

At present MATTHEW BRAYTON, the hero of these strange adventures, is residing with his father and brothers, and has become somewhat reconciled to civilized life. He has abandoned his design of returning to the Indians, and is endeavoring to fit himself for the different lot now assigned him. He has attended school as frequently as the state of his eyes permitted, and can now read a little, as well as converse very readily in the English language. After his thirty-four years of wanderings and hardships it is to be hoped that he will now be content to remain among his family and partake to the full of the blessings of civilization.

Narrative of Larsena A. Page

Garland Publishing, Inc., New York & London
1977

Copyright © 1977
by Garland Publishing, Inc.
All Rights Reserved

Bibliographical note:

this facsimile has been made from a copy in the
Newberry Library
(Ayer.256.P13.1860)

Library of Congress Cataloging in Publication Data

Page, Larsena A
  Narrative of Larsena A. Page.

  (The Garland library of narratives of North America
Indian captivities ; v. 76)
  Issued with the reprint of the 1860 ed. of Bone,
J. H. A. The Indian captive. New York, 1977.
  Reprint of an article entitled The Indian captives,
originally published in the Oquawka spectator, v. 13,
no. 16, 1860.
  1. Apache Indians--Captivities. 2. Page, Larsena A.
3. Indians of North America--Captivities. 4. United
States--Biography. I. Series.
E85.G2 vol. 76 [E99.A6] 973'.04'97s [970'.004'97] [B]
ISBN 0-8240-1700-5   76-54524

Printed in the United States of America

Short Narrative of James Kimball

Garland Publishing, Inc., New York & London
1977

Copyright © 1977
by Garland Publishing, Inc.
All Rights Reserved

Bibliographical note:

this facsimile has been made from a copy in the
Newberry Library
(Ayer.256.K48.K48.1930)

Library of Congress Cataloging in Publication Data

Kimball, James P   b. ca. 1829.
  Short narrative of James Kimball.

  (The Garland library of narratives of North American
Indian captivities ; v. 76)
  Issued with the reprint of the 1860 ed. of Bone,
J. H. A. The Indian captive. New York, 1977.
  Reprint of the 1930 ed. printed for friends of C.E.
Heartman, Metuchen, N.J., which was originally published
in the Cleveland weekly plain dealer, Jan. 30, 1861.
  1. Shoshoni Indians--Captivities. 2. Kimball,
James P., b. ca. 1829. 3. Indians of North America--
Captivities. 4. United States--Biography. I. Title.
II. Series.
E85.G2 vol. 76 [E99.S4] 973'.04'97s [970'.004'97] [B]
ISBN 0-8240-1700-5   76-54520

Printed in the United States of America

NARRATIVE
OF
JAMES KIMBALL

SHORT NARRATIVE

OF

JAMES KIMBALL

ELEVEN YEARS A CAPTIVE

AMONG THE

SNAKE INDIANS

DISCOVERED IN THE
CLEVELAND WEEKLY PLAIN DEALER
OF WEDNESDAY, JANUARY 30, 1861

TWENTY-EIGHT COPIES REPRINTED FOR
FRIENDS OF CHARLES F. HEARTMAN

METUCHEN, NEW JERSEY
1930

No. .... OF TWENTY-THREE COPIES PRINTED

IN the Spring of 1848 when the California gold fever was at its height, a company of sixty-four persons, five of them being wives of members of the party, formed at Syracuse, N. Y., for the purpose of seeking the Golden El Dorado by crossing the Plains. Among the company was a young man named James P. Kimball, then nineteen years of age, and his wife Jane, to whom he was married on New Year's day of that year. At the time he was married he was working a farm near Onondaga Hollow, a village a few miles south of Syracuse. His father, Major Newell Kimball, was a merchant in Syracuse. The late Philo Rust, long proprietor of the Syracuse House and one of the most popular landlords in the country, was his uncle. The father of young Kimball's wife, Rev. James McNeil of Bloody Run, Bedford Co., Pa., a Missionary, was also of the party. The company was composed of men like Kimball, young and adventurous, with strong hands and bold hearts eager to solve the problem of life through toil and peril. The young wife who had been reared tenderly amid the refinements of life gave up her comfortable home without repining and went cheerfully forth with her husband, sharing with him both toil and danger. The company was mostly from Onondaga Co. On the first day of April, 1848, they left Syracuse followed by the prayers and good wishes of their friends, and after they began their journey across the Plains they were never again heard of. It was believed that they all perished by the hands of the hostile Indians.

On Saturday morning last there arrived in this city on board a freight train from Toledo a man with weather beaten visage and long bushy hair sweeping over his shoulders, accompanied by a pale and emaciated woman, sick and worn out with hunger, exposure, and fatiguing journeys on foot. They were James Kimball and his wife, who eighteen months ago escaped from the Snake Indians, with whom they had been captives eleven years, and made their way on foot for thousands of miles, suffering hunger, sickness and danger, to the States. Both were poorly and thinly clothed and bore numerous evidences of what they had passed through in making their way thus far. They remained at the depot all day, and their story becoming known they were provided with food by some of the depot men, and were furnished by the Lake Shore Road with free transit to Buffalo en route for Syracuse, on the night express. Our reporter had an interview with them on Saturday afternoon and obtained the following narrative of their adventures:

STORY OF THE CAPTIVES

The company of sixty-four persons, to which Mr. Kimball belonged, left Syracuse April 1st, 1848, crossed the Mississippi at Quincy and Missouri at Brownville, proceeded to Fort Scott, and thence to Independence, going 212 miles out of their way for the purpose of joining a train which they learned was soon to leave the latter place on the overland route. When they arrived at Independence they found that the train had been gone four days. Being provided with teams and all the necessary outfit for the journey, they hired a mountain pilot and pushed on, hoping to be able to overtake the train. They crossed the Plains by way of Salt Lake and thence proceeded to the Chillicothe Valley, in Oregon. At 3 o'clock one afternoon the little train stopped while passing through the Chillicothe Valley, and prepared to encamp for the night beneath an overhanging cliff. While they were preparing their camp they were suddenly fired upon from the cliff above, where a large force of Indians of the Snake tribe—Indians particularly hostile to the whites and the terror and scourge of overland travellers—were in ambush.

The little band of adventurers prepared to resist the attack as well as circumstances would admit. The women were protected from the shots of the Indians by one of the wagons, while the men carried on the unequal contest (the Indians were nearly two thousand in number) from behind the other wagons. The battle continued without intermission until 10 o'clock the next morning. On the afternoon of the attack about half of the whites were killed. During the night firing continued, but only one man was wounded. The Indians adopted their own peculiar manner of warfare, skulking among the timber which grew upon the cliff, and picking off the men with rifles, with which they were well provided. When the fight ended, only thirteen of the company were alive and they immediately became prisoners. A sister of Mrs. Kimball was among the killed. Mrs K. was badly wounded. The Indians took their prisoners up on what they called Rattlesnake Mountain, seventeen miles from the scene of the fight, and many of the whites being grievously wounded the march was a painful one in the extreme. Arrived there a council was held to decide what disposition should be made of the prisoners. It was decided that all but two should run the gauntlet. One of those exempted was the Mountain Pilot hired at Independence, who was part Indian; the other was the Missionary McNiel, Mrs. Kimball's father, who was reserved to be burned at the stake to appease the spirits of the warriors who fell in battle. Mr. Kimball ran the gauntlet, first for himself and again for his wife. He was allowed a club and a pistol, the rules of the race permitting him to shoot down any person who stepped in front of him while he was running. He shot one Indian who jumped in front of him. He escaped both races with but two blows from clubs, one on the back of his head and the other on the back of his neck.

Mr. McNiel was burned before the eyes of his friends amid dreadful tortures. His body bristled with pine splinters which were driven into his flesh before the fire was built about him, causing fearful agony when they caught fire. His daughter was forced to witness the horrible spectacle, the Indians dancing around their victim with fiendish yells.

The next day the Indians continued on with their prisoners to the territory principally inhabited by their tribe. The whites there joined the tribe as Warriors, Kimball taking the name of "White Cloud." His wife was treated with much cruelty by the Indians during the first years of their captivity. She had a son born shortly after falling into the hands of the Indians, whom they called Warrior, and had three other children during the eleven years following, all of them girls.

After being with the Snakes two years, joining them alike in the hunt and on the war path, Kimball became what the Indians call a "Palmora," meaning a student with the Medicine man of the tribe. The latter was an old man, and after studying with him four years, Kimball succeeded him as Medicine Man, and held that honorable position in the tribe until his flight. The Snakes ranged through Oregon, Washington territory and sometimes upper California.

The other members of his company who joined the tribe became scattered and some of them he has not seen in four years.

During the eleven years that he was a captive Kimball had contemplated escape, but he was watched so closely that no opportunity for successful flight with his family offered for years. He tried to appear perfectly contented, and in the latter years of his stay with them their vigilance relaxed greatly and he was permitted many liberties. He was allowed to take his family and go off on hunts, and coming back always within the time specified, all suspicion was at rest and they believed that he had no desire to leave them. About eighteen months ago Kimball determined on flight, and pretending that he was going off on a two weeks' hunt, he made all the preparation he could for what must be a long and arduous journey to the States.—We neglected to say that some time previous to this Mr. Kimball had met Kit Carson who intimated to him the way in which he could escape from the Snakes and it was upon Carson's suggestions that Kimball acted in going on hunts with his family, thereby accustoming the Indians to his absence. He had had numerous opportunities to escape, but none before with his family.

The tribe was then located about four days' ride from the mouth of the Columbia river, which separates Washington Territory from Oregon. He started on the pretended hunt with his wife and four children. Himself, wife, and "Warrior," who was about eleven years of age, were all armed with rifles. K. had a revolver, and a single barreled pistol, very heavy, which was used by his father, Major Kimball, in the war of 1812. On the fourth day of their flight they were met by five Snake Indians, and Kimball, resolved at once that they must die. They skulked behind trees and as the Snakes advanced they fired upon them killing three. The remaining two skulked behind trees and fired at the whites, one of the shots taking effect in Kimball's left arm and breaking it. (Mr. Kimball exhibited to our reporter the scar caused by the bullet and a scar by the side of it where he had cut the bullet out with his knife.) K. dispatched another of the Indians with his revolver and then followed a contest between himself and the remaining Indian, each trying to take the other at a disadvantage, while preserving his own body from a shot by skulking behind trees. In the meantime Mrs. Kimball had released her rifle and when the Indian intent upon watching Kimball exposed his body to her range she fired and wounded him; as he fell Kimball rushed out and endeavored to dispatch him with the single barrelled pistol, but it wouldn't go off. He then struck him a blow on the head with the butt of the pistol which dispatched him, crushing in his skull and breaking the stock of the pistol nearly from the barrel. He still has the pistol in his possession, broken, and rusted with the blood of the Indian.

Kimball scalped all of the Indians after the style of the Wallawalla tribe, in order that the Snakes, when they discovered the bodies, would think they had fallen by the hands of the Wallawallas, with whom they were at war. On the failure of himself and family to return, they might also conclude that the above Indians had taken them prisoners. The Snake cut off the scalp in a circular and the Wallawallas in a triangular form. They proceeded on their way, and the next afternoon they came upon a company of United States Surveyors—Kimball called them Mountaineers—nearly 150 in number.—One of them set his broken arm. They were going to Fort Laramie, and the fugitives accompanied them there. From thence to Muscatine, on the Mississippi river, they continued on foot, a distance between three and four thousand miles from mouth of the Columbia from whence they started. They suffered incredible hardships during that journey, which consumed several months. A volume might be filled with an account of all they passed through. They were once 5 days without tasting food, and some of the time their way was obstructed by almost impassible snows. Two of his girls died on the way; one, an infant, almost, died in his arms as they were journeying along. The other girl, six years old, died not far from the Muscatine. At a settler's house, where she died, the settler took Kimball's overcoat in payment for keeping the family over night. This was in December last. At Muscatine they remained seven weeks, Mrs. Kimball being sick with a fever brought on by suffering and exposure. They stopped with one John G. Stines, who kept the Pennsylvania House. Our reporter asked Kimball if he had money to pay his bills there. He replied that he had had only two dollars and fifty cents since 1848, about twelve years.—Stines was very kind to them, and trusted them to pay him when they were able. While at Muscatine, his son "Warrior" dropped down dead one evening in the bar-room. The toil and privations of the journey caused his death. They proceeded thence to Fulton, on the Mississippi, and have performed the remainder of the journey by railroad, being furnished with passes by railroad Superintendents to whom they had made known their story.—Their oldest daughter, and now only child, 9 years old, being sick and worn out, was left with a kind family near Iowa City.

Mr. Kimball had a brother named Charles Decatur Kimball. While at the Girard House in Chicago, Mr. K. heard that a man of that name lived in Cleveland. He made inquiries for him here on Saturday, but learned that he had left town.

They failed to obtain a pass from Toledo here and started to walk, but a conductor of a freight train, who had heard their story, took compassion on them and brought them down on his train.

In conversing together in the presence of our reporter they both talked in the Indian tongue. Kimball says he can speak the language of several different tribes. None of his children could speak English.

The woman bears fearful evidence of the suffering she has endured, although there are still traces of former good looks. She exhibited a dent in her skull made by an Indian bullet when the train was attacked. She was wounded in many places during that contest, and her arm was broken by an Indian war club. Her husband set her arm very imperfectly, as our reporter, to whom she exhibited it, could readily perceive. Her condition excited much sympathy among the ladies, on Saturday, who listened to her story in the sitting-room at the depot.—A lady, to whom Mrs. Kimball exhibited her feet, says they are an excruciating sight, the nails being gone entirely, and thick callous places on the bottoms of them, the effects of that terrible journey on foot from the shore of the Pacific, almost, to the Mississippi river.—Mrs. Kimball says she has seen Olivia Oatman, who was for many years a captive among the Indians, and whose interesting narrative has been published and extensively read. Kimball is of medium stature and rather slight in build. He has a most determined grey eye, and his hair is long and bushy. He has alarming spells of spitting blood, caused by the hardships and exposures attending his escape. His narrative, which we have no reason to doubt, is deeply interesting and worthy of a prominent place among narratives of adventures among the Indians.

The Life of Jacob Persinger

Joseph Persinger

Garland Publishing, Inc., New York & London
1977

Copyright © 1977
by Garland Publishing, Inc.
All Rights Reserved

Bibliographical note:

this facsimile has been made from a copy in the
Newberry Library
(Ayer.256.P46.P461.1861)

Library of Congress Cataloging in Publication Data

Persinger, Joseph.
　　The life of Jacob Persinger.

　　(The Garland library of narratives of North American
Indian captivities ; v. 76)
　　Issued with the reprint of the 1860 ed. of Bone,
J. H. A. The Indian captive. New York 1977.
　　Reprint of the 1861 ed. printed for the author by
Moody & M'Michael, Sturgeon? Mo.
　　1. Shawnee Indians--Captivities.　2. Persinger,
Jacob.　3. Indians of North America--Captivities.
4. United States--Biography.　I. Title.　II. Series.
E85.G2　vol. 76　[E99.S35]　973'.04'97s　[970'.004'97] [B]
ISBN 0-8240-1700-5　　　　　　　　　　　　　76-54521

Printed in the United States of America

THE LIFE
-OF-
JACOB PERSINGER

WHO WAS TAKEN BY THE SHAWNEE INDIANS WHEN AN INFANT; WITH A SHORT ACCOUNT OF THE INDIAN TROUBLES IN MISSOURI; AND A SKETCH OF THE ADVENTURES OF THE AUTHOR.

By JOSEPH PERSINGER.

* * *

STURGEON, MO.

Printed for the Author by Moody & M'Michael.

1861.

Reprinted

THE LIFE AND ADVENTURES
OF
JACOB PERSINGER.

The subject of the following memoir, Jacob Persinger, was born in Virginia about the year 1735. When an infant he was captured by the Shawnee Indians and carried to Old Chillicothe, in the State of Ohio, with thirty other children. The squaw who adopted him had two sons. She took great pains to rear them according to Indian usage. Never expecting to give up the white child, she raised him as her own sons. Every morning she would immerse them in water, at all seasons of the year, and make them run about until they were dry, and then take them into her wigwam. When they were young, during several years, she would tie boards to their backs in order that they should grow straight. She took great pains in learning them to swim, and hunt with the bows and arrows; and in a few years she gave her white son a gun. The Indians were still hostile to the whites; they told them that "the whites were cowards and would not stand fire."

When he was about twelve years old, as he supposed, there was a treaty entered into between the whites and Shawnee Indians, by the conditions of which the Indians were under obligations to give up all the white prisoners, both male and female, taken about the time he was. Accordingly, the chief selected a guard to take them through the Alleghany Mountains to the head waters of James river. When they arrived at the place appointed, they informed the whites that they had brought the prisoners. Parents who had lost their children immediately collected to see if they could recognize theirs. It appeared, at that time, that no person claimed him; he became dissatisfied and ran back to his Indian mother. When he arrived, his Indian mother was so rejoiced to see him that she almost went beside herself. She did not conceal him at that time and the chief discovering him, called his warriors together and made to them a speech; the purport of which was, that the treaty be held sacred, and they must take the young man back to his people." The warriors opposed him, stating that they had taken him back once and that was enough. They then retired to their wigwams.

Some time after, the chief summoned his warriors in council, and made another powerful effort to have him sent back; but without avail. The Chief, after some time, concluded he would make one more effort: he called his whole nation togther, and told them that "the treaty should be fulfilled at all hazards." So he appointed three warriors, who took him to the head waters of the James river. During his absence it was ascertained that there was yet a boy held missing; but before the woman who had lost a child got to see him he had made his escape, and went back to the Shawnees a second time. When he returned, his Indian mother concealed him for a considerable time. The chief finally discovered him; whereupon he called his nation together and spoke in quite a different manner. He told them that "the captive must be taken back; that the pale faces were getting powerful; that if they kept him the treaty would be violated and he would be responsible": so they were constrained to consent. The prisoner, hearing that he must be taken back to his people, concluded that his Indian friends had forsaken him, and that he never would return to them again. They commenced their journey through the mountains and arrived safely at the same white settlement from which he had previously made his way back to the Indians. It was soon known in the settlement.

The woman that supposed him to be her son was of German origin, about four and a half feet high; the prisoner, when grown, was about six feet four inches. This woman came to see him, and stated that if he were her son he had a scar on his ancle caused by the bite of a rattlesnake, when hay-making, having taken him into the meadow with her and laid him in the shade. Upon examination no scar was found, consequently she did not believe him to be her son; she also thought him to be too large: notwithstanding she adopted him into her family. There being a Dutch school in the neighborhood, they prevailed on him to go; he went a short time, but could not learn their language. Some time after they sent him to an English school. When going to school he always carried his tomahawk, butcher knife, rifle, and bow and arrows. Teachers in those days being very severe, he concluded that if his own made an attack on him he would kill him and make his escape to the Indians. The teacher discovering, perhaps, that he was a perfect Indian in custom and manners, endeavored to conciliate him by occasionally giving him a piece of money. The whole time he went to school was only three months.

The woman that adopted him, whose name was Persinger, did not treat him as kindly as she did her own children; consequently he became dissatisfied, and concluded he would shift for himself. He left them and went to Stony Creek, and built a wigwam after the Indian fashion. He followed hunting. Everybody wore buckskin then; so hunting was a tolerably good business in those days. He killed a great may bear and deer, and found a ready market at home for the peltry he saved, and made it very profitable. Some time after he discovered a man measuring the land with a chain for some one of the company. He supposed it was intended for hunting ground. He found that this man was paid with money for his surveying; so he concluded that he would have some measured off for himself, and had several surveys made. All a man had to do in those days was to pay the surveyor for his work, eight dollars, for which he gave you a warrant; and that document gave you a good title to the lands, and these surveys would sometimes cover several hundred acres of land.

People, shortly afterwards, began to go in and build cabins, clear the ground, plow it, and raise corn and and vegetables for their own family consumption; when their corn ripened they gathered it, then invited all their neighbors to aid in husking, they would then dance to the merriment of all present. It seems that Jacob Persinger was a particular guest; I presume, because he was raised with the Indians. They took great pains in exhibiting to him the manners, customs and usages of the whites. He at last became better satisfied and built himself a wigwam on one of his surveys, but still followed hunting. It was not long until the young people began to marry in the settlement: he generally received an invitation. He discovered that the couple would stand upon the floor and that ceremony would be said to them, but still he did not understand it. After the marriage ceremony was over they would have a feast, and after the feast they would go to dancing, and enjoy themselves the most of the night in all the mirthful enjoyments of life.

About these times he began to understand the English tongue, and talk so that he could be understood; so after having seen a great many marriages, and having begun to understand the meaning of these weddings, he concluded to get a wife himself, and afterwards married and took a wife to his own wigwam. After they were married, she asked him where his bed was: he pointed to a couple of *black bearskins.* She then told him he must go down to the store and buy some blankets, and have better beds; that she was not accustomed to such beds as bearskins; so he went several miles to a store and traded skins for blankets, with which she made a bed. She told him they must have a house like their neighbors; so he cut logs and built a cabin. I will stop here, and refer back to the time he was given up until he married.

For some cause, I know not what, there was another war commenced between the Shawnees and whites, and General Lewis with his army went against the Indians. This white person was then know by the name of Jacob Persinger, after the name of this Dutch woman's child.

When General Lewis started out against the Shawnees, Jacob Persinger volunteered under Captain Arbuckle and Lieutenant Ganway; all under the command of Gen. Lewis. The officers all discovered that he would make a good spy, and appointed him and a man by the name of James Mooney. Persinger recollected the boasting of the Indians in regard to the cowardice of the whites, and thought, as he said, that he would see whether the whites were cowardly or not, and whether the Indians would not run first. So they started over the Allegany Mountains to the seat of the war, and on their trip they met with many hardships. The Indians had stationed themselves near the junction of the Kanhawa river with the Ohio river; General Lewis made his way over the mountains and established his head-quarters on the point between the two rivers. Persinger and Mooney were put on the scout every morning to reconnoitre the army of the Indians.

Lewis had a strong fort built between the two rivers. The Indians, finding out where the whites were stationed, determined to make a vigorous attack. The chief made three divisions of his army; they crossed the Ohio river in the night, and made arrangements so that one division was to go down the Kanhawa, one down the Ohio, and the third between the wings. The centre was to attack the fort and keep the whites engaged until the two flanks could surround the fort; and at a certain signal they were to charge over the breastworks. But fortunately for the whites, those two celebrated *spires* were on the alert, and discovered the enemy at daylight. Two men were out that morning hunting their horses, and met the Indians marching towards the fort, about the time the spies discovered them. The Indians fired upon them and wounded one of the men, who then ran to the fort and gave the information. A great many men of the army were still in their tents. The scouts ran to the General's marquee and reported to him that the Indians were marching in full force against the fort.

The General ordered all the captains to parade their men on the spot, and to count sixteen men out of every company to march forthwith and meet the Indians before they could get to the fort; the balance of the army the General kept in the fort. The troops that were ordered out marched up the bottom with Persinger and Mooney in company, who, on being discovered by the officers, were directed to take the lead. They ran along in front the lines until they met a strange company with but few in it, about which time they met the beef cattle running in great affright, when Persinger spoke and said, "Now, boys, we will have fun." Some one of the company wished to know who that chap was, and what he knew about it. He told him the cattle had smelled the Indians, and that was a sure sign of their being near at hand.

Immediately a gun was fired to the right of the company, and in a few minutes there was a general peal of rifles all along the lines. Persinger said that when he ran along the lines, he met some of the men running to and fro in every direction, and blood was flowing freely from some of the men. He said he stopped to see if he could see any Indians, and knowing that the Indian mode of warfare was to take a tree as quick as possible, he started and ran to one tree and then to another, and had started to run to a third, when he discovered the feet of an Indian that was lying behind it. He then knew that he was compelled to make his way to the tree and shoot first, if possible; but on arriving at the tree he discovered that some man had given the Indian a dead shot: his gun was lying by his side cocked, and his horn well filled with powder; so he took the Indian's horn, filled his own, then gave it to a man by the name of Ezekiel Johnson, who supplied himself also, and soon afterwards ran to a tree. About this time he said he turned his head and discovered three Indians behind another tree, and one of them could not well conceal himself; he took up the gun of the Indian that was killed, and shot one of the three dead on the spot, and made his escape to another tree farther off for safety.

He said the battle raged hot all day, and late in the evening he saw an Indian shoot a man from behind the roots of a fallen tree; after which he crept as near to him as he possibly could unperceived, and got behind the roots of a large elm that had blown down, from which he saw a man standing behind a tree, who projected his head beyond it, he supposed, to see if he could get sight for a shot at an Indian; when in an instant he heard the report of a rifle, and saw the man fall with a large hole in his forehead. He discovered it was the same Indian that he first saw behind the roots of a tree, loading his gun, but could see nothing but his arm. About the time this Indian got his gun loaded, Persinger said there was a man by the name of David Gleason, standing behind a tree not far off, who stepped out a little to discover the Indian he was trying to get a shot at. The Indian fired, and the ball struck Gleason in the breast; he broke and ran to the fort. Gleason, however, survived the wound, and lived to the good old age of eighty-nine years.

While Persinger was lying behind the roots of the elm he first reached and was watching for an opportunity to discover the Indian's head, another Indian discovered him and fired, the ball striking directly under him; he then jumped up and left the place. Every time an Indian would fire and kill or wound a man, he would give the war-whoop. He then retreated, and had come back some distance before he saw any white, but at length he found several lying behind a log; they said the Indians had retreated, and they had stopped there to rest. He said the first time he noticed any thing except the battle, was the croaking of the ravens that came to deveour the dead; when he looked up, and discovered that the sun was setting. "I did not (said he) think we were engaged more than two hours." He said he then made his way back to the fort, and had no gloomy feelings until he heard the groans of the wounded and dying.

About sunset Persinger went out from the fort and sat down upon a log, when a young Indian came along and hailed him in the Indian tongue: he answered it, and the Indian came to him, who proved to be one of his Indian mother's sons. He said they talked about the war. The Indian told him that he had been sent there to see if there was any chance of attacking them with success, and that the fort would be attacked the next day. He said he told him how near he was being killed, when the Indian gazed upon him for some time, gave a long sigh, accompanied with a loud shriek, shook his head and departed with all the friendship that could be expected from an enemy, by saying that he hoped the next day would settle the matter between them forever.

That night Col. Christy marched into the fort with a battalion of fresh troops: he had the day previous stationed his troops on the mountains, and heard the roaring of the battle, but so indistinctly that they could not account for it; but finally became satisfied that a battle had taken place. By the influence of Colonel Christy they agreed to make a forced march that night at all hazards, which they did. Some time in the night they got safely in the fort, which caused great satisfaction to General Lewis and his army. Before Colonel Christy's arrival Lewis considered himself in imminent peril; because the day after the battle neither army with propriety could claim the victory.

Before the chief had any information of a reinforcement, he sent an interpreter with a message to Lewis that he intended to decide the matter the next day, which caused great alarm in the fort; but an Indian spy who laid in ambush that night, counted Christy's men as they marched into the fort four men deep, went back to his chief and reported the fact of Lewis's reinforcement, which caused the chief to abandon the idea of attacking the fort.

So, on the next morning, every thing was arranged for a general engagement by the whites; but when the spies came and reported that the Indians had re-crossed the Ohio river, and were stationed on the opposite bank, they went out and hallooed to the Indians, wishing to know why they did not give them battle as they promised to do. The old chief took hold of a small sprout, twisted it into a knot, after which he went to a sapling and tried to twist that, but could not do so; that was done to show that he had twisted them the day before, but could not do so now; and also showed to the army of the whites that he had discovered Christy's battalion when it made its appearance the night before. But if the Indians had renewed their attack immediately after the battle they would have undoubtedly captured all the men in the fort; for they were hungry, weak, fatigued, and nearly destitute of ammunition, save the horn of powder that Jacob Persinger took from the Indian found at the foot of the tree. The Shawnee chief's plan was exceeding wise for attacking the fort next day. He intended to divide his army in three divisions, as he did the day before: let the two wings at night march in silence on either side of the fort and conceal themselves so close, that when they made their appearance the next day the fire of the guns could do but little execution, until they could storm the fort; and the chief, with his chosen band of warriors in the centre, could so distract the whites, by firing upon them first, and divert their attention so much that few Indians would be killed from either wing. But, fortunately, by the reinforcement of Christy's army, and the alacrity and skill of the two celebrated spies, the men in the fort were inevitably saved from a horrid massacre and torture by the Indians. The war was, for that time, settled with the Shawnees. The wounded men were put in charge of the two spies, and conveyed by them in safety up the Kanahawa river to their relations. Jacob Persinger returned to his residence. Thus ended that campaign.

Some time after he returned to his home he courted and married a fine and amiable lady, by the name of Mary Kimberlin, and then turned the most of his attention to his little farm. It seems, from the manner in which he conducted his farm, that he was endowed with some supernatural power to aid him in that capacity; for he conducted it with such skill and ingenuity that one might believe he was reared a farmer. He raised all kinds of vegetables to supply all his neighbors bountifully, and had plenty of other things to keep his family supplied with every thing needful. After the cropping season was over, every year, Jacob Persinger was always found in search of *bear* and *deer,* while he was able to walk over the mountains, and kept his family well supplied with all kinds of game. It is rather remarkable that, as fond of hunting as the subject of this was, he kept his farm in the most elegant style, and allowed nothing noxious to grow on it. His fencing was well built; his house though rough was neat, his cattle and horses always fat; and no creature around or about him ever suffered in want of anything as long as Jacob Persinger had any thing to contribute to their wants. His neighbors thought that whatever he said was law, and that any calculation made by him was correct. Notwithstanding, the only three months' education he ever received entitled him to all the confidence and respect of his friends, together with his stability, integrity, and firmness. He was always, to the end of his life, the self-same Jacob Persinger. He was a man fond of civil, social, and mirthful enjoyment; and would frequently invite his friends and neighbors to come and partake of a sumptuous repast, and divert themselves with one of the common pleasures of those days, which was "to trip on the fantastic toe."

Amidst the height of his farming, and, as he supposed,, of his peaceful retirement to the society of his beloved wife and children, the Revolutionary war began; and thus feeling the endearment of family ties, the welfare of his lovely children—to see them oppressed by the tyrannical yoke of Britain he could not endure. He related the condition of his country to his beloved Mary; and told her how his blood ran when he thought that his and her children should become subjects to such despotism. His emotions he could not control. His wife saw them and earnestly entreated him to withhold from the war if possible; but if his country needed his service, as much as it would grieve her to part with him, it was nothing but right that he should go. And she further said, "Now go, Jacob, and God be with you; myself and children can make a good support for me and them, and have something for you after your return." And Jacob Persinger did go. What man after receiving the encouragement he did from so lovely a wife, and possessing a spark of patriotism, would not then shoulder his gun and march in defense of his country's rights? Jacob Persinger did, so he took his gun and proceeded to the army immediately, and there received a commission; but what commission I am not able to say, and fought bravely in defence of his country; and after the war he retured to his family. Jacob Persinger raised a respectable family; but for the want of sufficient means he failed to give them a good common education. The name of his sons were Andrew, Alexander, Joseph, and John.

Alexander and Joseph emigrated to Missouri, in which state they have ever since lived; both married and raised respectable families. Alexander moved to Montgomery county, in this state. Whilst living in that county he was elected several times to the Legislature; and then afterward was judge of the same county for nine years; and then moved to Boone county, and presided as one of the county judges until August, 1860.

Joseph was of a different temperament from Alexander, entirely; he was fond of hunting, dancing, and fishing. It seems that the backwoods or frontier life was most suitable to him. He once became a candidate for the Legislature of Boone county, against one of the most conspicuous men of those days, and was defeated by only a small majority; the cause of his defeat was that he was the candidate of the weaker party, but outrun his ticket by three hundred. He has been enrolling clerk of the Legislature, sergeant-at-arms, and doorkeeper of the Senate for several consecutive years. Whilst not engaged in his public pursuits, he would be found closely engaged in what he desired above all pleasures—hunting bear or deer, or dancing. He is a great violinist, and amuses to the present day all persons with whom he associates. He is a large man, weighs about two hundred and seventy pounds. He has killed more bear, deer, and caught more beavers, than any other man in Missouri. There is something more about this man Joseph Persinger; he was taught by his father that it is the duty of every man to love, revere, and respect his country and his country's rights.

In an early day the Sioux Indians became very troublesome, and did a great deal of mischief in Howard and other adjoining counties, and committed depredations of the worst kind. Joseph Persinger was ever ready to take up his gun and follow them as far as any man. The Indians once stole some horses from Howard county, and at the same time took with them a negro man from a man by the name of Baxter, and made their way east. Baxter and his son went in pursuit of them, and followed their trail over the Grand Prairie until they came to a branch which is now running through Audrain county, eight miles west of the county seat, called Mexico; there they discovered fresh traces of the Indians, which proved the Indians were near. Baxter alighted from his horse and told his son to hold him, and not let him make a noise, for he would soon come back. So he went into the hazel brush, on the south side of the stream and discovered the Indians building up a fire; after which time, he immediately returned and told his son to keep as still as possible, and also to keep the horses still; that, if the Indians knew they were there, there would be no possible chance of escape from them. They kept still untill it had become dark; then Baxter went to the edge of the water and sat down. Shortly afterwards an Indian came to the stream, sat down and stayed there sometime, then got up and went back to the camp, wrapped his blanket around him and laid down near the other Indians. There were eight in company with the negro. Baxter waited after that for some time, until he found they had full time to get to sleep; his weapon was nothing but a tomahawk with a spike on the pole of it, which was very sharp. He then proceeded to cross the creek very easily, which was about waist deep, crept up the bank very cautiously, until he reached the top, stood for a few minutes, like a tiger watching his prey; and then, with all the power and ability he could possibly summon, he pounced upon them and soon dispatched the whole of the Indians, by sticking the sharp poll of his tomahawk in the heads of every one. He then awoke his negro man, and told him to go and tell his son to come to the camp. The negro went and told his young master what his old master had done; they both then returned to the camp, and with the old man, all three laid down and slept upon the ground on which the Indians were captured. The next day they gathered their horses and made their way back to Howard county, the place of their abode. The circumstances above related was the cause of that branch, which is now meandering its course through Audrain county, being called Skull Lick.

Several years after this transaction of Baxter's took place with the Indians, the people began to hunt and then to settle there. They discovered skulls lying about on the creek, and saw large holes in them; they concluded them to be the skulls of the Indians that Baxter killed, and called the stream "Skull Lick." I presume this stream will bear that name as long as time lasts.

I will tell you of another battle that took place shortly after Baxter killed the seven Indians on *Skull Lick*. Again there were more horses stolen from the whites. They collected together a small company, and started immediately in pursuit of them, in order to recover their property. They followed after them as far as St. Charles county, and then lost all traces of them; when they concluded to return. On arriving at Loutre Lick, (not suppossing any danger;) they travelled unguarded. At the prairie fork of Loutre, where it empties into the main stream of Loutre creek, there is a high bluff on the north side of the stream that runs back from it several yards. The whites were between prairie fork and the main stream. Upon this bluff the Indians were lying in ambush, and fired upon the whites. They saw no possible chance of escape, but to swim the main stream so those who could swim pitched into the creek, but few, if any, ever got across—those who stayed behind were massacred and killed by the merciless hands of the savages. Thus ended one of the most brutal murders that was frequently committed by the Indians in Missouri in those days.

At another time the same company of Indians came in and stole several head of horses, besides other property. Colonel Cole had command of the rangers at that time. He collected them together, as quick as possible, and started in pursuit of the Indians, and overtook them on the waters of the *Salt river,* and demaded their stock. The old chief met them very friendly. Cole asked him why he allowed his warriors to take their horses? The Chief said there were some of his men he could not control and they should have all their horses without any difficulty, and readily gave them up. The whites started back with their stock, traveled until night overtook them.

The Colonel was unwilling to camp; but his men remonstrated, and told him they entertained no danger; but Colonel Cole said to them that he knew the customs of Indians too well to stop at that time; that they were sure to follow them, and probably, if they did camp, kill several of them. The men, feeling themselves greatly fatigued, opposed Cole very much; even his four brothers, who were in company, seemed desirous that they should camp; and also charge him with cowardice. Cole then remarked if they were willing to risk their lives he was willing to share the same fate with them; so he immediately ordered them to strike camp, let the result be as it might. About midnight the Indians made the attack. The camp-fires of the whites were blazing up greatly, and made every man a good target for the Indians. The Indians came up behind the men, and, as soon as they got near enough, they let off a volley of guns, which killed and wounded together nearly every man in the camp. Col. Cole was slightly wounded: he saw his four brothers fall at the first fire. The Indians rushed in the camp with their tomahawks and knives to kill all that were left alive, and to scalp all they could kill. One Indian attacked Cole with a knife, but Cole, being a very athletic man, kept the Indian from killing him for some time: but the Indian still pressed on him, and at length stabbed Cole five or six times. Cole knew that it was death or victory; and, notwithstanding the loss of blood he had sustained, he clinched the Indian, threw him into the fire, and held him there until he burnt to death.

Whilst Cole was holding the Indian in the fire he hallowed manfully for help; but the other Indians were so closely engaged in murdering and scalping the whites they paid not attention to the burning Indian, if they heard him. Cole seized his gun, hurried out of camp, and sat down by the root of a tree, quite faint and weary. Afterwards the Indians came back to the fire and began to scalp those of the whites they had missed before. The blood was running from Cole's wounds very profusely; he discovered a large Indian, about the fire, making gesticulations and motions, throwing and brandishing his hatchet in the air in every direction. Cole thinking at that time, death was certain; so, weak as he was, he raised his gun and shot the Indian dead, who went tumbling into the fire. From that report the Colonel expected every minnute to be killed; but the shot seemed to alarm the Indians, and they shortly moved off out of the reach of the ear. Cole started to travel, in order to get as far from the battle ground as possible by daylight. He traveled until he became so weak that he laid down expecting never more to rise a live man; but, after resting until the following evening, he found he could travel again, and attempted to rise, but found his clothes so stiff with blood that it was almost impossible to walk; so he threw away his gun and started out again. He had not traveled far when he heard a sharp whistle, which he immediately knew to be the whistle of a hunter. He answered it. A white man came to where he was and assisted him in getting home.

The man told Cole that he had gone out hunting that day and had discovered the battle ground, and saw some traces of blood leading off from the place; he concluded to follow them up and aid the one that needed it—and this is the way he found Cole. He got well of his wounds, and lived many years afterwards, and made a useful man during his life. This same Cole is the man for which Cole county in this State is named. A short time after this massacre of the whites took place the chief came to the whites and made proposition for a treaty with them; but told them that he had about fifty young warriors who would not come into any treaty they could make, and that he would not become responsible for any depredations they might commit; but probably, through his influence, the warriors would become less reckless, and they might, at some future time, become willing to go into treaty. However, the whites concluded to make a treaty on as amicable terms as possible; and thus concluded a treaty with the chief.

Not long after this treaty was made some hunters went down on the Bon-Femme creek to find some game and, in traveling down an Indian path in pursuit of game, they discovered the head of a white man sticking upon a pole; they became alarmed, immediately went back and reported what they had seen. The whites collected together as quick as possible, made arrangements to catch the murderers, and started off to where the head was found; they found two men had been killed, which exasperated them very much. They then entered into a compact that they would hunt from day to day until they found the murderers; and seek revenge by taking the lives of those who committed the atrocious deed. They started and travelled over a considerable scope of country, and at length saw an Indian alone; took him prisoner, and interrogated him in regard to the murder of the two men; but he stoutly denied having any knowledge of the murder at all. They then asked him if he knew of any Indians; he told them he did; that they were then stationed on the point between the creek and the Missouri river.

The white men immediately set out to march against them. They proceeded to get as close as possible unobserved, and they succeeded. They crossed over the creek as easy as possible, and formed a line that extended from the creek to the river. When they marched upon the Indians they found them playing *bandy*. They made a rush and got between them and their guns. The Indians knew their only chance for safety would be either to swim Bon-Femme creek or the Missouri river; but the whites were too fast for them; they made a charge and killed off forty-nine, all except one; he escaped with a broken arm. After the battle was over, the whites took the Indian prisoner upon the bottom or low ground on the Missouri river, told him if he wished to save his life, he could get clear by out-running any one man in the company. The Indian readily acceded to this proposition, and started off at full speed; but a man by the name of Fuget started after him, caught him immediately, and led him back to the company. The whites told him they would give him another chance; that he might commence running, and after he got a certain distance from them they were to commence firing—and if none of the balls struck he should go uharmed.. The Indian started at full speed again; after he got to the required distance he ran in an angular direction; but the poor creature did not get far until he fell dead, with seven bullet holes in him. This defeat of the Indians settled the war with them for some time.

The next Indian war was with the Indians that lived on the North Grand river. The people from the northern parts of Howard and Boone counties had suffered considerably from the thefts that had been committed upon their borders, and concluded to raise a company and find out the locality of the Indians. Colonel Field Trammel commanded the company. After reaching the waters of Grand river, they understood that many depredations had been committed there; they immediately went in pursuit of them and found them encamped on Chariton creek, near the boundary line of Missouri and Iowa. Trammel marched up to the Indians' camp, and called out the chief, (Big Neck), and insisted upon his coming out, which he did. Trammel then told him he wanted him to give up all the stock they had taken from the frontier settlers. The chief replied that all the stock they had was about paid for at that time, and also made a great preliminary speech in regard to the stock. By this time the Indians had collected entirely around Trammel's men, when the chief ordered his men immediately to cock their guns. A man by the name of Myers saw that the Indians were about to fire upon them, so he made a rush and took the head of their interpreter off; thus the conflict commenced, and in a short time there were several whites killed. Those that were left alive made a rush, broke the Indian lines and made their escape, but were hotly pursued by the Indians for many miles. On the return of the Indians to the battle-ground, they piled logs together and burned all the bodies of the dead.

Some time after this, General Owen Crawley started in search of the Indians, together with M. Horner, commander of a company, and Joseph Persinger, commander of another company. After marching several days they overtook the Indians, who, finding themselves over-powered, retreated towards Rock Island, on the Mississippi; but some of the whites pursued and overtook them. The chief surrendered unto them with all his warriors. They were confined and taken to the Howard county jail to await their trial at the regular term of Howard Circuit Court. The trial came on, and the Indians proved the whites to have been the aggressors, and were acquitted according to law; thus they were released.

After this trial there were some white men that went and traded with the Indians, and bargained with them for all their wives, upon the condition, that if they, the Indians, would let them have their squaws, the whites

LIFE AND ADVENTURES OF JACOB PERSINGER   19

would, at a certain time, give up all their white women. The Indians readily acceded to the proposition, and presently went to the white women and claimed them as their property; but the women treated them with disdain and refused to have anything to do with them. These refusals greatly enraged the Indians, and they swore they would take revenge; so they commenced retaliating by killing all the hogs they could find, and stealing all the horses they could lay their hands upon.

The next trouble between the Indians and the whites was the war with Black Hawk. This chief and his tribe committed many depredations in the State of Illinois; in fact all the ravages were confined to that State. But the people of Missouri, hearing of these butcheries and thefts, concluded at once to assist her sister State in repelling her savage foes, if they should perchance cross the Mississippi river. A detachment of men was sent to the Des Moines river, to be in readiness to receive the Indians should they at any time attempt to cross the Mississippi; these troops being commanded by Austin A. King and Sinclair Kirtley. The only fear entertained by these commanders was, that if Black Hawk should cross over into Missouri, he would be aided by his brother-in-law who was living in this State and commanded many warriors, although he held out the idea that he was not interested in this war. While the Indians of Illinois were preparing for a general war, Generals Scott and Atchison were moving towards them for an attack; but the Indians timely discovered their movements, and retreated up the Mississippi. The whites pursued and overtook them immediately on the bank of the river, and had them so completely surrounded that their only alternative was to swim the river, which they undertook to do; but the sharpshooting whites picked them off, one by one, so fast, that in a short time there was scarcely an Indian to be seen in the water except Black Hawk and a few others, who made their escape up the river; but were captured by some friendly Indians and taken back to Scott and Atchison, who took them and kept them until a treaty was made by Black Hawk with the whites.

I will now go back and relate a strange circumstance that took place a short time after Jacob Persinger was married. In those days the people of the western part of

Virginia would search the caves in the mountains for black bear; and whenever they killed one they would make bacon of it, which is very fine indeed. The bear is a very singular animal. About Christmas, it generally takes up its winter quarters, which are generally in a cave; but, before finally entering for the winter, it lays out for several days without eating, until all the excrementitious matter is ejected from its bowels, then it enters the cave, and remains there until spring. A short time after the female enters her cave she brings forth her young, which are generally from two to four in number. The cubs, immediately after their birth, crawl to the teats and suckle, and do not let it out of their mouths until spring. At the time they are first brought forth they are not larger than a mouse, and are entirely destitute of hair.

Jacob Persinger and a son of the German woman spoken of previously, concluded they would go in quest of bear. It was not long after they started that they came to a small cave, which they proceeded to examine, and soon discovered in it a very large one. They fired their guns, and, after waiting until they thought the bear was dead, made preparations for hauling him out. Jacob Persinger took a rope and went into the cave, while the German boy stood on the outside. As soon as Jacob got in, he told the German that the bear was dead, for he then tied the rope around the bear's hind leg and came out; but just as he got to the entrance of the cave, the bear ran out past him and made its escape.

I will now tell you something about the beaver, an animal with which I am well acquainted. I got my first information about the beaver from William Baxter, the gentleman that killed the Indians on *Skull Lick,* of which mention has already been made. I was then young, and the idea of trapping beaver was my greatest delight. Baxter invited me to go with him, and promised to show me how to catch beaver. Baxter had but one trap; I managed to get another from Nathan Boone, which his father (Daniel Boone, the pioneer of the western country) had left him.

Baxter and I started up the Perche and soon found signs of the animal: we set our traps and soon caught five. From there we went to a place on the Missouri called the Thousand Islands, situated just below Nashville, there set our traps, and caught eleven. By this time I thought myself perfect in trapping beaver, but I still continued with my old preceptor. The greatest mystery in catching beaver is procuring the bait. The beaver has at the extremity of its intestines from four to six lumps, about six inches long and one inch in diameter; these are called castors. You take one of these and fasten it on your trap, and place it about five inches above the water. As soon as the beaver gets scent of the bait, which it can do at a goodly distance, it proceeds forthwith to the trap, and is caught by the foot. If it is in deep water, it drowns; but if it should fail to get into deep water, it gnaws its own foot off.

The beaver cuts down trees with its teeth from four inches to two feet thick, which I have myself seen. One beaver cannot do much by itself; but they assemble together in la.ge numbers, and build dams across small streams to float their timber into larger streams, where they build their houses. I have seen logs cut off eight feet long, but how they got them to the water I have never been able to learn. The Indians think they pull the logs into the water with their tails. These dams will stand for several years. The manner in which they build their dams shows that they have great instinct: they set the timbers endwise in the mud with the top leaning down stream, so that the water and mud, pressing upon them, give them greater strength. The beaver's hind feet are webbed like those of a goose, but its forefeet are not; its tail very much resembles that of a fish, having scales, but rather darker in color.

Isaac Vanbiber and myself were once trapping on Big Loutre creek: we caught eleven. We knew there were more there; but they became so shy that they would not come out of their houses. We then left, returning again in about two weeks, and again set our traps. One more was caught but it cut its foot off and made its escape. Van Biber said if we would change the bait, we could catch more; so we took fresh bait taken from the beaver, set our traps, and that night caught the same beaver that had its foot cut off, and one other that we had left from the first trapping. This shows that the beaver will risk its life for the musk other beavers contain.

I will now give you an idea how we caught young

buffalo and young elk. We would take gentle milch cows out on the prairie, and when we found a herd of buffalo or elk we would get behind the cows and drive them towards the herd; the old buffalo of the herd would then run off and leave the calves lying in the grass; we would then drive a cow up to a calf, when it would immediately jump up, run to the cow, and suckle it just as if she was its mother.

I will also show how we captured the black bear and the cubs. Priestly H. McBride, John Ashby Snell, and myself, went out on a hunting excursion on Salt river. Shortly after we crossed it, we discovered a large bear standing on its hind legs, shot it and McBride and I ran up to it, and McBride shot it in the head. While we were skinning it we heard a noise up a tree, and on looking up, we discovered a cub, which immediately jumped down and started off: it came near falling on Snell. I started after it and caught it, but had to kill it with my knife. We began then to look around, and discovered another in a lynn tree. I proposed to them that if they would cut the tree, I would tie it, as I had a rope with me. They set to work and soon had the tree down: just as the tree fell, I threw the rope around its neck and threw and held it down, when it began to bite and claw me considerably; I then let it up, and tied the rope to a tree standing near by; after which it became quite gentle. Before we were done butchering the first bear that was killed, another came down a tree; when I started after it and ran it up another tree, and McBride shot it. McBride and I put the live cub upon Snell's horse, behind him, to carry it home. After they got there, we took it off and put in the yard with our dogs: it immediately became attached to them, and during its stay it never did any harm—only, when the family would leave the house it would go in, pull off all the bed coverings, place them on the floor, get upon them and go to sleep. This bear became very fond of hunting; sometimes when we went on a hunt it would follow the dogs. One morning we went out on a fox hunt; the dogs started one, the bear followed, and in the chase it got so far from us that it never returned.

I was once in the Alleghany mountains hunting. I discovered a large female bear under a chestnut tree, with two cubs, feeding on chestnuts. In trying to get a shot, I saw her strike one of the cubs on the head, which caused it to run up a tree; when she immediately struck the other, which caused it to also climb a tree, and as soon as they were up she ran off. I then knew she had scent of me; but she soon came back, and I killed her and both the cubs.

I was once in the mountains fishing for trout, along with a man by the name of Tucker. I saw the track of a bear not far from us. He replied, as he had never seen a wild bear, he would be glad to get a shot at it, and took his gun and started off. I told him he had better be cautious, for if it should chance to be a dam with cubs, she might prove very dangerous. He started out towards a small piece of bottom land not far from us, and as soon as he got out of sight I heard a gun fire and a cub squall; and directly I saw Tucker coming full tilt, and the bear close after him. On coming to the water, he jumped in up to his neck. The bear stopped on the bank and looked at him; and while standing there I levelled my gun and shot her dead. I then endeavored to prevail on Tucker to go with me and show me where the cubs were; but he would not go. So he left his gun and would fish no more that day.

At another time, a young man by the name of Harmon and myself started out for a deer lick, and whilst going thither we saw a young bear coming down the hill to get water. Harmon said he wanted a pet, and would try to catch it; so he started after it and ran it up a tree. He said he would climb the tree and tie the cub if I would watch for the old one, and started up. As soon as he got near the cub, it began to bawl; and immediately the old bear came full tilt, ran past me, and commenced climbing the tree; but, being small, it was difficult for the bear to reach Harmon. As Harmon looked down at the old bear, I saw he would soon fall; so I quickly raised my gun and shot the bear dead. Harmon and the bear both fell together. The cub fell shortly afterwards; when I caught it, took it to Harmon's father and made him a present of it. He kept it until it was full grown, and then killed it: it weighed four hundred pounds. But young Harmon never entirely got over his fright from the old bear.

On another occasion, a man named Edgar and myself went to the mountains to gather chestnuts; he had a dog with him. We had not gone far into the mountains when the dog gave us to understand that game was near. Edgar said he thought it was a panther, and would hiss the dog on that he might tree it, as they were very easy animals to tree. We heard the dog bark once, and presently we saw him coming back as fast as he could, and a bear close at his heels, snapping at him at every jump. The dog, in order to save himself, ran between Edgar's legs; and the bear ran against him and knocked him over. The bear soon discovered that she was among enemies and, starting off, ran some distance from us before I could shoot; but I soon "drew a bead," when a shot from my gun laid her dead. A bear will fight harder and more bravely for their young than any other animal. The panther is a very cowardly animal; a small dog can run one off at any time. I once found in a cave seven young panthers, and took hold of them, upon which they made a great noise; but the old ones, although they showed themselves, would not come near enough for me to get a shot. A young panther, when as large as a full grown cat, is spotted like a fawn.

In conclusion, I will give a brief account of a battle that Linsy Carson, had with the Fox Indians at a place on Black Water creek, (now in Macon county,) Missouri. The Indians had stolen several horses from some of the citizens of Howard county. Carson, with his rangers, went in pursuit of them, and found them encamped on Black Water. Carson sent one James Cockeral as a spy to reconnoiter the Indians, who reported, on his return, that the Indians were playing baudy. Carson then ordered that one man to every five horses should stay and hold them, while the others should go into battle. As there were two Indians to one white man, three of the latter concluded that it would not be safe to go into action, so started off and took a position on a neighboring height from whence they could see the fight. Carson's attack took the Indians by surprise; but they soon rallied, and the warriors divided into three bands, and came very near surrounding the whites. Cockeral first saw the danger and gave instant notice to Carson, who at once ordered a retreat towards their horses, which was safely effected; but just as they reached them, an Indian fired and the ball took off two of Carson's fingers. The Indians came on shouting and laughing, expecting an easy capture; but Cockeral assisted Carson in getting on his horse, and all made their escape but the three men who would not fight.

In Captivity

Samuel J. Brown

Garland Publishing, Inc., New York & London
1977

Copyright © 1977
by Garland Publishing, Inc.
All Rights Reserved

Bibliographical note:

this facsimile has been made from a copy in the
Newberry Library
(Ayer.*f256.B795.B795.1896)

Library of Congress Cataloging in Publication Data

Brown, Samuel J   1845-1925.
   In captivity.

   (The Garland library of narratives of North American Indian captivities ; v. 76)
   Issued with the reprint of the 1860 ed. of Bone, J. H. A. The Indian captive. New York, 1977.
   Reprint of an article entitled Reminiscenses of the Sioux massacre and war of 1862, originally published in the Daily & weekly review, Mankato, Minn., 1896?
   1. Dakota Indians--Wars, 1862-1865. 2. Dakota Indians--Captivities. 3. Brown, Samuel J., 1845-1925. 4. Indians of North America--Captivities. 5. United States--Biography. I. Title. II. Series.
E85.G2 vol. 76   [E83.86]   973'.04'97s [977.6'04] [B]
ISBN 0-8240-1700-5   76-54522

Printed in the United States of America

IN CAPTIVITY.

The Experience, Privations and Dangers of Sam'l J. Brown, and Others, while Prisoners of the Hostile Sioux, during the Massacre and War of 1862.

Also, an Account of the Perilous Ride made by Mr. Brown in 1865, to save the Frontier Settlement from Attack.

The following historic sketch, written by Mr. Brown, was published in the Daily and Weekly REVIEW, and embraces the only authentic account of the Sioux Massacre and War from the Indian side. Mr. Brown, his mother, and sisters and brothers were prisoners with the hostile Indians from the beginning of the massacre, August 18th, 1862, until the release of the captives by General Sibley the latter part of September of the same year.

The writer is a son of the late Major Joseph R. Brown, probably the brainiest man among the early settlers of Minnesota. At the time of the Sioux outbreak Major Brown's family was living in their comfortable home within a short distance of the Sioux agencies, and south of the Minnesota river. The writer has a remarkable memory, which, with the aid of a diary kept at the time, has enabled him to recall some intensely interesting incidents of captivity, and the dangers attending their retention in the hostile country.

The incidents have never before been published, they are told in an interesting manner, he writes fluently and his descriptive powers are graphic, and the article is a valuable contribution to Minnesota history, and especially the exciting period incident to the Sioux massacre and war.

FOR SALE AT REVIEW OFFICE, MANKATO, MINN.
PRICE, 10 CENTS EACH.

REMINISCENSES.

Of the Sioux Massacre and War of 1862.

Thrilling Incidents of Captivity With the Indians—By Saml. J. Brown, Esq. of Brown's Valley.

JOHN C. WISE, ESQ., Mankato, Minn.

MY DEAR SIR:—In furnishing you with the following papers relative to the captivity of myself, mother, sisters and brothers, among the Indians during the Sioux outbreak of 1862, and of my ride during the war following the outbreak, I wish to say that the material was gleaned principally from diaries kept by myself and other members of the family, and the notations are supposed to be correct. These papers were originally prepared for the late Gov. Marshall, who wanted them for the Historical Society, but his death ended the idea of furnishing them as contemplated, and I take pleasure in submitting them to you for publication.

A Brief History of the "Sioux of the Mississippi"

so called in contradistinction from the "Sioux of the Missouri"—seems necessary to a proper understanding of the subject in hand. At the time of the outbreak the Mdewakanton and Wahpekoota bands, under the leadership of Little Crow, the Sioux chief, the Sisseton and Wahpeton bands were living upon a reservation, and had an agency exclusively their own on the Minnesota river, above or north of the Yellow Medicine creek, and these bands were known as the Upper Sioux and the agency as the Upper or Yellow Medicine agency. Below or south of the Yellow Medicine creek, and also on the Minnesota river, were the Mdewakanton and the Wahpakoota bands also owning a reservation and an agency; these were known as the Lower Sioux and the agency as the Lower or Redwood agency. The Upper and Lower agencies were about 30 miles apart, and the business affairs of both were conducted under the supervision of one agent. These Indians were accustomed to meet at their respective agencies each year to receive their annuities, and were gathered in 1862 for this purpose. Owing to the delay of the disbursing agent they were kept in great distress for lack of food for nearly two months, waiting for their annuities.

The lower bands becoming impatient and because of wrongs, either real or supposed, which it is not worth while to mention in this connection, finally broke out and the dreadful massacre of 1862 followed. A few of these (lower) Indians remained loyal to the government, and some of them became scouts, but the bands, as bands, were engaged in hostilities. While a few of the young men of the upper bands joined in the hostilities the bands, as bands, were loyal to the government. They were principally instrumental in bringing about the final release of the captives, joined and did good service with the expeditions sent against the hostile Indians, rendered most valuable and efficient service as "avenging angels" of Fort Wadsworth or Totanka Republic, killing many Indians who were on hostile raids, and finally by the terror they inspired among the hostile Indians, stopped all hostile expeditions against the whites. The number of persons, according to the census, upon which the upper bands were paid their annuity money in 1861—last payment—was 4,524, and of this number seventeen were condemned to death. The number of persons, according to the census, upon which the lower bands were paid their annuity money in 1861—last payment previous to outbreak—was 3,213, and of this number 286 were condemned to death. Of the upper bands two were hung, and of the lower thirty-six.

At the time of the outbreak I was residing with my parents in a fine stone house, elegantly furnished, twenty-five miles above the lower or Redwood agency, and seven miles below the upper or Yellow Medicine agency, on the opposite side of the Minnesota river. This house was totally destroyed by the Indians, during the first week of the massacre, and the entire family (except my father who was absent looking after his steam wagon venture) made captives by Little Crow.

The following particulars connected with the affair are mainly notations taken from my old diaries and I do not hesitate to vouch for its absolute correctness.

FIRST INTIMATIONS OF OUTBREAK.

On Monday, the 18th of August, I went to Yellow Medicine with my sister Nellie, to get some washing done. On the way an Indian named Little Dog came out of his house, as we passed by, and beckoned to us to stop. We did so and he approached us and as he came up we could see that he was troubled. He told us breathlessly that the lower bands had broken out and killed everybody at the agency, and were slaughtering the whites in the vicinity of Beaver Creek, and that they were killing everybody without mercy and without regard to age or sex, and intended to sweep the country as far as St. Paul. He begged us to turn back, tell mother, and get out of the country. He said that he warned us at the risk of his life. Little Dog was a "farmer" Indian, one of that band of Sioux braves who had their hair cut, their scalp locks taken from them by Uncle Sam in 1858, who discarded the Indian dress for that of the white man—the breech cloth for the pantaloon—who lived in a brick house instead of a skin tepee, drove oxen instead of horses, and depended for his subsistance upon the plow and hoe instead of the bow and arrow. As Little Dog has attributed his present prosperous condition with this change to my father when he was Indian agent from 1857 to 1861, he naturally had a warm spot for his family. But the Indian was an inveterate liar. Indeed he was regarded as one of the greatest liars in the country, and besides, "Indian scares" had become so frequent that we paid no attention to the warning and drove on. This was about noon, and as we were passing the agency headquarters, one and a half or two miles further on, George Gleason, the government clerk there, came out to our carriage and chatted with us. He said he was going away that afternoon with Mrs. Wakefield—wife of the agency physician—he to visit his people in the east, and she to visit with friends at Shakopee, Minn. He promised that when he got back he and Hon. James W. Lynd would visit with us at our home, and spend the fall hunting, fishing, horseback riding, etc. About three miles further on we arrived at the washerwoman's—near Dr. Williamson's old mission station. As we were coming away an old Indian woman came up and told us (in a whisper) that we had better be getting away, as there would soon be trouble. We drove rapidly to the agency and stopped at John Fadden's for dinner. We there asked an Indian woman, who was doing washing at the hotel, if she had heard any news, and if there was any trouble among the Indians. She said she had not, but when we told her what we had heard she said that all this talk grew out of the report that the Missouri Indians were coming over on a horse stealing expedition, and that the people were excited over it.

We left the agency at about half-past three. George Gleason and Mrs. Wakefield had just left. When we reached home that evening we told all we had heard. My brother Angus and brother-in-law, Charles Blair, pooh-poohed the idea of trouble with the Indians, but mother was scared. After we had all gone to bed she locked and bolted the outside doors and then retired.

MORNING REST DISTURBED.

About four o'clock the next morning, Tuesday, August 19th, while lying half awake in my bed, I heard someone outside, directly under my room window. (I was up in a back room in the third story.) I heard someone outside calling in a loud voice a number of times for "Brown! Brown! Brown!" But I was tired from the trip to Yellow Medicine the day before and was sleepy and therefore did not feel disposed to answer the call. An ox train from Forest City on the way to the agency had camped the evening before on the hill just back of the house, and as I kept a ferry I thought the voice came from one of the teamsters, who wanted to cross on the ferry. I lay abed perfectly still, half awake, and listening, when Charles Blair, who was occupying a room adjoining mine, raised the window and called out: "What do you want this time of night," and the answer came: "For God's sake hurry, Indians are burning everybody at the agency. The Yanktonnais are burning the stores and killing everybody. I have barely escaped with my life—for God's sake hurry."

This brought me into a wakefulness. I lost no time in getting into my clothes and hastening down stairs. I do not know how I got down two flights of stairs, but think I slid down most of the way on the banisters, for I was very soon at the bottom, and in the dining room, listening to the particulars of the attack on the stores—of the burning, plundering and killing—from the lips of old Peter Rouilliard, an old Canadian Frenchman, who had lived with the Indians for many years.

PRESSING OXEN INTO SERVICE.

We became very much alarmed. Mother told me to awake Lousman, the hired man, and send him at once for the horses. I rushed to Lousman's room, but found it locked, and I pounded and kicked, and finally I succeeded in waking him and getting him out of bed. He immediately started for the horses (they were running loose on the prairie) and after chasing them around a bit and failing to catch them he went to the cattle yard, where we had over 100 head of oxen and cows, and yoked three pair of oxen and hurried hitched them to three lumber wagons. By this time five or six families, neighbors of ours arrived, two Ingalls girls, Charles Holmes, Leopold Wohler and his wife, Garvie's cook and two or three others whose names I cannot now recall. We gave them two of the teams and kept one for ourselves. All got into the wagons and started for Fort Ridgeley, thirty-five miles below us. We started up the hill back of the house and then took the Ridgley road. My brother Angus and brother-in-law, Charles Blair, caught a horse apiece and remained behind intending that should any Indians be seen approaching the house to mount and gallop after us. We had gone but a mile or so, however, when they caught up to us—concluding it was not safe to stay. They had ridden out to the teams camped back of the house on the Forest City road and told the men to unload their teams and hurry back—that the Indians were killing the whites and they would surely be killed if discovered. There were two teams and both were loaded with flour for the agency. (The drivers made good their escape.)

We jogged along pretty fast—the oxen being kept on a trot—and calculated that we would reach the Fort about noon or little after. When we had gone about six miles we saw some people a mile or two to the right of us, near the timber on the brow of the hill, but supposed they were white men working on their farms. (The Yanktonnais whom we were afraid of lived above us.) These people were running back and forth. They soon began to run towards us, or rather to scatter out toward the road ahead of us. Very soon an Indian half-naked and on horseback popped up before us from behind a knoll, and began to beckon the others toward him, and before we knew it we were surrounded.

THE AWFUL CUT-NOSE—RECIPROCAL FRIENDSHIP.

Mother at once grasped the situation. Little Dog had told the truth. We were in the midst of the murdering Indians. She knew that to save us she must speak and make herself known. She must do so quickly or we would be killed. So she stood up in the wagon, and waving her shawl she cried in a loud voice that she was a Sisseton—a relative of Wannatan, Scarlet Plume, Sweetcorn, Ah-kee-pah and the friend of Standing Buffalo, that she had come down this way for protection and hoped to get it. We immediately saw swarms of Indians around us. They were popping out of the grass on every side and in every direction—every blade of which seemed to have suddenly turned into an Indian, all running towards us; some with blackened faces and bloody hands, came up and demanded that we be killed. The awful Cut Nose, the terrible Shakopee or Little Six, and the imprudent Dowannive, three of the worst among the lower Sioux, came to us first, shaking their bloody tomahawks menacingly in our faces. They were the most savage looking of the lot—perfect man-eaters in appearance. We had brought along two shot guns, but no ammunition. The barrels were empty and we were completely in the power of the Indians. But there happened to be one in the crowd that took our part. He rushed up to our wagon with gun in one hand and uplifted tomahawk in the other intending to massacre us, when he happened to recognize my mother. This Indian had once (the winter before) come to our house when he was freezing, and mother took him in and warmed him. He told the other Indians of this and said he remembered it and would show his appreciation of the kind act by protecting us. Upon recognizing mother he jumped into our wagon and shouted at the top of his voice: "This woman," pointing to mother, "saved my life last winter, and I shall save her's now," and in an impassioned speech declared that not a hair on our heads should be molested. The others then withdrew sullenly, saying "they would kill the white men anyway." There were five of these white men besides Blair and Lousman, and each Indian had selected his victim—the particular one he was to shoot. But mother knew the Indians too well to allow any killing to be done Besides her desire to save the lives of these white men, she knew that if they once got to killing and scalping in her presence their savage natures would become uncontrolable and we would all meet the same fate. So she begged that their lives be spared She begged them not to kill these unoffending white men who had come to her for protection. When she saw that they were not disposed to turn from their purpose she angrily demanded that their lives be spared—telling them plainly and eloquently that unless they did so the vengeance of the upper Sioux would fall upon them. "Save them, save them, what do you mean?" says Cut Nose, with bloody hands and face and arms. "Save them," he replied, "are you not grateful that your own life is spared?"

A BRAVE WOMAN—A HUSBAND'S AFFECTION.

"Remember what I say, if you harm any of these friends of mine, you will have to answer to Scarlet Plume, Ah-kee-pah, Standing Buffalo and the whole Sisseton and Wahpeton tribe," continued mother, and then appealed to her friend for help. Whereupon he with Cut Nose, Shakopee (or Little Six), Dowanniye, and all the other Indians, repaired to a mound close by and held a council. They soon came running back to the wagons where we were all huddled together (twenty-six of us) and informed us that mother and her family, including Blair and Lonsman, could all live but the rest must die. They had vowed at the commencement of the outbreak, the day before, they said, to spare no white man, and should they spare these, Little Crow and the Soldiers' Lodge would have them (the warriors) all shot. Mother again pleaded and then argued and at last threatened, and all went to the mound again to talk the matter over. After much bitter wrangling, and mainly through the persuasive eloquence of our friend, they reluctantly decided to accede to the wishes of my mother, that is, to spare the lives of the white men and let them go. Holmes, Wohler and Garvie's cook and one other, were ordered to start off at once across the prairie in the direction of the big woods, while old Peter Rouillard was ordered back to his Indian wife at Yellow Medicine. The three women—Mrs. Wohler, Misses Jennie and Amanda Ingalls—were ordered to remain still in their wagon. Then all the men ran off—our in one direction and one in another. Immediately one of the four Mr. Wohler) turned and ran back to get his boots. Cut Nose ran up to him, while mother was screaming for elp, and cocked his gun and threatened to shoot him if he did not hurry ff. Leopold picked up one boot and started off, but turned again and ran back for the other, when in the midst f mother's screaming, the Indians again drove him away. But this was not all. Leopold went a little ways and returned the third time. It so happened that in the excitement he had not offered to kiss his wife good-bye. Cut Nose was leading her off when Leopold ran up, bareing his breast, saying: "Shoot me, but I shall first kiss my wife." Mr. Wohler was but rrecently married and was desperately in earnest. This act completely paralyzed the Indians, for they stood like statues while Wohler embraced his pretty young wife and showered her with kisses, then broke loose and ran away. With the exception of Blair and Lonsman the men were now all gone. Lousman, the Indians said, must stay and drive the oxen and do chores for my mother, while Blair would be attended to later on. The white women—Mrs. Wohler and the two Misses Ingalls—were then parcelled out among the Indians and ordered to follow them. One beautiful young girl of about 17 years of age refused to alight from the wagon when ordered to do so. Cut Nose had told her he wanted her for his wife, and to get out of the wagon and follow him. She screamed and resisted, when he drew his knife and grabbed her by the hair and threatened to scalp her and frightened her so that she got out and he led her away. Presently the Indians came back with the women and ordered them all to get into one of the wagons—our family and Lonsman and Blair, sixteen in all, being in the other—and started, for we knew not where, the Indians ordering us to follow them.

INDIAN PRANKS.

One hideous looking fellow—Dowanniye by name—who was on horseback, rode up to our wagon and snatched my sister's hat from her head and placed it upon his own and then commenced singing the war song. He was very merry. He would shout and yell at the top of his voice and say that the Indians would have a good time now, and that if they got killed it would be all right; that the whites were trying to starve them to death to get rid of them and were delaying the payment for that purpose; that he preferred to be shot and to die as becomes a Sioux rather than to be starved to death. He jerked off Lonsman's vest and put it on inside out, Lonsman got very angry at this, and demanded its return. He wanted it back he said, because there was a twenty dollar gold piece in one of the pockets—all the money he had in the world—and the Indian might lose it. He was making a great fuss over this, when Blair ordered him to shut up or he would throw him out of the wagon. Lonsman quieted down and muttering something about "making that Indian pay for this some day." Shakopee or Little Six, who was also on horseback, would now and then galop ahead and then suddenly turn and with a whoop and a yell dash toward us and cock his gun and eye us fiercely. Mother did not like this. She told him that she wanted none of his foolishness around her, and that he must either shoot and kill or stop his antics. He would reply that we were his prisoners and should not talk so much, and then commenced singing the war song. He would shake his tomahawk at Blair and Lonsman and then repeat the war song that got so familiar afterwards, viz:

"Iaxica-canze-maye-ca-e.
Niyake-bawahunbun-we."

The English of which is: "The Dutch have made me so angry, I will butcher them alive." When he saw that mother was not afraid of him he quit his fooling.

SAVAGE BRUTALITY.

We had proceeded but a little ways when we came upon four dead bodies—three men and one woman—all horribly mutilated. Our captors had committed the murders. The men had been mowing, and the woman had been raking hay. Their scythes and pitchforks lay near—the woman had a pitchfork sticking in her person, and one of the men had a scythe sticking into his body. Cut Nose gleefully told that he had killed this man and described how he did it. The man was mowing, he said, and he went up to him in a friendly manner and offered his hand, and as the white man threw down his scythe and reached out his hand the Indian drew his knife and like a flash plunged it into the white man's breast, just under the chin, whereupon the white man grasped him around the waist and both struggled for the mastery, when they fell—the white man on top. In working the knife into his breast the Indian got his thumb into the white man's mouth and "got bit." The knife in the hands of the Indian soon touched a vital spot and the white man rolled off, dead. Cut Nose held up his bitten thumb. It was bitten and chewed, and was lacerated most horribly.

THE FIEND CUT NOSE.

This fiend in human shape, this man Cut Nose, presented a most forbidden, horrifying spectacle. With his bloody thumb he had besmeared his naked body, with his blackened face and long bushy hair like a Zulu's, and a half nose (one of his nostrils was missing) he was by far the ugliest looking and most repulsive specimen of humanity I had ever seen.

He was hung at Mankato along with thirty-seven others Dec. 26, 1862, and my father was the signal officer on that occasion—tapped the drum that cut the rope that held the trap that sent Cut Nose to the happy hunting grounds.

MASSACRE OF CAPT. MARSH'S MEN.

Our Indian captors then took us to their camp on the Rice creek, about seven miles above the lower or Redwood agency on the Minnesota river, which we reached about noon. Here we learned that on the day before all the soldiers sent out from Fort Ridgley had been massacred at the lower agency ferry. An Indian had a mule team which he said he had captured there. He had them hitched to a wagon, but was afraid he could not manage them, so Angus and I drove them about awhile.

HIDING UNDER DIFFICULTIES.

We remained at this camp but one hour or two, when it broke up and all moved toward the main or Little Crow's camp, seven miles below. We stopped at the house of John Moore, a mixed blood Sioux, while the train moved on and camped on the hill across the Redwood river. At Moore's we were put up stairs in a dark room and told to remain quiet, for bad Indians were around, and if we were seen we might be killed. Several captive women were there besides ourselves, but owing to the darkness we did not recognize them. In a few minutes three savage looking Indians came up and ordered us away, saying that we could go to the camp on the hill. They ordered the other captives to remain, while we groped our way in the darkness down stairs and out of the house, got into the wagon and drove off, following the Indians. When we got about half way to the camp and as we were crossing the Redwood creek, we suddenly missed our Indian guides. We supposed they crawled into the bushes on the bank of the creek and hid from us, so we waldered on toward the camp.

MORE HARDSHIPS.

At foot of the hill a few hundred yards further we passed a white woman with six children, the eldest not more than ten years of age, two in her arms, two on her back and two traveling on behind. She was accompanied by a half-naked Indian with a gun on his shoulder and a tomahawk in his hand. We stopped and asked the woman to get in, but the Indian would not let her. He said the woman was his and would do as he pleased with her and ordered us to hurry on. He looked so fierce and ugly that we were afraid he might make quick work of us, so we passed on and went up the hill. About a half a mile further on we arrived at the camp, but were sternly told to "go on"—onto Little Crow's camp, a few miles further on. Mother begged to remain until morning, but the Indians were obdurate. She was told to "go on, go on, no Dutchman wanted." This was a heavy blow to mother, and she for the first time that day broke down and commenced to cry. She gave up all hopes and told Lonsman to drive down the road. There was no escape and we must all die. It was quite dark and Indians were returning from their bloody work. We felt that death was staring us in the face as we drove along.

A FRIEND.

But we had not gone more than a mile when an Indian woman, standing on the road side in front of her house as we were passing along, recognized mother and hailed her and we stopped. She asked us in. We drove up to the door and all quietly alighted. Indians passing along—going to and coming from Little Crow's camp below and the camp above—would stop and ask all sorts of questions—who we were, what we wanted, etc. The Indian woman would not allow Lonsman to enter the house, saying that his presence would endanger the lives of the rest of us. She advised him to run through the corn field and into the woods back of the house and follow the river down to Fort Ridgely—about sixteen miles. He laughed at the idea, saying that he was not afraid of the Indians, and started off in the direction of the camp we had just left.

GETS A SITUATION.

It so happened that he reached the camp in safety and entered the first lodge he came to, and went in and found an old Indian woman there. She was delighted to see the white man. She had no one to live with and wanted some one to cut wood, bring water, etc., and set at once to work and prepared supper. Lonsman had not tasted a mouthful all day and was hungry and he ate heartily, and then went to bed, laying down on a buffalo robe and went to sleep. After a hearty breakfast the next morning the old woman gave him the ax and told him to chop some wood in the timber just back of the lodge, which was at one end of the camp. While at work there was quite a stir at the other end of the camp—great excitement and everybody running until not a soul was left in his immediate neighborhood. Lonsman dropped the axe and ran into the woods and made good his escape.

CRUELTY OF INDIAN BOYS.

The excitement was caused by a white boy being stoned, clubbed and beaten to death, and shot with arrows by Indian boys. Lonsman says he went back to the old home that we had left so suddenly the day before and killed a pig, threw it on his back and walked to Henderson, a distance of some sixty miles.

AT LITTLE CROW'S CAMP.

As soon as we got into the house the good Indian woman hurried us up stairs out of the way, and got something to eat for us. We had not eaten a mouthful all day, and the children particularly were overjoyed when supper was announced, after which and as soon as we had donned the Indian dress—the leggins and blankets—which had been given to Angus and I, two of Little Crow's head warriors who happened in advised mother to send her sons to the Chief's camp. Fearing treachery she at first demurred, but finally consented and Angus and I and the two Indians started for Little Crow's camp, three or four miles down the river. Our mission was to call upon the chief and deliver to him a message from mother. The mission was a delicate one, for we did not know what would be our fate, Little Crow being regarded as a very dangerous man. We arrived at the camp some time after dark. It was all excitement—singing, dancing, shouting, yelling and the beating of the tom tom. We walked through the crowd and into the chief's house unnoticed by the rabble. Little Crow was in his own house and the great camp was pitched around it—numbersome 250 or 300 lodges.

We found the chief at home, with his three Indian wives and five white women that he was keeping. H greeted us very cordially and at once asked about mother, and gave us blanket apiece and told us to g after her immediately, for he wanted to see that she was properly cared for—made comfortable. He ordered one of his head warriors to return with us.

Of course we were delighted over the success of our mission. Mother was afraid we might be killed, but now we had good news for her. We hurried back and hitched up the oxen and all got into the wagon and started for Crow's camp. It was now very dark, but we had no difficulty in keeping the road. We were constantly meeting Indians who were returning from the attacks on New Ulm and Fort Ridgely. They would stop and peer at us through the darkness and act threateningly, but after an explanation by the warrior who was our guide we would be permitted to pass on. But on one occasion our lives were in imminent danger. We met a party of drunken Indians who wanted to kill us, and our friend, the warrior-guide, interceded and saved our lives. Upon telling them who we were and that Little Crow had sent for mother and that he would defend his charge with his life, if necessary, they sobered up and let us go.

We finally reached the camp, which was in a perfect uproar as before, and all got out of the wagon and proceeded in Indian file through the camp to the chief's house, which we reached at about 10 o'clock at night.

LITTLE CROW'S ANXIETY AND PLANS.

When mother entered the chief arose from his couch and stepped up and greeted her very cordially, and then handed her a cup of cold water and told to her drink, saying that she was his prisoner now. We were all hurried up stairs and told to remain quiet. The chief gave us robes and blankets and told us to lie down and go to sleep He would sneak up stairs and ask mother (in a whisper) if she was comfortable, how the children were, etc. He was anxious to get into conversation with her, and finally said to her that he wanten her to know all about the troubles that have so suddenly come upon his people, and he wanted to tell her about it. He said in substance that his young men had started to massacre; that he at first opposed the movement with all his might, but when he saw he could not stop it he joined them in their madness against his better judgment, but now did not regret it he said and was never more in earnest in his life; that the plan was for the Winnebago Indians to sweep down the Minnesota river from Mankato to St. Paul the Chippewa Indians down the Mississippi from Crow Wing to St. Paul, and the lower Sioux down between the two rivers from lower agency through the big woods at St. Paul; that all would meet in the neighborhood of the confluence of the two rivers and make a grand charge on Fort Snelling; that this was a stone fort and might take a day or two to batter the walls down.

METHOD IN HIS KINDNESS.

The chief was very kind to us, and assured us that we would not be harmed, that he would take as good care of up as he would if we were members of his own family.

The wily old fellow! He was working for the aid and support of the Upper Sioux. He knew of mother's influence over Standing Buffalo, Waanatan, Scarlet Plume, Sweet Corn Red Iron, A-kee-pah. and other influential Sisseton and Wahpeton chiefs. He was afraid, he said once, that he could not keep Blair alive until morning, that the young men outside were bloodthirsty and desperate, and should they learn that a white man was in camp there was no telling what might happen.

The chief got some vermillion and daubed Blair's face with the red paint, and gave him a new red Mackanac blanket and a pair of red leggins, and pulled off his own moccasins and put them on Blair's feet, and then cautioned us to remain quiet, as bad Indians were near by, and then went back down stairs.

OUR SCALPS DEMANDED.

About midnight someone came to see Little Crow. He told the chief that it was rumored about camp that a white man and some strangers were in the house,—that the warriors were very angry about it, and he wanted to know if there was any foundation to the rumor. When told that there was, and that we were Sisseton mixed bloods and his friends, the man got very angry and insisted that we should all be killed at once. He said that no prisoners ought to be taken—that the Sissetons were a different people and had no claim whatever on the Lower Sioux and the mixed bloods of that tribe are no better than white people, and should be treated the same as the whites.

A COUNCIL DEMANDED.

He wanted Little Crow to call a council at once. But the chief told the man that we were his friends, that Standing Buffalo, Scarlet Plume, Ah-kee-pah, and Sweet Corn were his friends, and he would protect us, that it was too late for a council that night, and then compelled the man to leave.

BLAIR SPIRITED AWAY.

As soon as the man had gone away, Little Crow came quietly upstairs and told mother that he had just had a stormy interview with his (Crow's) private secretary, that the secretary had just left the house in a very angry mood. We had heard through a stove pipe hole all that had been said, so that we were prepared. Mother and Little Crow talked over the matter, and they both agreed that not only was Blair's life in danger, but the lives of all of us, including that of Little Crow himself. The only hope was to get Blair away—send him off in the dark. My mother and Mrs. Blair resolved to do this. They at once went to work to get him ready. They gave him what crackers they had, and Little Crow gave him a shawl to wrap around his head, and then summoned his head warrior and instructed him to lead Blair down stairs and out through the camp, and down through the woods to the river bank—a few hundred yards back of the house—and leave him there to make his escape as best he could. Little Crow said to Mrs. Blair: "I have known your mother for many years. She is a good woman, and in sending your husband away I am risking my life for her and for you all to-night. Be brave, your husband shall live."

After a sad farewell, Blair was taken away. He was dressed in full Indian costume.

PRIVATION AND SUFFERING.

Fort Ridgely was but about fifteen miles away, and yet the poor fellow was seven days getting to it. He was a consumptive and could not stand any hardships. He forded the Minnesota river a few minutes after the Indian had left him and crawled into a thicket where he remained until the next night. He then traveled until exhausted from hunger and fatigue. He lay in the tall grass on the flats opposite the Lower Agency, near the road. Indians on the warpath were constantly passing and he could not go on. Finally becoming crazed with hunger and from sheer desperation, and after five days and six nights of hiding, he got up at daybreak one morning and staggered out to the road and started out for the fort, about ten miles distant, which he reached after the lapse of seven days and eight nights from the time he left Little Crow's house.

The exposure was too much for his naturally weak frame and he kept sinking until February following, when at Henderson with his wife and children around him, death claimed as a victim.

SUSPECTED AND UNDER ARREST.

It has been said that upon Blair's arrival at the fort he was terribly emaciated, weak, and hardly able to walk or to speak; that he could only mutter a few words and that with difficulty and incoherently; that upon learning that he was a son-in-law of Major Brown, and because he was dressed in full Indian costume and had his face painted—a la Sioux brave—he was looked upon with suspicion and placed under arrest, as a spy; that he was kept in durance vile until the arrival of Gen. Sibley, who ordered his release instanter, and severely reprimanded the commanding officer. In justice to Col. Tom Sheehan, who was then, I believe, the officer in command at the fort, I will say that he denies this story in toto.

THE TERRORS OF THE NIGHT.

We passed a miserable night, did not sleep a wink. We were afraid that we might be attacked and massacred, that we might at any moment be fired upon by the half crazed Indians outside. The night passed, however, without any attempt to take our lives.

A FRIEND IN NEED.

The next morning (Wednesday, the 20th) old Aunt Judy (Hazatonwin) a good old Indian woman whom we had known for many years, and who was now the mother-in-law of Little Crow's head warrior, came to the house and took us away. She took us to her daughter's te-pee or lodge, near by, and gave us something to eat, She kept us there and took as good care of us as she could. I shall never forget the crackers and molasses she used to feed us on. We had all we wanted. She would never let us go hungry. She was always asking about our comfort—was afraid mischievous Indians might attempt to scare us or drunken Indians might shoot us. She got her son-in-law to guard us at night.

SERVED HIM RIGHT.

One evening as my sister (Mrs. Blair) had just been frying hard bread or crackers, and had just put away the frying pan half filled with hot grease near the doorway or entrance to the lodge, when a drunken Indian came in and squatted there. He made insulting remarks and then turned to go out, and as he did so accidentally placed his hand in the hot pan of grease. With a yell of pain he rushed out and disappeared in the darkness. He never came back.

INDIAN BRAVERY AND ELOQUENCE.

On Saturday, the 23rd, Ah-kee-pah arrived from Yellow Medicine. He had heard that Little Crow held us captives, and had come back to take us away—to take us back to Yellow Medicine, where our relatives and friends were living. Soon after his arrival one of Little Crow's warriors taunted the Wahpeton chief with cowardice, saying, among other things that (Ah-kee-pah) had not so much as killed one white man—not even a babe. He stepped in the midst of the crowd that had gathered around him and made a speech that opened their eyes. He declared that there was no bravery in killing helpless men and women and little children, but that it was simply cowardice, and cowards would only boast of it—that if he had found that any of his relatives had been harmed he would have gone about tomahawking the whole camp, "slaughtering the braves (?) like slaughtering a lot of beaver on dry land." He said, "when the sun arose that was to witness the horrors of an indiscriminate massacre of the whites in the valley of the Minnesota, regardless of age or sex, by the lower Sioux, the upper bands were peacefully attending to their crops on their own reservation, or hunting the buffalo on the distant prairies, the report of that day's work reached our ears in a more astounding tone than that of the voice of the Great Spirit issuing from the "dark clouds of the west."

RESUMING OUR JOURNEY.

The next morning, on Sunday, the 24th, we left Little Crow's camp and started for Yellow Medicine, Ah-kee-pah putting us all into one wagon and driving, his head soldier armed to the teeth and on horseback accompanying us. We were now in the hands of our relatives and friends and felt safe.

RESULTS OF THE MASSACRE.

Near the Redwood river we saw the dead body of poor George Gleason (whom we had seen but a few days before,) lying in the road with a stone imbedded in his skull. We saw no other dead bodies near or in fact between that and the upper agency.

It appears that when Mr. Gleason and Mrs. Wakefield came along they met some Indians who shot the man and took the woman prisoner.

AMONG OUR FRIENDS.

We reached Yellow Medicine that afternoon and at once moved into one of the vacated agency buildings, the residence of Dr. Wakefield, and remained there until Thursday, the 28th, when Little Crow's whole camp moved up from the Lower Agency. They passed by and ordered us to follow them, which we did. We moved up and located our camp near a creek west of the Hazlewood mission station, lately vacated by Rev. S. R. Riggs. The Upper Indians made this their camping ground, while the Lower Indians pitched their camp on the opposite side of the creek, the two camps being about a mile apart.

GOVERNMENT BUILDINGS BURNED.

On that day the government buildings at Yellow Medicine, and all the stores and other buildings there were burned and totally destroyed by the Indians. Our house followed suit.

ATTEMPTS TO COERCE FRIENDLY INDIANS.

In the evening several hundred of Little Crow's warriors came over to our camp on horseback, whooping, yelling and firing off their guns. They surrounded our camp and ordered the Upper Sioux to move at once to the camp of the Lower Sioux on the opposite side of the creek, saying that this was the will of the Soldiers' Lodge and must be obeyed; that unless we complied *instanter* our lodges would be cut up and destroyed, and we would be punished severely. The Upper Sioux protested against this most vigorously. They said plainly that they would not only not comply with the insolent demands of the Lower Sioux, who inaugurated the outbreak and must assume all responsibilities connected with it, and who moved into the country of the Upper Sioux without invitation, but would take up arms against them and die on the spot rather than move into the camp of the insane followers of Little Crow. Bitter wrangling followed, and the visitors finally left with threats of returning in the morning with a larger force and compelling obedience.

DEFENSIVE MEASURES.

The Upper Sioux, immediately upon the departure of the Lower Sioux warriors, sent out runners to the several camps and houses of the farmer Indians near by, and called in the people. In an incredibly short time several hundred half-naked and painted Indians came running into camp, armed to the teeth with guns, bows and arrows, knives, and pitchforks, ready for a fight. They at once set to work and pitched a large teepee or lodge, in the center of the camp, and formed a "soldiers' lodge"—a sort of committee of ways and means, composed of warriors of the tribe, from whose decision there is no appeal—and immediately decided upon taking some offensive action—to let Little Crow and his warriors understand once for all that they would not be permitted to ride rough shod over the whole Sioux nation, and that they were tresspassers upon the lands of the Upper Sioux and had better behave themselves, or they would be ordered and driven off.

This was the *nucleus* of the friendly camp that was afterwards so instrumental in saving the lives of the captives.

DISCRETION BETTER THAN VALOR.

On the next morning, the 29th, the lower Indians, some 300 or 400 half naked and painted warriors, came again, all on horseback, whooping and yelling as before, and surrounded our camp, but on noticing the soldiers' lodge in the center the visitors hastened away. They had evidently come for mischief—to carry out their threats of the day before—but the business appearance of the big lodge in the center opened their eyes and scared them away.

STANDING UP FOR THEIR RIGHTS.

Immediately after they left, the "friendlies" (hereafter I shall call them that instead of Upper Sioux) got their chiefs and warriors together, painted their faces and bodies, took their guns, bows and arrows and knives, mounted their horses, and proceeded to the camp of the Lower Sioux. They were going to demand all the property in the hands of Little Crow and his people belonging to the Sisseton and Wahpeton mixed bloods. The Lower Sioux had cattle, horses wagons, carriages and other property belonging to my mother, and I was taken along to identify them. There were 75 or 100 in the party and all went singing, shouting, yelling, and firing guns. We entered the camp amid great excitement, and proceeded direct to the Soldiers' Lodge, pitched on a mound in the center of the camp. We rode up to within about fifty feet of the lodge, and surrounded it and then dismounted, and held our horses by the bridle bits, while Little Paul, the spokesman for the friendlies, stepped to the front and delivered a speech in which he demanded the property. There were upwards of 100 of the chiefs and warriors of the hostiles (hereafter I shall call them that instead of the lower Sioux) lounging about in and around the big lodge. They were savage looking fellows, but that fact did not deter Little Paul from expressing himself without any fear whatever, Objections to the demand were at once interposed and bitter wrangling, followed, and, for a time the interview seriously threatened a bloody termination. The demands were, however, finally acceded to, after finding that the friendlies were determined to have their own way. The hostiles suggested that we should go through the camp and hunt up our property. We did so and discovered a horse belonging to my mother standing near a lodge, tied to a wagon. I pointed it out and the party went up to take it when the Indian rushed out of the lodge and ordered us not to touch the animal. The friendlies said they must have it and one of them went toward the horse when the hostile drew a bow from its quiver and quickly fixed an arrow in it and vowed he would pierce it through and kill it on the spot rather than let it go. The friendlies told him that we were warriors and belonged to the soldiers' lodge and must not be fooled with, and one of them dismounted and ran up to the horse, cut the rope or halter with which it was tied and led it away, the hostile not daring to make good his threat. It looked serious for a few moments. If the hostile had shot the horse the friendlies would surely have shot him to pieces, and there is no telling where the troubles would have ended.

[EXPLANATORY—In the introductory chapter of "Reminiscences" in defining the relations of the Upper and Lower Sioux tribes it was stated that seventeen of the former and 286 of the latter were condemned to death. This was the finding of the court, as we understand it, afterwards modified by President Lincoln's review and decree, but Mr. Brown wishes the words "or imprisonment" added, which would correctly read "condemned to death or imprisonment." Of the Indians hung at Mankato two belonged to the upper bands and thirty-six of the lower bands. In addition Little Six and Medicine Bottle were hanged at Fort Snelling in 1863 or 1864, and John Campbell at Mankato in 1865, making in all thirty-nine of the lower bands hung during the Indian war, which commenced Aug. 18, 1862, and ended June 1, 1866, according to official records. Inquiry has also been made as to the fate of Standing Buffalo. He was killed in a fight with the Crow Indians, Mr. Brown thinks, in 1866. "He was always a friend of the whites—loyal to the last—a truly good Indian."]

A SLENDER THREAD.

The fate of the captives hung on a very slender thread. When the hostile was told we were warriors and belonged to the soldier's lodge and must not be fooled with he pointed to me and sneeringly remarked: "Is he not a captive? You must be hard up for warriors."

WHAT WE OWED TO THE FRIENDLIES.

We next went where our carriage stood and took that away, and then to another place and secured another one of mother's horses. We then went singing and whooping and firing off guns back to our camp. Here we remained for some days, the friendlies and hostiles camping apart. But for the dangers braved by these friendlies, but for the firm stand taken by them, not a captive would have been saved—all would have been killed, including mixed-bloods and "farmer" Indians. As it was we barely escaped massacre at the hands of the hostiles on any occasion.

BOASTING OF EXPLOITS.

The Indians are fond of telling of their adventures, their exploits on the warpath. It is sickening to hear them boast of their devilish deeds. They say it is like play to fight the whites. Little Crow, who comes whenever he can to chat with mother, remarked one day that since the second attack on Fort Ridgley he had been suffering with a headache.

MADE HIS HEAD ACHE.

"What gave you the headache, were you scared so much as that?" she asked.

"Why," says he, laughing. "I was lying on the brow of a hill near the fort taking a nap when we were teasing the whites, shooting them through the windows of the fort and hearing them scream and cry like babies. I lay with my head on a huge rock for a pillow, and hearing the boom of a big gun I woke suddenly and peered over the rock to see

7

what the matter was, and saw a cannon ball coming. I quickly dodged and struck my head on the rock and have had a pain ever since. "But seriously," he went on, "I am worried—ammunition is giving out. We could of course use clubs, sticks and stones, and drive the whites out of the country, but they are numerous like the grass on the prairies—that it would take a long time." (These boasts were made to keep up the courage of the young men.)

A FRIEND ARRIVES.

On Saturday, the 6th of September, Scarlet Plume, a leading Sisseton chief, arrived from above, from his camp at the head of Lake Traverse. He assured mother that she would not be detained as captive much longer, that as soon as the Sissetons returned to their planting grounds on Lake Traverse from their buffalo hunt on the plains northwest of there, where they now are, they would come down in a body and take us away by force, if necessary, and deliver us over to the whites.

FEATHERS AND ALL.

I witnessed a singular spectacle today. One of Little Crow's warriors swallowed a bird whole, feathers and all. The warrior's son, a boy about ten years old, had shot and killed with his bow and arrow a little bird that had been hopping about on the prairie, and brought it home in triumph, when the father, in honor of the feat, and as an encouragement for the little warrior to preserve in that line and perform greater deeds, called the crowd together and taking the bird and dipping it in grease swallowed it and then smacked his lips with gusto and relish.

MOVING CAMP.

On Monday, the 8th, the camp criers of both camps went around telling the people to break camp the next morning and proceed up the river. We had camped here since the 28th of August. Very early Tuesday morning, the 9th, both camps broke up and started, making a train five or six miles long, and arrived at Red Iron's village that afternoon.

STOPPING THEIR PROGRESS.

When we approached the village, which was afterwards known as Camp Release, Chief Red Iron and his warriors came out to meet us and there came very near being a serious row between the Red Iron faction of the Upper Sioux and Little Crow's people. The former came up whooping and yelling and firing off guns and ordering the latter to halt. They were told to proceed no further into the Sisseton country, saying, "you commenced the outbreak, and and must do the fighting in your country. We do not want you here to excite our young men and get us into trouble," and so the whole train stopped and went into camp.

NEWS FROM THE FORT.

The Robertson boys, whom the friendlies had dispatched to the Fort on a mission of peace a few days ago returned today and we were informed the father was sick there, suffering from a gun shot wound received in the battle of Birch Coolie.

HOW THEY ENJOYED THEMSELVES.

The afternoon was lively. No sooner were the camps pitched than dancing and feasting was commenced. Some rode about on horseback, singing war songs. Charley Crawford, with father's uniform on and a prancing steed, made a fine appearance. George Washington on charger was "nowhere." The dancers had the long red whiskers of a white man dangling from a pole in the center of the ring around which the half-crazed warriors and their women and girls danced. One after another the half-naked and painted warriors would spring into the ring and make a speech. Each would boast of the exploits, relate his daring deeds. Then all would join in a the demoniac dance, with yells, whoops and songs and the beating of the tom-tom.

KILLED A WHOLE FAMILY. HELLISH BRUTALITY.

One hideous looking fellow jumped into the ring and gave the drum a tap with the flat side of his tomahawk, which act was a signal for the drummers to cease beating, and proceeded to narrate his adventures that day. He said he had despatched three—a man, a woman, and a child —and then proceed to act out the sufferings of his victims. He declared that he had destroyed a whole family for which he deserved much honor. That he went into a stable and shot a white man in the back and then beat his brains out with the but of his gun, then rushed into the house where he found the wife kneading bread and a babe in a cradle near by. He grabbed the shrieking woman by the hair of the head and threw her violently against the wall, then took the babe, put it into the bread pan, and shoved it into the hot oven, then turned and shot the woman as she was trying to get up, then set fire to the house and hurried away and joined his comrades.

GOOD PURPOSES DEFEATED.

On Wednesday the 10th, six of the friendlies with some captive women and children started from the fort, but were discovered by some of Little Crow's warriors and brought back. This has intensified the feeling of bitterness existing between the opposing factions, and "do not speak as they pass."

CROW'S INTENTIONS.

Little Crow is fast losing his hold upon the young men and this fact worries him greatly and the old warrior is getting heartily discouraged. He told mother today that he intended to spend the coming winter in the Green Lake region of the big woods and kill as many whites as he could, but if he should get killed himself it would be all right. He did not want to be caught and hung.

WISHED WE WERE BACK AGAIN.

Frank Robertson—one of the captives—and I took a long walk on the prairie today. We wished, and wished and wished that this "cruel war was over," and that we were back with the boys at "old Seabury" again.

TROUBLE THREATENED.

On Sunday the 14th, the friendlies and the hostiles got into a rumpus again. There came near being bloodshed. Ah-kee-pah's life was threatened. He has refused all along to join in the dances or take part in any demonstration against the whites. His band today struck their lodges and moved out and away from the main camp and established one of their own, and declared that they would fight and die like men rather than tamely submit to the insults and indignities heaped upon them by Little Crow's warriors.

A FRIENDLY CHIEF'S DEMANDS.

On Monday the 15th, Waanatan, the Charger, an influential chief of the Upper Sioux, arrived from the north. He told mother that most of his people were out on the buffalo ranges and had brought but few of his warriors with him and did not expect to accomplish much. His mission was, he said, principally to consult with Little Crow about the captives and to suggest that they be released and sent to the fort (Ridgeley)—at least such of them as were taken on or in the vicinity of the upper reservation—also to demand the restoration of such goods, provisions and other articles that the hostiles took from the government supply house and traders at Yellow Medicine.

A FRIENDLY COUNCIL—A BRAVE CHIEF.

On Thursday the 18th, the friendlies met in council for the purpose of taking some action towards rescuing the captors and delivering them over to Col. Sibley. Some favored taking our family alone to the fort on the ground that it would not be practicable to include all the captives—that to include them all would excite bitter opposition on the part of the hostiles — who out-numbered the friendlies five to one—and might result in a general massacre and the death of every captive in camp. Little Paul and others, however, opposed this plan, saying that no distinction should be made between the captives —that to take one family only would endanger the lives of those left behind.—that all should be taken from the hostiles and delivered over to the whites at once, that with proper management and pluck and earnestness on the part of the friendlies, the hostiles would quail and every captive could be taken away and delivered over to their friends. But the idea was dropped for the time being —the council concluding that the time was not yet ripe enough for any open action in behalf of the captives. They all came and danced around our lodge that night. This was done as a mark of respect for mother.

PLANNING TO RESCUE WHITES.

Waanatan told mother today that he was going to start back north tomorrow and would return in fifteen days with all his warriors and take us away, by force if necessary, and deliver us to Col. Sibley.

QUARRELS BETWEEN FRIENDS AND ENEMIES.

On Friday the 19th, the hostiles and the friendlies quarreled and came near fighting. The quarrel was ostensibly over the division of the plunder, but really over the captives. The latter wanted to take all the captives away and deliver them to the whites at the fort, while the hostiles wanted to massacre the whole outfit. The quarrel got very hot—threats made and guns fired. Tomahawks were shook at us and our situation was critical indeed. Poor mother! She has been crying all day, and has not tasted food since yesterday morning. She tries to hide her feelings, and the danger that confronts us, but we know it all and feel anxious for her.

The day was a most sad and gloomy one for us. Night came but we could not sleep.

A BRAVE PROTECTOR.

Lame Jim's son came to our lodge with his gun and tenderly cared for us during the night. He vowed he would shoot the first man that undertook to harm us in any way. Saturday the 20th, was another bad day for the captives. My brother and I and all who were kept advised of the situation of things sat up with others of our friends to watch for prowling Indians. Faithful Taxunkemaza (Lame Jim's son) with gun in hand walked around our lodge all night long ready to kill "two at a blow." Lame Jim was a brother of "Old Bets" and was well known in early days in and about St. Paul.

FEAR OF THE FRIENDLIES SAVED US.

Little Crow was very angry to find that the captives were apprised of his plans to massacre them during the night, and that they were prepared to defend themselves. In the morning he threatened our lives—said that the captives must all be killed. He ordered his warriors to massacre us, but no one dared to execute his order—no not one.

HOPEFUL NEWS.

News came that the troops were sighted at the Redwood and that they would reach the Yellow Medicine bottom about Sunday, the 21st.

WHITES TO BE WIPED OUT.

The Soldiers' Lodge (from whose decision there was no appeal) had solemnly decreed to attack the troops there and to slaughter them— wipe the white marauders from the face of the earth. Little Crow wants the Sissetons to go along—take teams and help haul away the plunder. But they refused, saying they did not care to be mixed up in the quarrel.

PRIZES FOR SCALPS AND "OLD GLORY."

On Monday morning, the 22nd, Little Crow's camp crier went around saying that the Soldiers' Lodge had decreed that every man in camp must go at once to Yellow Medicine and meet the troops, that anyone bringing in the scalp of Sibley, Brown, Forbes, Roberts, or Myrick, or the American flag, would receive as a present from the tribe all the waupum beads in camp and be showered with all the honors within the gift of the people, and be thereafter looked up to as the hero and chief warrior of the tribe.

PREPARING FOR SELF-DEFENSE.

In the afternoon of that day there was nobody left in camp but old men and boys and old women and girls, and most of the captives. As we were told by the friendlies to be prepared to defend ourselves against the hostiles upon their return from Yellow Medicine, we immediately set to work digging holes in the center of the lodges big enough for the women and children to get into, and ditches outside and around for the men.

MOST BEAUTIFUTLY THRESHED.

On Tuesday the 23d, the Indians returned from Wood Lake. They had met the troops there instead of at Yellow Medicine and been most beautifully threshed that day.

CAN'T ACCOUNT FOR IT.

Little Crow was despondent. He was almost heart broken. He stepped outside his lodge and spoke to the people. He told them that he was ashamed to call himself a Sioux. "Seven hundred picked warriors whipped by the cowardly whites,", he said. "Better run away and scatter out over the plains like buffalo and wolves," he continued. "To be sure," he went on, "the whites had big guns and better arms than the Indians and outnumbered us four or five to one, but that is no reason we should not have whipped them, for we are brave men while they are cowardly women. I cannot account for the disgraceful defeat. It must be the work of traitors in our midst"—meaning the friendlies.

HOW THEY WERE COUNTED.

There were 738 Indians on the battle ground at Wood Lake, and the actual number was ascertained in this way: At the crossing of a creek near Dr. Williamson's mission house, two trusty warriors were stationed on the road leading to the battle ground. As each brave passed he handed to the warriors a stick. When all had reached Yellow Medicine bottoms, a few miles from where the battle took place, these sticks were counted and found to number 738. Little Crow told mother this in my presence.

TO FLEE, BUT MUST KILL CAPTIVES FIRST.

On Wednesday, the 24th, Little Crow called all his warriors together and told them to pack up and leave for the plains and save the women and children, the troops would soon be upon them and no time should be lost. "But," he said, "the captives must all be killed before we leave.

They seek to defy us," he went on. "and dug trenches while we were away. They must die."

DESERTING THEIR LEADER.

The camp of the friendlies, where trenches were dug and earth works thrown up, and where the captives had been secreted, was pitched a little way from the main or hostile camp, and was rapidly increasing in numbers so that the captives felt comparatively safe. Indeed, when the friendlies had threatened to take Little Crow and his whole camp and turn them over to the troops and several hundred of the hostiles had come over into our camp with their captives and vowed they would stand by us, we simply laughed at Little Crow's bombastic talk.

DEPART LIKE THE ARABS

Upon realizing the condition of things Little Crow and some two or three hundred of his followers hurriedly fled, "folded their tents and stole quiety away."

RESCUING CAPTIVES.

On Friday morning, the 26th, Gabriel Renville, Joseph Lu Tramboise and two or three other friendlies took, at the risk of their lives two white captives, a girl and a boy, that were being carried off by a party of nine of the hostiles. This party had been to the Big Woods in the vicinity of Hutchinson and were on their way back and passing the camp with these captives when intercepted.

RELIEF COMING—SUDDEN CONVERSIONS.

About noon the entire camp was all excitement. The troops were approaching. Every man and woman in the camp, and every child old enough to toddle about, turned out with a flag of truce—every Indian became suddenly good. All were were friendly to the whites and anxious to shake hands with Sibley, Brown, Forbes, Robert and Myrick, the five for whose scalps reward has been offered. White rags were fastened to the tips of the tepee poles, to wagon wheels, cart wheels, to sticks and poles stuck in the ground, and every conceivable object and in some grotesque manner and ludicrous way.

NOVEL FLAG OF TRUCE.

One Indian who was boiling over with loyalty and love for the white man threw a white blanket on his black horse and tied a bit of white cloth to its tail, and then that no possible doubt might be raised in his case he wrapped the American flag around his body and mounted the horse and sat upon him in full view of the troops as they passed by, looking more like a circus clown than a "friendly" Indian.

JOY INDESCRIBABLE.

When the troops suddenly appeared on an eminence a mile away and there was no doubt that they were coming to our rescue the captives could hardly restrain themselves —some cried for joy, some went into fits or hysterics, and some fainted away. It was a joyful, yet most sad and gloomy.

NO GRANDER SIGHT

ever met the eyes of anybody than when the troops marched up with bayonets glistening in the bright noon day sun and colors flying, drums beating and fifes playing. I shall never forget it while I live. We could hardly realize that our deliverance had come. The troops passed by and pitched their tents a quarter of a mile from us and at once spiked their guns which commanded our camp.

VISIT FROM THE GENERAL

Very soon Col. Sibley with his staff and a body of guard came over into our camp and after calling the Indians together made formal demand for the captives which were readily given up.

FATHER'S ARRIVAL.

Then my father and Major Cullen, Doctor Daniels and one or two other personel friends came. We went with them to the soldiers' camp and remained there until sent to Henderson a few days subsequently—my father and I only of the family remaining with the expedition.

THE CAPTURED CAMP.

There were about 150 lodges in the Indian camp at the time of the arrival of the troops. But a few days subsequently the camp had increased to 243 lodges. Some had been captured and brought in, while others came in of their own accord, and including the captives (and exclusive of the soldiers there were at Camp Release 2188 souls, as follows:

Indians....................................1,918
Captive white men......................4
Captive white women and children 104
Captive mixed bloods.................162

The names of the four white men who made kept captives by Little Crow were as follows:

1—George Spencer.
2—Peter Rousseau.
3—Louis La Belle.
4—Peter Rouillard.

I mention this to correct the impression that there was but one white man (Spencer) made prisioner by the Indians.

PRMOTED TO SCOUT.

Upon my release from captivity I was at once put upon the U. S. scout roll and detailed for duty with Major Thomas J. Galbraith, United States Indian Agent. I acted as interpreter.

On the 4th of October I was ordered to inform the Indians that such of them as were not required as witnesses in the trial then going on must at once break camp and proceed to Yellow Medicine.—that this was rendered necessary on account of the stock of provisions running out, and that I was to go along as intepreter. We left the camp, (Camp Release) the same day under the escort of some soldiers under Capt. J. Whitney of the Sixth regiment, Minnesota Volunteers, and proceeded to our destination. The large number of cattle, horses, wagons, carriages, and buggies, and about 1250 Indians, (286 were men, the residue women and children) and about 150 soldiers, with their provisions and baggage wagons, made the train a long one.

RESUMING FARM WORK.

At Yellow Medicine, which we reached the same day, the Indians were all put to work digging potatoes and gathering corn. In a week we had filled several root houses and cellars—had housed about 6,000 bushels of potatoes and 1,500 bushels of corn.

WEEDING OUT THE GUILTY.

While thus engaged, and by exercising a justifiable piece of strategy, I assisted in causing the arrest and in safely detaining in custody all the Indian men (except forty-six who were above suspicion, and three or four who had "smelled a mice" and ran away during the night) and disarmed them and chained them in pairs together—that is, the right leg at the ankle of one was chained to the left leg at the ankle of another.

JUSTIFIABLE STRATEGY.

This successful and justifiable piece of strategy took place at the government warehouse, built by my father, when he was agent a few years before, a large two story building fifty feet long, which the hostiles had burned and destroyed when they passed up on the 28th of August, but the walls of which were still standing, and was accomplished in the following manner: About a hundred yards from this building the soldiers had pitched their tents, while the

Indians camped under the hill along the Yellow Medicine creek, a half or three quarters of a mile distant. I was ordered one day to proceed to the camp and inform the Indians that the annuity roll was to be prepared the next morning, and that they must all come at an early hour and present themselves to the agent at the warehouse and be "counted." They were delighted to learn that they were at last to get their money. The annuity payment for that year had not yet been made, and this ruse worked like a charm.

HOW IT WAS DONE.

About 8 o'clock the next morning the Indians flocked to the warehouse anxious to be "counted." Major Galbraith, Captain Whitney and two or three "clerks" were found seated at a table behind one end of the building with pens, ink, paper, etc., hard at work on the "rolls" while one of the officers and myself were stationed in a doorway at the opposite end and further end. As each family would step up to the table one of the "clerks" would rise and count or number them with his finger, one, two, three, etc., and after announcing the result with a flourish and motioning for them to pass on, a soldier would step up and escort the Indians to the other end of the building where I was stationed. As they reached the farther end and turned the corner and came in front of the doorway, I would tell the men to step inside and allow the women and children to pass on to the camp, telling them, as I was instructed to do, that the men as heads of families must be counted separately, as it was thought the government would pay them extra. I would then take their guns, tomahawks, scalping knives, etc., and throw them into barrels, telling them they would be returned shortly. In this way we succeeded in arresting and safely detaining in custody 234 of Little Crow's fiercest warrior. And since the Indian men outnumbered the soldiers two to one and were fully as well armed, I think that in this case "the end justified the means."

RECAPTURED.

In the evening of that day and before the Indians were put in irons, one of them broke from the guard and escaped to the camp where he was captured by the friendlies and brought back.

RETURNING.

We remained at Yellow Medicine until the 12th, when we left for the lower agency, arriving there on the 15th—the entire expedition from Camp Release arriving at the same time.

TRIAL OF CAPTIVES.

Here we remained for upwards of three weeks, the time being consumed in the trial of the ind cted Indians.

SEPARATING THE GOOD FROM THE BAD.

On the 9th of November, the uncondemned Indians and their wives and families, and the wives and families of the condemned and absent Indians, numbering in all 1,658 souls, were started off for Fort Snelling, Lieut. Col. Marshall of the Seventh regiment, Minnesota Volunteers, with an escort of three companies of soldiers, being in command.

MANKATO'S ALLOTMENT.

At the same time 392 condemned Indian men and seventeen Indian women as cooks, laundresses, etc., four papooses, and four of the friendlies, as assistants in the care of the prisoners, were started off for Mankato, making 417 in all, Col. Sibley and the main portion of the 'expedition and Major Brown, superintendent in charge of the Indian prisoners, accompanying these.

AN ANGERED MOB.

I went along with Col. Marshall's detatchment—the train measuring about four miles in length. At Henderson, which we reached on the 11th, we found the streets crowded with an angry and excited populace, cursing, shouting and crying. Men, women and children armed with guns, knives, clubs and stones, rushed upon the Indians, as the train was passing by, and before the soldiers could interfere and stop them, succeeded in pulling many of the old men and women and even children from the wagons by the hair of the head, and beating them, and otherwise inflicting injury upon the helpless and miserable creatures.

AS BAD AS SAVAGES.

I saw an enraged white woman rush up to one of the wagons and snatch a nursing babe from its mother's breast and dash it violently upon the ground. The soldiers' instantly seized her and led or rather dragged the woman away, and restored the papoose to its mother—limp and almost dead. Although the child was not killed outright, it died a few hours after. The body was quietly laid away in the crotch of a tree a few miles below Henderson and not far from Faxon.

THE LAST OF A TRIBAL CUSTOM.

I witnessed the ceremony, which was, perhaps, the last of the kind within the limits of Minnesota; that is, the last Sioux Indian "buried" according to one of the oldest and most cherished customs of the tribe.

MORALIZING UPON HUMAN DEPRAVITY.

And here my thoughts reverted to the case of the Indian brave at the dance who boasted in "ghoulish glee" that he had roasted a babe in the oven, and I contrasted it with the case before me. An uncivilized heathen in the one case, and a *civilized christian* white woman in the other!

A BRAVE MAN AND A BRAVE ACT.

There was another incident that took place at Henderson which is worth mentioning. I refer to a brave and noble act by one of the bravest and noblest of men—Lieut. Col. Marshall, afterwards governor of Minnesota.

While the train was passing through the town one of the citizens with blood in his eyes and half crazed with drink rushed up with a gun levelled at Charles Crawford, one of the friendlies, and was about to fire, when "the bold charger of the plains," Lieut. Col. Marshall, who happened along on horseback, rushed between them and struck down the gun with his sabre and got Crawford out of the way, thus saving a life at the risk of his own.

PLAYING MAJOR GENERAL.

Prior to the outbreak my father was a major general of the state militia and had a uniform of that rank in his house at the time it was ransacked and plundered by the Indians. Crawford secured this and wore it in camp, at dances, feasts, etc. He was a tall, broad shouldered man, a good rider and fine figure on horseback, and having pants with stripes down the legs, a coat with epaulettes, a cocked hat, sash, sword, spurs, and a prancing steed, he was a noticeable figure at all gatherings. The captives noticing this, and not knowing it was done for their benefit, naturally supposed he was a hostile of the worst kind, and hence the feeling against him.

TWICE TRIED AND ACQUITTED.

As the records of the military commission that tried the Indians—of which Gov. Marshall was a member—shows that Crawford was brought before it twice, and underwent a most searching examination each time, and was adjudged "not guilty" on every charge, there ought to be no doubt of the man's innocence.

FROM SOLDIER TO MINISTER.

Crawford rendered valuable service in the war following the outbreak, and is now pastor of the Presbyterian church at Good Will, South Dakota.

AT FORT SNELLING.

On the 14th we reached Fort Snelling and placed the Indians in camp.

WHAT BECOME OF THEM.

Here most of them remained—in charge of the military—until the following spring, when they were turned over to the interior department, put into steamboats and taken down the Mississippi river to the Missouri, and up the latter stream to a point called Fort Usher or Usher's Landing, but afterwards as Fort Thompson or Crow Creek Agency, D. T., about 200 miles above Yankton. In 1866 these Indians were removed down the Missouri to a point now known as Santee Agency, Nebraska.

MANKATO'S ALLOTTMENT DISPOSED OF

Of the condemned Indians sent to Mankato thirty-eight were hung there on the 26th of December, and the residue—except those that died from sickness—remained there until the following spring when they too were dumped into a steamboat and taken down the river to a military prison near Davenport, Iowa, where the most of them remained in *durance vile* until 1866, when they were released and returned to their friends and relatives on the Missouri.

SERVING UNCLE SAM.

I continued in the government service from the time of my release from captivity in 1862, with but little intermission, until the occurrence of my disabilities in 1866, a period of more than three years—half of which time I was stationed at Fort Wadsworth, D. T., and acted at different times as post interpreter and as scout, chief of scouts, and inspector of scouts in the "frontier scout force." Most of the time I had charge of the escort and courier service, and also of the patrolling service in the vicinity of the Fort, and was under the immediate command of the commandant of the post and of the 3rd sub-district (District of Minnesota, Department of the Northwest)—Major Robert H. Rose, of the Second Minnesota Calvary.

OF WHAT COMPOSED.

The "frontier scout force" was a special military organization composed of Sisseton and Wahpeton Indians, mixed-bloods and white men, the latter trappers, hunters and frontiersmen, employed by Gen. H. H. Sibley in the war following the Sioux outbreak of 1862, and commanded by Major Joseph R. Brown of the Third Regiment Minnesota Militia, until March 31, 1866, when he resigned and I, as inspector of scouts took charge of the same under Lieut. Col. C. P. Adams, of the Independent Bataillon Minnesoca Cavalry, who, under the general recognition of the forces operating against the hostile Sioux Indians, had been given the command of the third sub-district with headquarters at Fort Abercrombie, D. T.

IN COMMAND.

On the 13th of April following I was ordered to relieve the military agent, and to assume control (under the Lieut. Col. commanding) of all scouting operations and all Indian matters within the region described as follows: On the east by a line running from the foot of Big Stone Lake to the head of Lake Traverse, thence northwardly to the Twin Lakes, thence on a direct line to the Cheyenne river, on the west by a line running from the mouth of Snake creek up to the James river to the mouth of Moccasin creek, thence on a direct line to Willow Point on the Elm river, on the north by a line running up the Cheyenne river from where the east line strikes the same, until said line intersects a line crossing the Cheyenne river at the mouth of Bold Hills creek and running from the Red River of the North to the Willow Point on the Elm river, and on the south by a line running from the mouth of Snake creek on the James river eastwardly to Kampeska Lake, thence on a direct line to the foot of Big Stone Lake.

THE BUFFALO REPUBLIC.

On account of the immense herds of buffalo constantly passing up and down the James river flats and the coteau hills, this region was sportively called "Tatanka (Buffalo) Republic." In the fall of 1865 at a social gathering of some of the officers of the post, the "Republic" was declared "free and independent" with Major Robert H. Rose as president, Major Joseph R. Brown as secretary of war, Captain Arthur H. Mills as quarter master general, and Gabriel Renville as captain general of all the forces operating against "the woolly buffalo and the wily Sioux."

SERIOUS INJURIES.

While in the service as inspector of scouts and acting military agent, and in the line of duty, I contracted injuries which deranged my eyes, dimmed my eyesight, paralyzed my muscular powers, deprived me of the use of my legs, and of all natural power of motion, and permanently impaired my general health, the same having been superinduced by over-exertion and exposure to cold and wet weather in the following manner:

INDICATIONS OF A RAID.

On the afternoon of April, 19, 1866, at the military agency, near Fort Wadsworth, D. T., I received information that led me to believe there was imminent danger of an Indian raid. News was brought in to the effect that fresh moccasin tracks had been discovered in the vicinity of "where they cut bows," on the upper James river, a few days before, and that the tracks led in the direction of the Minnesota frontier.

STRINGENT ORDERS.

I immediately reported the matter to the commanding officer at the fort and informed him that I should at once leave for the Elm river for the purpose of putting the scouts there on the *qui vive*. I was under most stringent orders not only from the lieutenant colonel commanding at Fort Abercrombie, who required me to "see that all war parties are promptly pursued and intercepted in their hostile designs against the exposed frontiers of Minnesota and Iowa," (circular order No. 3, of April 5, 1866) but also from the major general commanding at St. Paul, who required me to "keep the scouts constantly on the *qui vive*." I therefore hurriedly drew on my buffalo skin suit—jacket, leggins and moccasins—buckled a Henry to my waist belt, hurriedly bridled and saddled my horse, which stood in the stable near by and always kept ready for any emergency of this kind that might arise, and mounting the animal and giving it the whip, started off on a brisk gallop for the Elm river scouting station—between fifty-five and sixty miles away to the westward.

ELM RIVER STATION.

This scouting station was occupied by seventeen lodges of scouts—regular and supernumerary—the former getting a per diem and rations and the latter rations only, and was under Joseph Rouillard, chief of scouts. The camp was located on the Elm river, west of the James, about where Ordway, Brown county, South Dakota, now is, and was regarded as one of the most important outposts in the service. Its location was far out in the hostile country and on the thoroughfare of travel for war parties from the northwest.

A PERILOUS NIGHT RIDE.

I left the fort, or rather the military agency half a mile east of it, at about sundown and before, I had gone far was enveloped in darkness. Indeed, when I had reached the western edge of the coteau hills—eight miles—utter darkness was upon me. The country from here on was a wild, level plain, and almost trackless. I tried to follow an old trail which led to the cottonwood grove on the James and could not. But I had been over this route before and had no trouble in making my way, and owing to the darkness I felt safe from ambush.

GUIDED BY THE NORTH STAR.

The north star, which peered through the clouds at intervals, was my main reliance. It was my only guide and comforter. I galloped on at a rapid pace across this wild and trackless prairie country without any interval of rest or let up whatever except when fording the James or pulling up the horse for a moment at a time to enable it to catch its breath, and arrived at my destination about midnight, making the distance—about fifty-five miles—in about five hours.

AT THE STATION.

Entering the camp and going direct to the chief's lodge I dismounted and proceeded to tie the horse to a wagon near by when Rouillard, who had been lying under it watching my movements, rose up and called out "hello, Sam! what's up." I hurriedly explained matters and was quickly informed that the Indians who had been sent north a month or so before as peace messengers to the hostile Sioux had that evening passed by on their return to the Cottonwood Grove, on the James, and that they had assured him peace had been made and there was no longer any danger from Indian raids.

GATHERING FOR PEACE CONFERENCE.

My father having been appointed a special agent of the interior department to collect the Minnesota Sioux and assemble them at Fort Rice to meet the U. S. peace commissioners there had dispatched some trusty Indian messengers to the north to endeavor to negotiate and bring them in. These were the peace messengers referred to.

A WILD GOOSE CHASE.

I was struck dumb with surprise and mortification, for I was satisfied I had come on a wild goose chase, and the alarm was a false one, that no war party was coming, and that the tracks or the trail of these Indian messengers had been seen and supapsed to be the tracks of hostile Indians. I at once decided to return without delay. I deemed it my duty to return at once and intercept the communication which I had sent in previous to my departure relative to hostile Indians, or to correct the same so as to not create unnecessary alarm at headquarters in St. Paul and throughout western Minnesota —the raid the spring before, particularly at the time of the murder of the Jewett family near Mankato, and the capture and hanging of the half-breed Jack Campbell there, having thrown the whole country into a feverish state of excitement and nervousness.

RETRACING MY STEPS.

Besides, it was considered hazardous and foolhardy in the extreme to attempt to cross the prairies by day, especially when alone, owing to the danger of being ambushed and waylaid by prowling Indians. So after securing Rouillard's fresh Indian pony, which stood picketed near the lodge, and which the chief had recommended as "tough and gamy," and saddling and bridling it, and giving my ow horse a parting tap with the whip, I mounted the pony and dashed away in the night—homeward bound.

NIGHT ON THE PRAIRIES.

There was no moon or star to be seen and I was enveloped in utter darkness. The north star which had peered through the clouds and had guided and comforted me on the way over, was no completely hidden behind heavy clouds and I was left with absolutely nothing to steer by except occasional faint flashes of lightning behind me in the west, and although the dark and heavy clouds overhead, as well as in the west, indicated a storm. I was not in the least disturbed thereby and pushed forward in the direction of the James. When I had been out an hour or so, however, and had reached the river, and had heard the noise of the rushing waters before me, and the rumbling of thunder overhead and before me, accompanied by sharp flashes of lightning, and felt a few drops of rain, I become somewhat nervous.

A FAMILIAR LOCATION.

But when I had forded the stream and had struck an old and well beaten trail and had recognized the spot where I, with a few scouts and a supply train, and Lieut. Jonathan Darrow with part of a company of soldiers, had camped a few nights before, and had found myself fairly on the James river flat, where the country before me was as level as a barn floor, and free from wolf holes or gopher knolls, or other impediments to fast traveling, I was not only delighted but highly elated and very much encouraged, for I felt that I could keep ahead of any storm that might come up from the west. I whipped up the pony and dashed forward at a break-neck speed, and kept on at a very rapid pace until I had reached "the old hay meadow" —a lake about half way between the James river and the fort.

THE VOICE OF THE GREAT SPIRIT.

Here I heard "the voice of the great spirit issuing from the dark clouds of of the west" in a more astounding tone than before. The flashes of lightning were so blinding and the peals of thunder so deafening that I made up my mind I would stop and crawl in among the tall weeds or rushes which skirted the lake, and wait there for the rain to pass by and pulled up.

CHANGED HIS MIND.

I was about to alight when the thought all of a sudden struck me that some war party passing along might already have taken refuge there, and acting upon the maxim that "discretion is the better part of valor" I struck the pony with my rawhide whip and went flying past the reeds and on over the prairie at a rate that would have put a Gilpin, a Sheridan or a Rankin to the blush. I had proceeded but half a mile or so when there rushed upon me from behind—Indians? No.

A TERRIFIC WIND STORM.

I was struck by one of the most terrific wind storms I ever knew. It rushed upon me with such suddenness and with terrific force and violence that I was started and nearly unhorsed.

A DELUGE.

Very soon the rain come. And such rain! It fairly poured. The floodgates of heaven seemed to have broken loose.

FROM RAIN TO SLEET AND SNOW.

Following the rain and close upon it came sleet, hail and snow, which in a few minutes turned into a snow storm—a genuine

DAKOTA BLIZZARD.

Death stared me in the face, and my situation was most awful. The terrible roar of the wind, the inky blackness of the night, and the thought of becoming lost or frozen or way-laid and scalped, and be given a sepulchre such as the wolves give, all combined, was terrible in the extreme. I need a "pencil and a pen divine" to describe it and do it justice. There was nothing to be seen, nothing to be felt or heard save wind and snow. But in spite of this I managed to keep the wind to my back and push on, or more properly speaking the wind kept to my back and pushed me on nolen-volens.

WITHOUT COMPASS OR BEARING.

Of course, no landmarks could be seen, but I knew, or thought I knew, that the range of hills known as the Coteau-des-Prairie was before me across my way, and that I needed only to be guided by the wind to reach it. I felt that once among the the hills I could find shelter in one of the numerous wooded ravines or coulies there and be safe.

COVERED WITH SLEET.

Very soon my clothes began to freeze, and notwithstanding my thick clothing, which kept my skin dry I was evidently uncomfortable.

A PLUCKY PONY.

My pony was truly "tough and gamey" as Rouillard had said it was, and it galloped on and on in the midst of the driving rain, sleet, hail snow, and through slush and mud, and across swollen streams, and frozen and icy places. The noble little animal would sometimes gallop through the rushing water, sometimes slip and slide on frozen and icy places, and sometimes break through soft ice and dump me into the water. Twice I was thus thrown, but fortunately my hair lariat—one end of which was fastened to the bridle bit and the other tucked in under my belt—prevented the pony from getting away.

STORM INCREASING IN FURY.

At about day break I found myself at the foot of the Coteau hills (the western slope) which I ascended. On reaching the top I found that the storms had not only not abated but seemed to have increased in fury—that is, the winds blew more furiously and the cold was more intense but the snow was lighter and the air much clearer.

SEEING LAND MARKS.

Land marks could be seen. I discovered several familiar and noteworthy ones. Away to the northwest and about a mile distant is the ravine or coulie where Lieutenant Thomas Thompson (I think) of the Second Minnesota Cavalry, with a detachment of fifteen or twenty soldiers and a dozen scouts and myself, camped of a night the spring before, after wandering about on the prairie all day in search of Indians. There just to the southeast and about five miles away is the butte or high peak overlooking the James river flats and called (in official dispatches,) Hawk's Nest or Buzzard's Roost, And there down on the flats and about three miles away is the spot where Gen. Corse and staff and party of hunters from St. Paul, and a number of the officers and some of the scouts and soldiers and Indian hunters from Fort Wadsworth, the fall before, struck an immense herd of buffalo—estimated at thirty thousand strong, where a sprig of an officer on the general's staff who had evidently never seen a buffalo before got excited and accidentally shot his horse in the back of the head with his revolver and felled it to the ground and lost the day's sport—a never ending joke on the fellow,—and where on the same hunt and chase a strange adventure befell me—was chased three miles and into camp by a wounded and maddened buffalo.

"WHERE HE WAS AT."

I found that I was about twenty-five miles southeast of the fort—fifteen miles or more off course. The wind having shifted from the west to the northwest or north, I had without knowing it changed my own course correspondingly. So fierce was the wind that I dreaded to face it—dreaded the long ride before me. The thought that possibly hostile Indians may be lurking in one of the wooded ravines near by destroyed ideas of seeking refuge there and whipping up the pony I dashed forward. The little fellow at first lagged and needed considerable urging. It, too, dreaded to face the piercing wind. But it finally pricked up its ears and took the "dog trot" and kept it.

SHIVERING WITH COLD.

I was now shivering with cold and had well nigh lost all hope. Giving the pony the reins and allowing it to jog along at its own gate and picking its own way I sat shivering and wishing I was at home. The noble little pony jogged along up hill and down, across frozen creeks, lakes, marshes, and swamps, until the fort —or rather the military agency which I had left the evening before—was reached about eight o'clock on the morning of April 20, 1866—having travelled about one hundred and fifty miles during the night.

A HAVEN AT LAST.

I proceeded direct to the agency building, or more properly speaking, the pony took me straight to it, and rode up to the stockade which was built of substantial oak posts or pickets ten feet high around the building with portholes for musketry, and bastions or blockhouses at the angles for the purpose of defense in case of attack from the Indians, and dismounted or rather rolled off the pony and fell in a heap on the ground bereft of

THE USE OF MY LEGS

The muscles were perfectly relaxed but I had no control over them. Gathering myself up by aid of the pony's forelegs and mane I unbuckled the girth, took off the saddle and bridle, and let the animal go. I was completely wet through and shivering with cold, was weak, and in an exhausted condition, and as the pony struck out for the stable and hay stack near by, I staggered towards the stockade gate and fell headlong through it and against the door of the house and burst it open. I crawled in and up to a bed tick in a corner of the room where for hours. or until late in the afternoon of that day, I lay in a condition of

SEMI-CONSCIOUSNESS AND STUPOR.

When I arose Rip Van Winkle like, and left the house and walked slowly and with difficulty, and in a staggering manner to the teepee or lodge of Francois Vasseur, an old French trapper, frontiersman and scout, about a quarter of a mile distant towards the fort, and there suffering with aches and pains, and from a weak exhausted feeling, and with all energy and courge lost, I sent for the commanding officer, Lieut. James E. Cochrane, of the Independent Battalion, Minnesota Cavalry, who immediately came to see me. I told him all about my trip, and asked to be relieved from further duty for the reason that I was no longer fit for service. He promised to send at once (by courier) to Fort Abercrombie and correct the report I had made the day before relative to hostile Indians and which had been forwarded that morning.

WHAT THE RIDE DID FOR ME.

Prior to the ride and the hardships encountered as herein set forth, I enjoyed good, sound physical health —was robust and strong, active and energetic. When a school boy I could lift more, run faster, jump higher and farther than of my schoolmates—at least I thought I could. The boys of "Old Seabury" at Faribault, and of "Dixon College" at St. Paul, can testify as to that. Today I am a physical wreck, not having taken a natural step since the incurrence of my disabilities. I am compensated in a measure, however, by the reflection that I did my duty.

In Mr. Brown's "Reminiscences" he speaks of a buffalo hunt enjoyed in the fall of 1865, with Gen. Corse and members of his staff, in which Mr. Brown had a thrilling encounter with a wounded animal. The following particulars of the encounter is published by him, as published in the Inter-State Tribune of Dec. 27, 1895:

"At the time of the Minnesota massacre, or Indian outbreak of 1862, or rather of the war following that tragic event, the region lying immediately west of Brown's Valley (as far as James river) was a paradise for the buffalo hunter. Countless thousands of these "monarchs of the prairie" were constantly found roaming over it, and for this reason, and also because the Sisseton scouts were constantly kept on the qui vive for war parties on their way to the settlements below, the region was jocosely termed "Tatanka (or Buffalo) Republic." One evening in the fall of 1865, at a social gathering of some of the officers of the post at Fort Wadsworth, and at which champagne flowed quite free, Major R. H. Rose was declared president and commander-in-chief; Major Joseph R. Brown secretary of war; Captain A. H. Mills quartermaster general, and Gabriel Renville captain general of the forces operating against the "wooly buffalo" and the wily Sioux."

"In the fall of 1865 Gen. Corse and staff came up from St. Paul on a tour of inspection. In order to give them a treat a number of the officers and soldiers, and some of the scouts and Indian hunters from the fort, numbering in all about one hundred, under the leadership of Gabriel Renville, escorted the distinguished party to the buffalo country about Buzzard's Roost, a high peak on the western slope of the Coteau desprairie, about forty miles nearly southwest from the fort and overlooking the James River flats. Near this point, about where the town of Groton is located, we struck an immense herd, a terror-inspiring one, from twenty-five to thirty thousand strong. A prig of an officer, a lieutenant or captain on the general's staff and named Scott, who had borrowed the most valuable and swiftest horse at the fort, and was going to teach the Indians how best to slay the buffalo, armed himself with a brace of Colt's revolvers, telling the Indians that the long gun was no good, and the very outset or onrush, when the Indians, at a signal from Gabriel Renville began yelling and whooping in a manner that would have put the Israelites at Jericho to the blush, got excited and dropped one of his pistols, and with the other accidentally shot his horse through the head and felled it to the ground, and thereby lost the day's sport.

"At this same hunt and chase a strange adventure befell me. But before relating it I wish to say that I never was an expert buffalo hunter —that is, I never could pick out the fattest and best in the drove and kill them one after another and as fast as one could fire, as the late Chief Renville or as Charles Crawford used to do. I have seen the former, armed with a Henry repeater, shoot and kill sixteen on one "run" and in less than that many minutes, and the latter fifteen, while four is the most I ever killed, and had a full hour to do it in. My forte was to single out the bulls, drive them from the herd and fill them with bullets. At the time I speak of I noticed in the midst of the scampering herd a big buffalo bull, a very shaggy fellow, and one of the ugliest looking brutes I had ever seen. I at once made up my mind to separate the big fellow from the drove and kill it if I could, or at least have some fun with it. I was mounted on a swift horse and armed with a Henry repeater. I rushed toward the big fellow and drove it from the herd and followed it for about three miles, peppering it as I went along, wounding it in several places and shooting off my last cartridge. It so happened that the buffalo, as if it knew I was out of ammunition and could do it no further harm, of the instant I discharged my last round, turned upon me and gave chase. I was going at full speed and passed the animal and circled around with the buffalo in hot pursuit, not more than twenty feet away. I put the whip to my horse and fled for dear life, and was soon far in the lead, a quarter of a mile or so from the buffalo. I galloped up to the top of a knoll and looked back. I saw the big fellow coming toward me slowly and leisurely. Thinking that perhaps the animal was not after me in particular, but was crazed from the wounds I had inflicted upon it, and was simply looking for a place to drop, thought I would give it the slip and see what it would do. I went down on the opposite side of the knoll and came back around under the mound and hid behind a hillock, where I could be seen only from the top of the knoll. The buffalo soon came jogging along up the knoll and ascending up to the top. Here it stood for some minutes looking around in every direction. At the instant it caught sight of me the big fellow bounded down and took after me as before. I again put the whip to my horse and started for camp, two miles away, and soon left the buffalo far behind. I would now and then look back and see it coming at a slow pace, and when about a mile from camp again tried to puzzle the animal by passing over a mound and showing myself, and then going down into a dry run and following it back and standing partially hidden from view by the tall grass and deep washout. Very soon the big fellow came jogging along, passed by and went up the mound, and on reaching the top stopped and looked around. He stood there for some minutes looking in all directions, and the instant it caught a glimpe of me through the tall grass it again gave chase, galloping slowly and then walking; as if it meant to catch me "if it took all summer." I became somewhat nervous. Indeed the thought that my horse might step into a wolf hole or gopher knoll or stumble and throw me off and be tossed in the air by a buffalo, and a mad one at that, made me fairly shake with fear, and I put the whip to old Dobbin and dashed off. Very soon the buffalo started on a run, and when I saw this I plied the whip more vigorously than ever, and made a "bee line" for camp, into which I went tearing, with the infuriated animal close at my heels. It so happened that Capt. Mills, the quartermaster general of "Tatanka Republic," who had just got in from the chase and had not yet dismounted, rode out and shot the buffalo, within a hundreds yards of the ambulance and baggage wagons."

REPORT ABOUT WAR PARTY, AND THE FEARS OF WHICH INDUCED MR. BROWN'S MEMORABLE RIDE.

MILITARY AGENCY,
FORT WADSWORTH, D. T.
April 19, 1866.
LIEUT. JAMES E. COCHRANE,
Post Commander.

SIR: I have the honor of reporting through you to the lieutenant colonel commanding that the chief of the Light Band has just arrived with the news that a war party is approaching the settlements. He says that on the 14th instant, or five days ago, fresh moccasin tracks leading in the direction of Big Stone lake had been discovered in the vicinity of the camp at "where they cut bows" on the upper James. I shall leave here tonight for the Elm to put the scouts there on the *qui vive*. I very much fear that for want of a scout at the mouth of the Snake or at Oak Grove on the James and a few at the mouth of the Moccasin, these rascals may be able to penetrate our lines and re-enact the horrors attending the "Jewett murder" near Mankato about this time last spring. I cannot urge too strongly the importance of at once establishing these stations. Very respectfully,

SAMUEL J. BROWN,
Inspector of Scouts, (Acting Military Agent.)

Taken captives by Cut Nose and Shakopee, Aug. 19, 1862:
Susan F. Brown, wife of Major Brown.
Lydia A. Blair, daughter of Major Brown.
Angus M. A. Brown, son of Major Brown.
Ellen Brown, daughter of Major Brown.
Samuel J. Brown, son of Major Brown.
Amanda C. Brown, daughter of Major Brown.
Emily A. Brown, daughter of Major Brown.
Augusta A. Brown, daughter of Major Brown.
Joseph R. Brown, Jr., son of Major Brown.
Sibley H. Brown, son of Major Brown.
Susie Brown, daughter of Major Brown.
Garvies' cook (name unknown.)*
Charles Holmes.*
Leopold Wobler.*
Peter Rouillard.*
Charles Blair, son-in-law of Major Brown. Liberated by Little Crow.*
Minnie Blair, daughter of Charles Blair.
Stuart Blair, child of Charles Blair.
Elizabeth Brown, wife of Angus M. A. Brown.
Edmund Brown, child of Angus M. A. Brown.
Lousman, (servant in Major Brown's family and real name unknown.)*
Mrs. Leopold Wohler, wife of L. Wohler.
Miss Jennie Ingalls.
Miss Amanda Ingalls.
Liberated through the efforts of Mrs. Major Brown marked thus *.
Besides there were two teamsters (teams with flour for the agency rom Forest City) warned and got away.

HISTORY OF MR. BROWN'S EFFORTS TO GET A PENSION.

A claim for pension was made in May, 1869, through Hon. Geo. L. Otis of St. Paul, and again in March, 1875, through Hon. D. Cooper of Salt Lake City, but owing to the difficulty of appearing with my witnesses before an officer of a court of record, no formal application was made until March, 1878, through Gen. John B. Sanborn of St, Paul. This application was made in the old log house at Brown's Valley, Minn., and before A. J. Parker, clerk of district court of Big Stone county, Minn. Mr. Parker drove up from Ortonville and did the job for $25. The claim was before the pension bureau upwards of three years when it was rejected on the ground that I had never been mustered by a mustering officer of the army. In December, 1881, I applied to congress for relief, but no progress was made beyond the introduction of the bill in the house and the reference of it to the committee on invalid pensions until February, 1884, when that committee reported it back to the house with the recommendation that it be referred to the committee on pensions. Here it remained without action until the winter of 1884-5 when it took up my case, but declined to report in my favor on the ground that I had not been a member of any military organization, notwithstanding the earnest and united efforts of Congressmen Nelson, Strait and Wakefield in my behalf. The committee decided unanimously that the proofs were ample and conclusive, that my injuries were received in the service of the government and in the line of duty, but the majority decided that the rule which barred civilians barred me, and that I was not entitled to a favorable report. I was thunderstruck when I heard of this. The idea that because I was not technically in the military service I was not entitled to a pension, that being practically in the army cut no figure, was inexplicable and perfectly preposterous to me. Acting upon the maxim that "thrice armed is he whose cause is just" I induced Congressman Nelson, at the next session of congress, to introduce another bill for my relief. This was promptly done, and the bill promptly referred to the committee on pensions in the house, and through the earnest and untiring labors of Congressman Nelson and many of the public men of the state—among them Gen. Sibley, Gen. Sanborn, Gen. Johnson and Gov. Marshall, all of St. Paul, and Gen. Corse of Boston, and the Emory Upton Post of the G. A. R. of Brown's Valley—the bill was taken up and reported favorably March 23, 1886, and went to the senate where it was referred to committee on pensions, which reported it favorably April 6, 1886, and passed that body April 21, 1886, and became a law May 9, 1886—twenty years after the incurrence of my disabilities.

EXECUTION OF
Thirty-Eight Sioux Indians.

AT MANKATO, MINNESOTA,

DECEMBER 26, 1862.

(From Mankato DAILY REVIEW, Dec. 26, 1896)

On Friday, December 26th, 1862, a few hours after the 38 Sioux Indians were hanged at Mankato, the *Mankato Record*, then owned and edited by the senior editor of the REVIEW, printed a special edition of that paper containing a very full report of the event and incidents of the preceding week pertaining thereto.

Several thousand copies of this edition were printed and sold, and many were sent to all parts of the country. In the thirty-four years intervening these papers have been lost or destroyed, and very few are in existence. We are able to recall only two in this city, one of which is in the bound volume of the *Record*, preserved among the files of this office. To gratify an often-expressed wish of many citizens to procure and preserve a report of the event which has always been esteemed of so much importance in the history of Mankato, we today reproduce so much of the special edition as pertained to the execution. The *Record* was the first paper in the state to publish a detailed report of the hanging, the writer being the only press representative present at most of the preceding interviews described, and indeed all the matter was specially prepared for the *Record*. Other papers in the state, especially the daily press of St. Paul, republished much of this matter—some without proper credit —and much of it passed into histories subsequently printed.

The original order directing that the execution take place was received here about midnight on the 17th of December, having been brought through by couriers from St. Paul. The writer put it into type immediately, and before morning copies were being carried by couriers to all the military posts in southwestern Minnesota. It was as follows:

SPECIAL ORDER NO. 11.

Headquarters Indian Post, }
Mankato, Dec. 17, 1862. }

The President of the United States, having directed the execution of thirty-nine of the Sioux Indians and half-breed prisoners in my charge, on Friday, the 26th instant—he having postponed the time from the 19th instant—said execution will be carried into effect in front of the Indian prison at this place on that day at 10 o'clock a. m. The executive also enjoins that no others of the prisoners be allowed to escape, and that they be protected for the future disposition of the government; and these orders will be executed by the military force at my disposal with utmost fidelity.

The aid of all good citizens is invoked to maintain the law and constitutional authority of the land on that occasion. The State of Minnesota must not, in addition to the terrible wrongs and outrages inflicted upon her by the murderous savages, suffer, if possible, still more fatally, in her prosperity and reputation, at the hands of a few of our misguided, though deeply injured fellow-citizens.
STEPHAN MILLER,
Col 7th Minn. Regt. Vols.,
Commanding Post.

The report as printed 34 years ago is as follows:

EXECUTION OF 38 SIOUX.

Reading of Death Warrant—Martial Law Declared.

CONFESSIONS OF PRISONERS.

Full Particulars of the Execution, Etc.—Prohibiting the Sale of Liquor to Soldiers.

On Monday afternoon the following order was read on dress parade, which the venders of spirituous liquors will do well to strictly adhere to:

GENERAL ORDER NO. 18.
Headquarters Indian Post, }
Mankato, Dec. 22d, 1862. }

All persons interested in Mankato and the adjoining distance for ten miles from these headquarters, are hereby notified to sell or give no intoxicating liquors of any description, including wine and beer, to the enlisted men of the United States forces in this valley or vicinity, unless it be upon an order from or approved by the colonel commanding.

Any violations of this order will be followed by the immediate seizure and destruction of all the liquors of the offender, and by such other punishment as the nature of the case may demand.

A vigilant patrol will be organized to visit suspected places, wagons, rooms, booths, etc., and to carry these orders into execution.
J. K. ARNOLD,
Adjutant 7th Regt. Minn. Vols., Post Adjutant.

GENERAL ORDER NO. 17.
Headquarters Indian Post, }
Mankato, Dec. 22d, 1862. }

Col. Benjamin F. Smith, of Mankato; Major W. H Dike, of Faribault; Hon. Henry A. Swift and H. W. Lamberton, Esq., of St. Peter; Edwin Bradley, Mr. E. H. Dike, Mankato, and Reuben Butters, of Kasota, together with such other good citizens as they may select, are hereby requested to act at this place on Friday, the 26th inst., as mounted citizen marshalls, Col. B. F. Smith as chief and the others as assistants

The colonel commanding respectfully recommends that they assemble at Mankato the previous evening and adopt such wholesome measure as may contribute to the preservation of good order and strict propriety during the said 26th instant.

By order of the colonel commanding.
J. K. ARNOLD, Post Adjutant.

CITIZENS' PETITION FOR MARTIAL LAW.

For the better preservation of order on the day of execution citizens of our town, on Tuesday last, addressed the following note to Col. Miller. requesting him to declare martial law in the town and vicinity:
STEPHEN MILLER, Col. 7th Regt., Minn. Vols.—

Sir: There is every probability that at the execution of a portion of the Sioux Indians on the 26th instant, now in your charge, there will be a large collection of people at this place, and in view of the excited state of the country occasioned by the outrages perpetrated by these Indians, it is apprehended that some disturbance may possibly occur on that occasion. Desirous to see law and order maintained, permit us to suggest to you the propriety of prohibiting the sale of all intoxicating liquor for three days, including the day before and the day after the execution, in the town and within a circle of five miles thereof. This, we presume, cannot be done without the declaration of martial law, and if this suggestion meets your views we will be happy to see you do so; and will use our influence to aid you in preserving the peace of the community and in maintaining the supremacy of the law. In making this suggestion we have no desire to intermeddle with your duties as a military officer, or to dictate to you what course you shall take on that occasion; our principal object being to inform you that in case you should take the same view of the matter that we do, that you may rely on our sustaining you in that course.

The above letter was signed by a large number of our citizens, including, we believe, nearly or quite all the dealers in intoxicating liquors in the town.

MARTIAL LAW DECLARED.

On Wednesday evening the following order in accordance with the above request, was issued by Col. Miller:

GENERAL ORDER NO. 21.

Headquarters Indian Post,
Mankato, Dec. 24, 1862.

The colonel commanding publishes the following rules to govern all who may be concerned; and for the preservation of the public peace, declares martial law over all the territory within a circle of ten miles of these headquarters:

1. It is apprehended by both the civil and military authorities, as well many of the prominent citizens and business men, that the use of intoxicating liquors about the time of the approaching Indian execution may result in a serious riot or breach of the peace; and the unrestrained distribution of such beverages to enlisted men is always subversive of good order and military discipline.

2. The good of the service, the honor of the state and the protect on of all concerned, imperatively require that for a specified period, the sale, gift or use of all intoxicating drinks, including wines, beer and malt liquors, be entirely suspended.

3. From this necessity, and for the said purposes, martial law is hereby declared in and about all territory, buildings, tents, booths, camps, quarters and other places within the aforesaid limits, to take effect at 3 o'clock on Thursday morning, the 25th inst.

4. Accordingly, the sale tender, gift or use of all intoxicating liquors as above named, by soldiers, sojourners or citizens, is entirely prohibited until Saturday evening, the 27th instant, at 11 o'clock.

5. The said prohibition to continue as to sales or gifts of all intoxicating liquors as before described, to enlisted men, in the service of the United States—except upon special written orders or permission from these headquarters—until officially revoked by the commandant of this post.

6. For the purpose of giving full scope and effect to this order, a special patrol will visit all suspected camps, tents, booths, rooms, wagons and other places and seize and destroy all liquors so tendered, given, sold or used, and break the vessels containing the same, and report the circumstances with the name of the offender to these headquarters.

7. This order will be read at the head of every company of the United States forces, serving or coming within said limits.

STEPHEN MILLER,
Col. 7th Regt. Minn. Vols.,
Official, Commanding Post.
J. K. ARNOLD,
Adjutant 7th Regt. Minn. Vols.,
Post Adjutant.

READING OF THE DEATH WARRANT.

On Monday last the thirty-nine Indians sentenced by the president were selected out and confined in an apartment separate and distinct from the other Indians.

About half past two o'clock Col. Miller, accompanied by his staff officers, ministers and a few others, visited them in their cells for the purpose of reading to them the president's approval of their sentence, and the order for their execution.

Rev. Mr. Riggs acted as interpreter, and through him Col. Miller addressed the prisoners in substance as follows: "The commanding officer at this place has called to speak to you upon a very serious subject this afternoon. Your Great Father at Washington, after carefully reading what the witnesses have testified in your several trials, has come to the conclusion that you have each been guilty of wantonly and wickedly murdering his white children; and for this reason he has directed that you each be hanged by the neck until you are dead, on next Friday, and that order will be carried into effect on that day, at ten o'clock in the forenoon.

"Good ministers—both Catholic and Protestant—are here, from amongst whom each of you can select your spiritual adviser, who will be permitted to commune with you constantly during the four days that you are yet to live."

The colonel then instructed Adjt. Arnold to read to them in English the letter of President Lincoln, which in substance orders that thirty-nine prisoners, whose names are given, shall be executed at the time above stated. Rev. Mr. Riggs then read the letter in the Dakota language.

The colonel further instructed Mr. Riggs to tell them that they have sinned so against their fellow-men that there is no hope for clemency except in the mercy of God, through the merits of the Blessed Redeemer, and that he earnestly exhorted them to apply to that as their only remaining source of consolation.

The occasion was one of much solemnity to the persons present, though but very little emotion was manifested by the Indians. A half-breed named Millord seemed much depressed in spirits. All listened attentively, and at the conclusion of each sentence indulged their usual grunt or signal of approval. At the reading of that portion of the warrant condemning them to be hanged by the necks the response was quite feeble, and was given by only two or three. Several Indians smoked their pipes composedly during the reading, and we observed one in particular who, when the time of execution was designated, quietly knocked the ashes from his pipe and filled it afresh with his favorite kinnekinnick; while another was slowly rubbing a pipe full of the same article in his hand, preparatory to a good smoke.

The Indians were evidently prepared for the visit and the announcement of their sentence—one or two having overheard soldiers talking about it when they were removed to a separate apartment.

At the conclusion of the ceremony Col. Miller instructed Maj. Brown to tell the Indians that each would be privileged to designate the minister of his choice, that a record of the same would be made, and the minister so selected would have free intercourse with him.

The colonel and spectators then withdrew, leaving the ministers in consultation with the prisoners.

The Indians under sentence were confined in a back room on the first floor of Leech's stone building, chained in pairs, and closely and strongly guarded.

NAMES OF THE CONDEMNED.

The following are the Indian names of the condemned prisoners, also the meaning of each, as translated by Rev. S. R. Riggs:

DAKOTA. ENGLISH.
Te-he-do-ne-cha.....One Who Forbids His House
Ptan-doo-ta, or Ta-joo..................Red Otter
Wy-a-tah-ta-wa........................His People
Hin-han-shoon-ko-yag-ma-ne.........
... .One who Walks Clothed in an Owl's Tail
Ma-ya-boom-doo..................... ..Iron Blower
Wan-na-doo-ta.................... ...... Red Leaf
Wa-he-kna............Don't Know the Meaning
Qwa-ma-ne.................... Tinkling Walker
Ta-tay-me-ma... ....Round Wind
Rda-in-yan-ka..................Rattling Runner
Do-wan-sa............... ....The Singer
Ha-pan ....Second Child if a Son
Shoon-ka-ska.................... ...... White Dog
Toon-kan-e-chah-tag-ma-ne...
.... One Who Walks by His Grandfather
E-tag-doo-ta........................Red Face
Am-da-cha........................Broken to Pieces
Hay-pe-dan.... . ....The Third Child, if a Son
Mah-pe-o-ke-ne-jin......Who Stands on a Cloud
Henry Millord.................. ....A Half-breed
Chas-ka-dan............The First Born, if a Son
Baptiste Campbell..................A Half-breed
Ta-tay-ka-gay..................... Wind Maker
Hay-pin-kpa..........The Tip of the Horn
Hypolite Ange.... ....A Half-breed
Na-pay-skin..............One Who does Not Flee
Wa-kan-tan-ka......................Great Spirit
Toon-kan-ko-yag-e-na-jin...........
One who Stands Clothed with his Grandfather
Ma-ka-ta-e-ne-jin..One Who Stands on the Earth
Pa-za-koo-tay-wn-nee.......................
.... One Who Walks Prepared to Shoot
To-tay-hde-dan...............Wind Comes Home
Wa-she-choon........................ . Frenchman
A-e-che-ga.........................To Grow Upon
Ho-tan-in-koo......Voice that Appears Coming
Chay-tan-hoon-ka........... The Parent Hawk
Chan-ka-hda........................Near the Wood
Hda-hin-hday........
.... To Make a Rattling Noise Suddenly
O-ya-tay-a-koo............The Coming People
Ma-hoo-way-wa.............He Comes for Me
Wa-kin-yan-ne................Little Thunder

CONFESSIONS OF THE CONDEMNED.

Rev. S. R. Riggs has kindly prepared for us the following synopsis of conversations held with each one of the condemned prisoners, wherein is contained much interesting information:

1. Te-he-do-ne cha (One who forbids his house), says he was asleep when the outbreak took place at the Lower Agency. He was not present at the breaking open of the stores, but afterwards went over the Minnesota river and took some women captives. The men who were killed there, he says, were killed by other Indians, whom he named.

2. Ptan-doo-ta, alias Ta-joo (Red Otter), says he had very sore eyes at the time of the outbreak, and was at that time down opposite Fort Ridgely. He was with the party that killed Patwell and others. Ma-ya-bon doo killed Patwell. He took Miss Williams captive. Says he would have violated the women but they resisted. He thinks he did a good deed in saving the women alive.

3. Wy-a-tah-ta-wa (His people), says he was at the attack on Capt. Marsh's company, and also at New Ulm. He and another Indian shot a man at the same time. He does not know whether he or the other Indian killed the white man. He was wounded in following up another white man. He was at the battle of Birch Coolie, where he fired his gun four times; he fired twice at Wood Lake.

4 Hin-han-shoon-ko-yag-ma-ne (One who walks Clothed in an Owl's Tail), says he is charged with killing white people, and so condemned; he does not know certainly that he killed any one; he was in all the battles. That is all he has to say.

5. Ma-za-boom-doo (Iron Blower), says he was down on the Big Cottonwood when the outbreak took place; that he came that day into New Ulm and purchased various articles, and then started home; he met the Indians coming down; saw some in wagons shot but does not know who killed them; he was present at the killing of Patwell and others, but denies having done it himself; he thinks he did well by Mattie Williams and Mary Swan, in keeping them from being killed; they now live and he has to die, which he thinks not quite fair.

6. Wa-pa-doo-ta (Red Leaf), is an old man; he says he was mowing when he heard of the outbreak; he saw some men after they were killed about the agency, but did not kill any one there; he started down to the Fort, and went on to the New Ulm settlement; there he shot at a man through a window, but does not think he killed him; he was himslf wounded at New Ulm.

7. Wa-he-hua (do not know what his name means), says that he did not kill any one; if he had believed he had killed a white man he would have fled with Little Crow; the witnesses lied on him.

8. Qua-ma-ne (Tinkling Walker) says he was condemned on the testimony of two German boys; they say he killed two persons; the boys told lies, he was not at that place at all.

9. Ta tah-me-ma (Round Wind) is a brother-in-law of the former well known Mr. Joseph Renville; he was the public cryer for Little Crow, before and during the outbreak; after the battle at Wood Lake he came over to the opposition, and was the cryer at Camp Release when the captives were delivered up; he was condemned on the testimony of two German boys who said they saw him kill their mother; the old man denies the charge —says he was not across the river at that time, and that he was unjustly condemned. He is the only one of the thirty-nine who has been at all in the habit of attending Protestant worship; on last Sabbath he requested Dr. Williamson to baptise him, professing repentance and faith in Jesus Christ; which was done on Monday, before he knew that he was among those to be hung at this time; may God have mercy on his soul.

10. Rda-in-yan-ka (Rattling Runner) says he did not know of the uprising on Monday, the 18th of August, until they had killed a number of men; he went out and met Little Crow, and tred to stop the murders but could not. The next day his son was brought home wounded from Fort Ridgley. He forbade the delivery up of the white captives to Paul when he demanded them, and he supposes he is to be hung for that.

11. Do-wan-sa (The Singer) says he was one of the six who were down in the Swan Lake neighborhood; he knows that they killed two men. and two women, but this was done by the rest of the party, and not by himself.

12. Ha-pan (second child, if a son) says he was not in the massacres of New Ulm nor the Agency; he was with the company who killed Patwell and his companions; he took one of the women; O-ya-tay-ta-wa killed Patwell.

13. Shoon-ka ska (white dog) says that when the outbreak took place he ran away and did not get any of the stolen property; at the ferry he talked with Quinn; first called to them to come over, but when he saw that the Indians were in ambush, he beckoned to Capt. Marsh to stay back; he says that his position and conduct at the ferry were misunderstood and misrepresented; that he wanted peace and did not command the Indians to fire on Capt. Marsh's men; that another man should be put to death for that; he complains bitterly that he did not have a chance to tell the things as they were; that he could not have an opportunity of refuting the false testimony brought against him; he says that they all expected to have another trial—that they were promised it; that they have done great wrong to the white people, and do not refuse to die, but they think it hard that they did not have a fairer trial; they want the presid-nt to know this.

14. Toon-kan-e-chah-tag-ma-ne (one who walks by his grandfather) says he took nothing from the stores except a blanket; he was at Fort Ridgley, but killed nobody; he is charged with killing white persons in a wagon, but he did not; they were killed by another man.

15. E tag-doo-ta (Red Face) said he was woke up in the morning of Monday, the 18th of August, and went with others, but did not kill any one.

16. Am-da-cha (broken to pieces says that he was doctoring a girl when he learned about the outbreak at the Lower Agency; he went with others and took some things from Mr. Forbes' store; he fired his gun only twice, but thinks he did not kill any one.

17. Hay-pe dan (the third child, if a son) says he was not at the stores until all was over there; he was with Wabashaw, and with him opposed the outbreak; he was afterwards driven into it by being called a coward; he went across the Minnesota river and took two horses, and afterwards captured a woman and two children; he tried to keep a white man from being killed, but could not; he was at the ferry when Marsh's men were killed, but had only a bow and arrows there; he was in three battles and shot six times, but does not know that he killed any one.

18. Mah-pe-o-ke-ne-jin(who stands on the cloud), Cut-nose, says that when Little Crow proposed to kill the traders he went along; he says he is charged with having killed a carpenter, but he did not do it; he fired off his gun in one of the stores; his nephew was killed at Fort Ridgley: he was out at Hutchinson when his son was killed; Little Crow took them out; he was hungry and went over to an ox, when there he saved Mr. Brown's family.

16. Henry Milord, a half-breed. Henry says he went over the Minnesota river with Baptiste Campbell and others; they were forced to go by

4

Little Crow; he fired his gun at a woman, but does not think he killed her; several others fired at her also; he did not see her afterwards. Henry Milord was raised by Gen. Sibley; he is a smart, active, intelligent young man, and as such, would be likely to be drawn into the Dakota rebellion; indeed, it was next to impossible for young men, whether half-breeds or full bloods, to keep out of it. They are to be pitied as well as blamed.

20. Chas-kay-dan (the first born, if a son) says he went to the stores in the morning of Monday; then he saw Little Crow taking away goods; he then went up to Red Wood with a relation of his; they were told that a white man was coming on the road; they went out to meet him, but the first who came along was a half-breed; They let him pass; then came along Mr. Gleason and Mrs. Wakefield; his friend shot Mr. Gleason, and he attempted to fire on him, but his gun did not go off; he saved Mrs. Wakefield and the children, and now he dies while she lives.

21. Baptiste Campbell is the son of Scott Campbell, who was for many years United States interpreter at Fort Snelling; he thinks they ought to have had a new trial; says he did not speak advisedly when before the military commission; he went over the Minnesota river with four others; they were sent over by Little Crow, and old to get all the cattle they could and kill every white man—if they did not the Soldiers' Lodge would take care of them; they went over to a farm between Beaver Creek and Birch Coolie, where they found a lot of cattle which they attempted to drive; the cattle, however, ran away, and then their attention was attracted to the owner; Campbell fired his gun first, but did not hit the man; he says his statement before the commission was misunderstood; he said he was a good shot, and if he had fired at the man he should have killed him; he fired over him intentionally; he fired because he felt compelled to do so by command of Little Crow. Campbell says that Little Crow compelled him and his brother, Joseph, to go out to Hutchinson; they tried to get away at the time of the attack on Capt. Strout's company, but were prevented; they were orced to go to the battle of Hutchinson; Little Crow told them if they did not kill white men they would be killed, but he did not shoot any men here.

22. Ta-ta-ka-gay (Wind Maker) is ite a young man, grandson of Sacret alker, who took care of Mrs. Josephine ggins and her children in their captivity; was one of those who killed Amos W. Higgins at Lac qui Parle; the other two, who are probably the most guilty, have escaped; says he was at Red Iron's village when he heard of the outbreak; another Indian urged him to go up with him and kill Mr. Higgins; he refused at first, but afterwards went; his comrade shot Mr. H. and killed him; he then fired off his gun, but held it up.

23. Hay-pin-kpa (the tip of the horn) is condemned because he boasted of having shot Stewart B Garvie with an arrow. As it is not known that Mr. Garvie was shot with an arrow but with buck-shot, it is probably true, as he said before the commission, that he lied about it. This is not the first time a man has been killed for lying; he now says that they determined to send off all the white people from the Yellow Medicine without killing any. Mr. Garvie refused to go; he did not shoot him; he dies without being guilty of the charge, and he trusts in the Great Spirit to save him in the other world.

24. Hypolite Ange is a half-breed; says he had been a clerk in one of the stores for a year previous to the outbreak; was sent down the Minnesota river with Baptiste Campbell and others by Little Crow; shot the white man, but not until after he had been killed by others.

25. Na-pa-shue (one who does not flee) says that at the time of the outbreak he was quite lame—that he was not engaged in any of the massacres; he was not engaged in any of the battles, but was forced with others to come down to the Yellow Medicine before the battle of Wood Lake; he dies for no fault of his.

26. Wa-kan-tan-ka (Great Spirit) says he was not present at the commencement of the outbreak; was along with the company which came down from New Ulm; saw the men in two wagons killed, but he did not kill any one; says one witness before the commission testified that he killed one of those men, but the witness lied on him.

27. Toon-kan-ko-yag-e-na-jin (one who stands clothed with his grandfather) says that he was in the battle of Birch Coolie; was also at the battle of Hutchinson, but does not know that he killed any one.

28. Ma-ka-ta-e-na jin (one stands on the earth) is an old man: says he has not used a gun for years; was down at New Ulm, but did not kill any one; had two sons killed; wants to have the truth told.

29. Pa-za-koo-tag-ma-ne (one who walks prepared to shoot) says he was out in a war party against the Chippewas when the outbreak took place; when he came back the massacres were over; he did not kill any one; says that his statement before the commission was misunderstood; when he was asked whether he was in a war party and fired his gun, he replied, "Yes, but it was against the Chippewas and not the whites."

30. Ta-ta-hde-dan (wind comes home) says that the men of Rice Creek were the authors of the outbreak; tried to keep them from killing white people, but only succeeded partially.

31. Wa-she-choon (Frenchman) says he did not know anything about killing white people; is to die for no crime; was very much affected.

32. A-e-cha-ga (to grow upon) is charged with participating in the murder of an old man and two girls; made neither confession nor denial.

33. Ko-tan-in-koo (voice that appears coming) says he did not have a gun; was at the Big Woods, and struck a man with his hatchet after he had been shot by another man; did not abuse any white women.

34. Chay-tan-hoon-ka (the parent hawk) says he did not kill any one; was down at Fort Ridgley; was also at Beaver Creek and took horses from there, but did not kill the man

35. Chan-ka-hda (near the woods) says he took Mary Anderson captive after she had been shot by another man; thinks it rather hard that he is to be hung for another's crime.

36. Hda-in-hda-day (to make a rattling noise suddenly) says that he was up north at the time of the outbreak and did not come down until after the killing of the whites was past; was at the battle of Wood Lake; he says he is charged with having killed two children, but the charge is false.

37. O-ya tag-a-kso (the coming people) says he was with the company that killed Patwell and others; he is charged with striking him with a hatchet after he was shot; this charge he denies.

38. Ma-hoo-way-ma (he comes for me) says he was out in one of the raids towards the Big Woods; did not kill anybody, but he struck a woman who had been killed before; was himself wounded.

39. Wa-kin-yan-wa (Little Thunder) says he is charged with having murdered one of Coursall's children, but the child is still living; has seen the child since he was before the military commission; he has done nothing worthy of death.

And now, not guilty or not guilty, may God have mercy upon these thirty-nine poor human creatures, and if it be possible, save them in the other world through Jesus Christ, His Son. Amen.

In making these statements, confessions and denials they were generally calm, but a few individuals were quite excited. They were immediately checked by others, and told that they were all dead men and there was no reason why they should not all tell the truth. Many of them have indited letters to their friends in which they are very dear to them but will see them no more. They exhort them not to cry or change their dress for them. Some of them say they expect to go and dwell with the Good Spirit, and express the hope that their friends will all join them there.

On Tuesday evening they extemporized a dance with a wild Indian song. It was feared that this was only a cover for something else which might be attempted, and their chains were thereafter fastened to the floor. It seems, however, more probable that they were only singing their death song. Their friends from the other prison have been in to bid them farewell, and they are now ready to die.

S. R. R.

LETTERS FROM CONDEMNED INDIANS.

The following is a copy of a letter from one of the condemned prisoners to his chief and father-in-law, Wabashaw. It was taken down in the exact language dictated by the prisoner, and excepting its untruthfulness, we think it an excellent letter:

"Wabasha: You have deceived me. You told me that if we followed the advise of Gen. Sibley, and give ourselves up to the whites, all would be well—no innocent man would be injured. I have not killed, wounded or injured a white man, or any white person. I have not participated in the plunder of their property; and yet today I am set apart for execution and must die in a few days, while men who are guilty will remain in prison. My wife is your daughter, my children are your grandchildren. I leave them all in your care and under your protection. Do not let them suffer, and when my children are grown up let them know that their father died because he followed the advice of his chief and without having the blood of a white man to answer for to the Great Spirit.

My wife and children are dear to me. Let them not grieve for me. Let them remember that the brave should be prepared to meet death; and I will do so as becomes a Dacotah. Your son-in-law,
RDA-IN-YOU-KUA.

The above Indian was convicted of participating in the murders and robberies at the Upper Agency; and the sworn testimony at Washington differs materially from his confession as given above.

AN AFFECTING SCENE.

On Wednesday, each Indian set apart for execution, was permitted to send for two or three of his relatives or friends confined in the main prison, for the purpose of bidding them a final adieu, and to carry such messages to the absent relatives as each person might be disposed to send. Maj. Brown was present during the interview, and describes them as very sad and affecting. Each Indian had some word to send his parents or family. When speaking of their wives and children almost everyone was affected to tears.

Good counsel was sent to the children. They were in many cases exhorted to an adoption of Christianity and the life of good feeling toward the whites. Most of them spoke confidently of their hopes of salvation. They had been constantly attended by Rev. Dr. Williamson. Rev. VanRavaux and Rev. S. R. Riggs, whose efforts in bringing these poor criminals to a knowledge of the merits of the Blessed Redeemer, had been eminently successful. These gentlemen are all conversant with the Dakota language and could converse and plead with the Indians in their own language.

Fun is a ruling passion with many Indians, and Ta-zoo could not refrain from its enjoyment even in this sad hour. Ta-ti-mi-ma was sending word to his relatives not to mourn for his loss. He said he was old, and could not hope to livelong under any circumstances, and his execution would not shorten his days a great deal, and dying as he did, innocent of any white man's blood, he hoped would give him a better chance to be saved; therefore he hoped his friends would consider his death but as a removal from this to a better world. I have every hope, said he, of going direct to the abode of the Great Spirit, where I shall always be happy. This last remark reached the ears of Ta-zoo, who was also speaking to his friends, and he elaborated upon it in this wise: "Yes, tell our friends that we are being removed from this world over the same path they must shortly travel. We go first, but many of our friends may follow us in a very short time. I expect to go direct to the abode of the Great Spirit, and be happy when I get there; but we are told that the road is long and the distance great, therefore, as I am slow in all my movements, it will probably take me a long time to reach the end of the journey, and I should not be surprised if some of the young, active men we will leave behind us will pass me on the road before I reach the place of my destination."

In shaking hands with Red Iron and Akipa, Ta-zoo said: "Friends, last summer you were opposed to us. You were living in continual apprehension of an attack from those who determined to exterminate the whites. Yourselves and families were subjected to many taunts, insults, and threats. Still you stood firm in your friendship for the whites, and continually counselled the Indians to abandon their raid against the whites. Your course was condemned at the time, but now we see your wisdom. You were right when you said the whites could not be exterminated, and the attempt indicated folly. Then you and your families were prisoners, and the lives of all in constant danger. Today you are here at liberty, assisting in feeding and guarding us, and thirty-nine men will die in two days because they did not follow your example and advice."

Several of the prisoners were completely overcome during the leave taking, and were compelled to abandon conversation, Others again (and Ta-zoo was one) affected to disregard the dangers and joked apparently as unconcerned as if they were sitting around a camp fire in their perfect freedom.

On Thursday the women, who are employed as cooks for the prisoners all of whom had relations among the condemned, were admitted to the prison. This interview was less sad but was still interesting. Locks of hair, blankets, coats, and almost every other article in the possession of the prisoners were given in trust for some relative or friend who had been forgotten or overlooked during the interview of the previous day. At this interview far less feeling was displayed than at the interview of Wednesday. The idea of allowing women to witness their weakness is repugnant to an Indian and will account for this. The messages sent were principally advice to the friends to bear themselves with fortitude and refrain from great mourning. The confidence of many in the salvation was again reiterated.

[In the preparation of the issue 34 years ago help was scarce, and much of the matter was printed without the usual formula of proof-reading. In the third paragraph of the article headed "An Affecting Interview," as originally printed it read: "There is a ruling passion with Indians," etc., but the reader is not told what that "ruling passion" is. It should have read: "Fun is a ruling passion," etc. In the republication of this article by newspapers, historians, etc., mostly without credit, this error is repeated, proving beyond doubts its first publication by the Record.]

THE PRISONERS ON THURSDAY.

On Thursday evening, we paid a brief visit to the condemned prisoners in their cell. The Catholic ministers were baptizing a number. All the prisoners seemed resigned to their fate, and much depressed in spirits. Many sat perfectly motionless, and more like statues than living men. Others were deeply interested in the ceremony of baptism.

THURSDAY NIGHT.

Thursday night passed quietly, at the quarters, nothing of special interest occurring.

RESPITE.

A special order was received by Col. Miller, night before last, from the president, postponing the execution of Ta-ti-mi-ma, reducing the number to be executed to thirty-eight.

THE CROWD.

Yesterday, last night, and up to the hour of execution this morning, persons were constantly arriving to witness the hanging. Our streets were densely crowded most of the night with soldiers and visitors. The sand bar in the river, the opposite bank, and all eligible places were occupied by spectators.

MILITARY PRESENT.

The following is a correct statement of the military force present:
h Regt., Lieut.-Col. Averill	200
h Regt., Col. Miller	425
h Regt., Col. Wilkin	161
th Regt., Col. Baker	425
apt. White's Mounted Men	35
t Regt. Mounted Rangers	273
Total	1419

THE GALLOWS.

The gallows, constructed of heavy, square white oak timbers, is located on the levee, opposite the headquarters. It is 24 feet square, and in the form of a diamond. It is about 20 feet high. The drop is held by a large rope, attached to a pole in the center of the frame, and the scaffold is supported by heavy ropes center-ing at this pole, and attached to the one large rope running down to and fastened at the ground. The gallows was afterwards sold to Mr John F. Meagher, who used the timbers in building a warehouse. Afterwards one of the timbers was donated to the State Historical Society, and the others have been lost sight of in the course of time, some having been burned in the incendiary fire of the old barn on the corner of Second and Walnut streets.

THE ORDER OF EXECUTION.

We visited the prisoners in their cell an hour before the execution. Their arms were tied, some were painted, and all wore blankets or shawls over their shoulders. They were seated on the floor, composedly awaiting the appointed hour. They seemed cheerful, occasionally smiling, or conversing together.

The last hour was occupied by Father Raveaux in religious service, the prisoners following him in prayer. Their time was thus occupied until the hour of execution.

Captain Burt was officer of the day and officer of the guard.

The prisoners were confined in a rear room, on the south side, first floor, of the old Leech stone building, the windows and doors of which were securely barricaded. At an early hour in the morning admittance was denied the public, and those permitted to spend the last hours with the prisoners were the ministers, priests, reporters and officers and men of the provost guard. The irons were removed from the limbs of the prisoners and their arms pinioned and other preparations were being made while the priests were conducting service or talking to the condemned.

While Father Raveaux was still talking to the prisoners, Capt. Redfield, of the provost guard, entered the prison, whispered to him that everything was in readiness, word was communicated to Henry Milford, a half-breed, who repeated it to the Indians, most of whom were sitting about the floor. In a moment all were upon their feet, and as the barricades were removed from the door, forming in single file, they marched quickly through the intervening room to the front door. On each side was a line of infantry, forming a pathway to the gallows, and as the prisoners caught sight of that instrument they hastened their steps, and commenced to sing a death song. The officer of the day received them at the gallows, then following the lead of Capt. Redfield, they ascended the steps, and eight men detailed to assist placed them in position, and adjusted the ropes and placed on their heads unbleached muslin caps to hide their faces. All this time their song was continued with a dancing motion of the body.

Maj. J. R. Brown was signal officer, stationed in front of headquarters, he gave three taps upon a drum, and the last was to notify Capt. W. J. Duly, stationed inside the gallows, to cut the rope which held the platform. His first blow failed to do it, but a second brought down the platform with a thud, intensified by the dancing motion of the prisoners.

To those near the gallows, evidences of fear and nervousness under this trying ordeal were manifest. One Indian managed to work the noose to the back of his neck, and when the drop fell he struggled terribly; others tried to clutch the blankets of those next to them; while with a spirit of defiance one went upon the gallows with a pipe in his mouth. Two clasped hands and remained in this relation in death when their bodies were cut down. In the fall, the rope of one was broken, but the fall broke his neck, and he lay quiet upon the ground, until his body was taken up and hung in place. After the lapse of nearly ten minutes one breathed but his rope was readjusted and life soon was extinct.

Drs. Seignorette, of Henderson and Dr. Finch of the seventh regiment, were detailed to examine the bodies, and after hanging for half an hour they were pronounced lifeless, and they were cut down.

Four teams were driven to the scaffold. The bodies were deposited in the wagons, and under an armed escort, conveyed to the place of burial—Company K, Captain Burke, without arms, acting as a burial party. The place of burial was the low flat between Front street and the river, which is overgrown by swamp willows. A trench wide enough to permit the placing of two rows of bodies, possibly thirty feet long, twelve feet wide and four to five feet deep, was dug in the sand on the river bank, their bodies were placed in with feet to feet, the layer was covered with coarse army blankets, and over this another layer of bodies, then blankets again, the whole covered with earth.

So great was the desire for relics that crucifixes, wampum and ornaments, were taken from the bodies before burial; others took locks of hair and a few cut off pieces of clothing. The burial escort and guard were under command of Lieut. Col. Marshall.

AN INCIDENT.

Among the soldiers doing duty on this occasion was a lad of possibly 18 or 20 years, a member of Co. K, Seventh regiment. His parents and several sisters and brothers had been murdered by an Indian on the gallows. The lad manifested great excitement throughout the proceedings, his face was pale and beads of perspiration stood upon his forehead. As the drop fell he pointed a finger trembling with excitement at the prisoner, and as the body dangled in the air, he gave utterance to a loud expressionless laugh, which was heard and taken up by the multitude in a shout of exulation, which could have been heard for a great distance.

"THE RESURRECTION."

On the day of execution a number of physicians from different parts of the state as well as army surgeons were here in person or represented by agents to procure bodies for scientific use. During the night the grave was opened and a number of bodies taken. Others were taken on subsequent nights until the grave was almost emptied. The bodies of Cutnose, named because of a slit in one side of his nose and noted for brutality, and the Indian who broke his rope, were secured by an eminent physician of an adjoining town, thoroughly scrubbed, and were their spirit to have returned they would not have known themselves.

In the scramble for bodies, one was dropped or hidden in the timber between the grave and the town, and next morning it was in the possession of a squad of soldiers. It was nude and frozen stiff, and the possessors were trying to place it in position for a mark. A squad from headquarters rescued and buried it before they succeeded in their intentions, they spending the day in the guard house.

THE CROWD.

The civilians who witnessed the hanging were variously estimated at from two to four thousand. The first is a very conservative estimate, and a divide of the figures would probably most correctly represent the truth. The windows, porches, house tops, sheds and even trees were occupied by anxious spectators, while those content to remain on the sidewalks and streets obtained good views.

INCIDENTS.

The order maintained throughout the exciting event was excellent, and both the military and civilians were specially complimented, in special orders issued afterwards by Col. Miller, commander.

The day was exceedingly mild for so late in December. In the month of November and the first part of December, cold weather had been experienced, and snow had fallen to the depth of several inches, but by execution day the latter had disappeared from the streets and highways, the temperature was mild, and in the afternoon several of the regiments indulged in dress parade on Second street.

The population of the village of Mankato was probably about 1,200 people at the time of the execution, including many families of men serving in the army—regiments in the south or doing service against the Indians. It had also become the temporary residence of many engaged in the military service of the department against the Indians, either of soldiers, scouts or employes.

The attempt to capture and murder the Indian prisoners at this city, created a profound impression, especially in military circles, and when the order for the execution of the Indians was made public, grave fears of further demonstrations by civilians were entertained. Gov. Ramsey was impressed with this fear, and Col. B. F. Smith being at Fort Snelling, and consulted as to the possibility of further efforts of civilians to attack the prisoners, he expressed his willingness to come to Mankato, where he resided and was well and popularly known, to assist the military department. Asked what force he would need to assist him he replied none, saying that he had no fears in the direction indicated from his fellow citizens. He came to Mankato, and after looking over the situation, named a number of prominent men of this section as his aids, they were appointed as such, and backed by a strong public sentiment, Col. Smith's confidence was more than verified, Not only was there no hostile demonstration, but the loyalty of the masses to civil and military regulations was so strong that it elicited the highest commendation from the authorities, Col. Miller especially referring to it in general orders.

Among those witnessing the execution was Baptist Lassuillier, head chief of the Winnebago Indians, whose reservation was in this county. He was a man of fine physical development, and dressed in citizens clothes, his presence was not known except to his intimate friends and acquaintances. Always a staunch friend of the whites and loyal to authority, his sympathies were of course on the side of law and order, and against those who had so cruelly murdered the white settlers. The military display, at the execution, was conceded to have been the finest ever witnessed in the state up to that time. The soldiers had been in the service long enough to be well drilled and disciplined, they were cleanly uniformed and equipped, and presented a fine soldierly appearance. They were entirely Minnesota soldiers.

Two lines of infantry was formed from the front door of the prison in which the condemned were confined to the foot of the gallows, between which the Indians passed to their doom. A line of infantry enclosed the gallows, in the form of a square; and the infantry was surrounded by a line of cavalry, kept in motion until the Indians had ascended the gallows, when they were formed into lines facing the gallows. The cavalry separated the civilians from the execution grounds.

There were present artists from Harper's *Weekly* and Leslie's *News* both of which papers published illustrations of the execution. The one we print today is the Leslie picture which is the best and most accurate —so much so that some of the figures were recognizable.

With the exception of a few one story structures, the buildings represented in the picture are as they existed then, and they are very accurate.

Capt. W. J. Duley, of the scouts was the man selected to cut the rope that held the platform on which the prisoners stood. His wife had bee a prisoner, taken from the Lake Shetek settlement, and liberated only a few days before the execution. Is said that his first blow failed to cut the rope, because of the excitement under which he labored, but the second blow was successful, and speedily sent the 38 murderers to the happy hunting grounds—if such characters are there admissable.

Abenteuer unter den Indianern (Captivity of the Haverland Family)

Garland Publishing, Inc., New York & London
1977

Copyright © 1977
by Garland Publishing, Inc.
All Rights Reserved

Bibliographical note:

this facsimile has been made from a copy in the
Newberry Library
(Ayer.256.H38.A14.1863)

Library of Congress Cataloging in Publication Data
Main entry under title:

Abenteuer unter den Indianern = Captivity of th
Haverland family.

(The Garland library of narratives of North
American Indian captivities ; v. 76)
    Issued with the reprint of the 1860 ed. of Bone,
J.H.A. The Indian captive. New York, 1977.
    Original t.p.: "Frei nach dem Englischen."
    Reprint of the 1863 ed. published by J. M. Hoffmann, Pittsburgh.
    1. Indians of North America--Captivities--Fiction. 2. Haverland family--Fiction.
3. Mohawk Indians--Captivities--Fiction. I. Title:
Captivity of the Haverland family. II. Series.
E85.G2 vol. 76 [PT2660.A1] 973'.04'97s
ISBN 0-8240-1700-5 [813'.008'0352] 76-57230

Printed in the United States of America

Abenteuer

unter den Indianern,

oder:

Ina's Gefangenschaft unter den Wilden und ihre wunderbare Befreiung.

Frei nach dem Englischen.

Pittsburg:
Verlag von J. M. Hoffmann u. Br.
1863.

Capitel 1.

Der Fremde.

Vor etwa 75 Jahren schallte durch die Stille des westlichen Urwaldes der Klang einer Holzart, geführt von einem Hinterwäldler, welcher die blitzende Schneide tief in's Herz einer Eiche begrub.

Alfred Haverland, so hieß der Mann, war vor mehreren Jahren vom Osten New-Yorks nach dem wilden, damals noch unbewohnten Westen desselben Staates ausgewandert, und hatte eine kleine Niederlassung gegründet, wo er mit seiner Frau und Tochter und einer Schwester einfach, aber glücklich lebte. Einsam, wie sie waren, sah Haverland im Geiste schon die Städte und Dörfer, welche später diese Gegenden schmücken, und den Indianer nach dem fernen Westen treiben sollten.

Haverland war in die Tracht der Hinterwäldler gekleidet. Dauerhafte Zeuge deckten den Leib, Mokassins die Füße und eine Mütze von Waschbärenfell den Kopf. Die breite Brust und die schwellenden Muskeln verriethen beträchtliche Stärke; dabei waren seine Glieder von schlankem Wuchse und die Züge seines Gesichtes anmuthig. Um die breite Stirn flossen Locken, welche in Schwärze mit den blitzenden Augen wetteiferten, und die ganze Erscheinung trug den Stempel, welchen die Natur zuweilen ihren Lieblingen aufdrückt.

Die Art war mittlerweile tiefer und tiefer in's Holz gedrungen, und der Riesenbaum fing an zu wanken. Langsam erst, dann rasch und immer rascher begann der Fall, bis die letzten Fasern krachten und das stolze Haupt im Staube lag.

Haverland wollte eben den Stamm von den kleinen Aesten befreien, als auf einmal ein verdächtiger Laut sein Ohr traf, und ihn veranlaßte, die Art mit der Büchse zu vertauschen, und spähend umherzublicken.

„Wie geht's, wie steht's? Hab Euch doch nicht erschreckt, hoff' ich? Ich bin's blos, Seth Jones, von New=Hampshire," sagte der Ankömmling, mit sonderbarer Betonung. Haverland erblickte ein seltsames Menschenkind vor sich, einen sogenannten Yankee von New=England. Er hatte eine lange, dünne, römische Nase, kleine funkelnde Augen, magere, aber sehnige Gliedmaßen und schlotternde Beine und Arme. Seine Kleidung glich der Haverland's, mit Ausnahme der starken Schuhe, welche er trug, seine Stimme war unsicher, wie die von jungen Leuten zur Zeit des Brechens; wenn aufgeregt, war sie sonderbar und unnachahmlich.

Haverland's erster erfahrener Blick sagte ihm, daß er nichts zu fürchten habe. Er nahm die Büchse in die Linke, und streckte die Rechte dem Fremden entgegen.

„Ganz und gar nicht!" antwortete er auf die Frage des Fremden, „aber Vorsicht ist besser als Nachsicht, wißt Ihr, zumal in dieser Wildniß, und zu solchen Zeiten."

„Sehr wahr, sehr wahr, Mr..... aber ich bin des Kuckuks, wenn ich Euern Namen weiß."

„Haverland!"

„Ihr habt Recht, Mr. Haverland, wie ich sagte, dies sind kitzliche Zeiten, und ich war beträchtlichermaßen erstaunt, als ich Eure Art hörte."

„Und ich nicht weniger beim Anblick Eures Gesichtes, Mr. Jones — sagtet Ihr nicht Jones?"

„Grad so! Seth Jones von New=Hampshire. Die Jones sind dort eine zahlreiche Sippschaft, ein bischen zu zahlreich für Gemüthlichkeit, deßhalb wanderte ich. Kennt sie vielleicht, die Jones?"

„Nein, ich kenne dort Niemand."

„Nicht? Dachte, Jedermann kennte die Jones. Viele Genies darunter. Aber, was zum Henker thut Ihr in diesem Heldenlande? Was hat Euch hergeführt?"

„Unternehmungsgeist. Ich war des Ostens müde, und mit solch' herrlichem Lande vor mir, hielt ich es für eine Sünde, die Gelegenheit zu versäumen. Nun aber, Mann, seid eben so ehrlich: was hat Euch hergeführt? Ihr schaut wie ein indianischer Jäger oder Kundschafter."

„Nu, ich bin so was der Art. Ich war unter Oberst Allen bei den Grünjacken; als Friede wurde, ging ich nach Hause und arbeitete eine Weile für den Alten. Da passirte was in der Nachbarschaft — kein Verbrechen übrigens — und ich hielt's für's Beste, mich zu drücken. Ich war ein paar Tage am River brunten, und faßte den Entschluß, 'nen Abstecher hierher zu machen."

„Das freut mich sehr. Wir sehen Weiße nur sehr selten. Nehmt bei uns fürlieb, und bleibt so lange, wie's Euch gefällt, wohlverstanden, je länger, je besser."

„Ich denke, ich werde bleiben, bis Ihr mich müde seid," lachte der excentrische Jones.

„Wenn Ihr von Osten kommt, könnt Ihr wahrscheinlich über die Gesinnungen der Indianer zwischen hier und dort berichten. Nichts Apartes, nach Euern Bemerkungen zu urtheilen?"

„Das wüßt' ich doch nicht!" sagte Jones, schüttelte den Kopf und schaute zu Boden.

„Warum, Freund?"

„Ich will Euch nur sagen, ich hörte furchtbarliche Historien unterwegs. Seit dem Krieg sollen die infamen englischen Rothröcke die Inschen aufreizen. Jedenfalls sind sie irgendwo am Werke."

„Seid Ihr sicher?" fragte der Hinterwäldler mit sichtbarer Angst.

„So ziemlich. Die kleine Niederlassung, ein paar Meilen von hier — wie heißt sie gleich? — ist rein niedergebrannt."

„Ist es möglich? Gerüchte von tödtlicher Feindschaft zwischen Rothen und Weißen sind mir schon seit Monden zu Ohren gekommen, aber ich glaubte es ungern."

„Glaubt's lieber, und wenn Euch die Alte zu Haus und die Engelchen lieb sind (werdet schon welche haben, he?) so nehmt meinen Rath an, und zahlt Fersengeld. Wie habt Ihr's nur so lange getrieben?"

„Ei nun, ich war immer freundlich und gerecht gegen die In= schen und sie gegen mich. Das ist Alles, worauf ich bauen kann."

„Ganz recht, aber 'n Insch ist eben 'n Insch. Such' sie, und sie sind nirgends zu finden, grad so, bei meiner Seele!"

„Ich fürchte, Euer Argwohn ist nur zu gegründet," erwiderte Haverland, in trübem Tone.

„Bin froh, daß ich über Euch gestolpert bin. Werd 'n bis= chen unruhig, und da ich Euch 'mal gefunden habe, will ich auch zu Euch halten."

„Danke, mein Freund; jetzt aber laßt uns nach Hause. Ich wollte arbeiten, aber Ihr habt mir die Lust vertrieben."

„Thut mir leid, aber besser ist besser, nicht wahr?"

„Ganz gewiß, es wäre Unrecht gewesen, wenn Ihr mich nicht gewarnt hättet. Jetzt kommt."

Mit diesen Worten zog Haverland seinen Rock an, warf Büchse und Art über die Schulter und schlug gedankenvoll den Weg nach Hause ein. Sein neuer Freund folgte ihm.

Capitel 2.

Die dunkle Wolke.

In einem anmuthigen Thale stand die Hütte Haverlands. Er selbst hatte den Grund „gekleart," wie es heißt, nach allen Seiten, so daß das Haus eine Strecke vom Walde lag, welcher sich Meilen weit erstreckte. Der Boden der Lichtung war beackert, und wenn auch hier und dort noch ein schwarzer Baumstumpf stand, gewährte doch Alles einen vielversprechenden Anblick.

Das Haus selbst war ein Blockhaus, mit einer Thür und einem Fenster. Inwendig waren zwei Zimmer, eines unten, das andere oben. Im untern wohnte, im obern schlief man. Haver=

land hatte wenig auf Vertheidigung gesehen, in der Hoffnung, daß dieselbe unnöthig sei. Auch hätte er selbst mit den besten Vertheidigungsanstalten keine lange Belagerung aushalten kön=
nen, und hatte deßhalb, wie gesagt, keine getroffen.

Als er in die Lichtung trat, erblickte ihn seine Tochter I n a, und sprang ihm entgegen.

„O Vater, ich bin so froh, Du bist da, das Essen ist fertig. Dachtest Du dran? Ich sagte eben zur Mutter —"

Sie hielt plötzlich inne, als sie den Fremden sah, und stand, mit der Hand auf dem Munde, stille, ungewiß, ob zu bleiben oder davon zu laufen.

„Nein, ich dachte nicht an's Essen, sondern bekam Besuch, und meinte, ich könne ihn zu Hause besser bewirthen, als im Walde. Aber, wo bleibt Dein Kuß, Kind?"

Der Vater beugte sich nieder und berührte die rosigen Lippen seiner Tochter mit den seinen, dann nahm er ihre Hand, und führte sie in's Haus.

„Ei!" rief Jones bewundernd aus, „hol' mich dieser und jener, wenn das nicht 'ne hübsche Blume ist. Ist sie hier gewachsen? Tochter, denk' ich, oder nicht?"

„Ja, meine Tochter, aber nicht hier geboren."

„Was Ihr sagt! Verzweifelt hübsch ist sie, und das macht, was ich sagte, doppelt —"

Ein Wink des Vaters gebot ihm Stillschweigen, und ohne Weiteres gingen sie auf die Hütte zu.

Es war übrigens kein Wunder, daß Ina's Anblick Jones solche Lobsprüche entlockte. Sie war wirklich ein reizendes Ge=
schöpf von 15 bis 16 Jahren, deren letztere sie in der Wildniß verlebt hatte. Sie war klein von Wuchs, aber schlank wie ein Reh, frei von dem Zwange der feinen Gesellschaft. Sie hatte schwarzes Haar, ausdrucksvolle blaue Augen, eine tadellose grie=
chische Nase, dünne Lippen, und ein volles Kinn, wodurch das Profil ganz gerade wurde. Ihr Gesicht war oval und die Farbe fast zu weiß für kernige Gesundheit. Ihr Anzug war halb bar=
barisch, ähnlich denen, welche wohlhabende Indianerinnen zu

tragen pflegten; auch trug sie Perlenschmuck nach indischer Art. Ina ging voran, und die Drei traten in die Hütte. Haverland machte den Freund mit Frau und Schwester bekannt und sagte, derselbe sei zufällig des Wegs gekommen, und werde einige Tage bleiben. Aber trotz des sorglosen Tones war Mrs. Haverland der nachdenkliche Ausdruck im Gesichte ihres Mannes aufgefallen, und obgleich sie nicht fragte, so fühlte sie doch, daß dieser Umstand einen tiefern Sinn verbarg.

Man unterhielt sich über Alltagssachen, bis der Tisch gedeckt war und Alle sich setzten. Ein Segen wurde gesprochen, und das Mahl ging seinen stillen Gang.

„Frau," sagte endlich Haverland zärtlich, „ich werde mit diesem Freunde ausgehen, und Du und Mary könnt unterdeß thun, was Euch am Besten dünkt. Wir werden vielleicht bis Abend ausbleiben; ängstigt Euch nicht unserthalben."

„Ich will mein Bestes versuchen, lieber Mann, aber geht nicht weit weg, denn seit Kurzem ist eine seltsame Furcht über mich gekommen."

„Fürchte nichts, liebe Frau, wir gehen nicht weit."

Haverland ging hinaus, und fand Jones, wie er Nase und Mund aufsperrte und Ina bewunderte, welche aus= und einging.

„Jerusalem! ich werde mich in das Mädel vergucken. Nichts dawider? hoffe ich."

„Nein," antwortete Haverland mit einem leichten Lächeln, „ihr Herz ist ungebunden und wird's hoffentlich noch lange bleiben."

„O, ich will sie nicht lieben, wie Ihr Eure Alte, nur wie meine Tochter, wißt Ihr! Sie ist noch zu klein, um an einen Schatz zu denken. Hütet sie noch fünf oder sechs Jahre vor solchen Uebeln."

„Ich will's versuchen, aber laßt uns gehen. Ich habe Euch was zu sagen, was sie nicht hören sollen."

„Schon recht; nur noch 'ne Minute."

In diesem Augenblicke erschien Ina mit einem Wassereimer, um aus der nahen Quelle Wasser zu holen..

„Wart 'nen Augenblick, schönes Kind," sagte Jones und nahm ihr den Eimer ab, „das ist zu schwer für Dich."

„O nein, gar nicht, ich schöpfe alle Tage."

„Diesmal laß mich's nur holen, blos um meine Galantheit zu zeigen."

Ina gab lachend nach und folgte ihm mit den Augen, als er mit langen, ungeschickten Schritten dem Walde zu ging.

„Wie weit ist's?" fragte er, sich umdrehend.

„Eine kleine Strecke," sagte Haverland, „der Pfad führt hin."

Seth gab eine unverständliche Antwort und verschwand.

Die eben erzählte einfache Begebenheit, obgleich unbedeutend an sich selbst, war eins jener Ereignisse, welche wichtige Folgen nach sich ziehen, und zu zeigen scheinen, daß eine allweise Vorsehung existirt, welche sie zu ihren Zwecken benutzt, um unser Wohl zu befördern. Jones beabsichtigte nichts, als eine kleine Unterhaltung, sah aber schon vor seiner Rückkehr, wie glücklich sich dieses getroffen hatte.

Er ging schnell vorwärts, und kam nach kurzem Verlaufe an die Quelle. Als er anhielt, glaubte er sicher ein Geräusch im Walde zu hören, und beim Eintauchen des Gefäßes in den klaren Wasserspiegel gewahrte er in dem Bilde eine Bewegung des Gebüsches. Er besaß übrigens zu viel Schlauheit, seine Bemerkung kund zu geben und füllte vielmehr den Eimer, ohne seinen Argwohn im Mindesten zu verrathen. Als er sich wieder erhob, warf er einen, wie zufälligen Blick umher, und sah nicht zwanzig Schritte von sich, die kauernden Gestalten von zwei Indianern. Bei'm Umdrehen ergriff ihn eine etwas ungemüthliche Empfindung. Er durfte jede Minute ein paar Kugeln in seinen Rücken erwarten, ging aber trotzdem nicht im Geringsten schneller, und zeigte durchaus keine Unruhe, als er in die Lichtung trat und Ina den Eimer überreichte.

„Kommt, laßt uns gehen," sagte Haverland, und ging auf die Quelle zu.

„In der Richtung? Noch lange nicht,"

„Warum nicht?"

„Ihr sollt's bald erfahren."

„Zum Flusse denn?"

„Das geht an, zumal wenn's nahe beim Hause ist."

Haverland sah ihn scharf an, sagte aber nichts, und schlug den Weg zum Flusse ein.

Der Fluß war nur einige hundert Schritte vom Hause und floß in der Richtung von Norden nach Süden. Er war hier glatt und enge, aber einige Meilen weiter unten mündete er in einen breiten, tiefen Strom. Die Ufer waren meistens mit dichtem, undurchdringlichem Gebüsche gesäumt, überragt von höheren Bäumen. Haverland ging nach einem Punkte, wo eine Art Landung war, und sagte dann:

„Nun, was meintet Ihr, als Ihr sagtet: **nicht weit vom Hause?**"

„Wartet 'n Bischen," antwortete Seth und lauschte. Haverland folgte seinem Beispiele, und Beide hörten ein Geräusch im Wasser, als wenn ein Canoe fortgerudert würde. Seth trat an den Rand des Wassers, schaute stromabwärts, und winkte Haverland, zu folgen. Beide sahen jetzt ein Canoe, welches von drei Indianern gerudert wurde und sich rasch entfernte.

„Versteht Ihr mich jetzt?" fragte Seth. „Die Spitzbuben waren an der Quelle, Euer Mädchen zu fangen."

Capitel 3.

Die dunkle Wolke platzt.

Auf Haverland's dringende Frage berichtete Seth das Erlebte, und fügte hinzu, daß, seiner Ueberzeugung nach, die Indianer am Abende in Menge wiederkommen würden.

„Das ist auch meine Meinung." sagte Haverland, „die Zeit des Handelns ist gekommen."

„Gerade so, und was gedenkt Ihr zu thun?"

„Ihr habt mir schon so großen Beistand geleistet, daß ich um Euren Rath bitte."

„Nun, der ist bald gegeben. Ihr sitzt hier in der Klemme, und je eher Ihr aufbrecht, desto besser. Zwanzig Meilen von hier ist die Ansiedlung, wie Ihr wißt, und Ihr solltet keinen Augenblick verlieren, Eure Sachen zu packen und die Reise dorthin anzutreten."

„Euer Rath ist gut; aber da wir zu Wasser gehen müssen, würde es nicht besser sein, auf den Schutz der Nacht zu warten? Wir haben eben gesehen, daß der Fluß Feinde birgt, die unsern Plan leicht vereiteln könnten, wenn sie Kenntniß davon hätten. Ja wir müssen auf die Nacht warten."

„Ihr habt Recht, und da wir einen wolkigen Himmel haben, so sind unsere Aussichten trefflich, zumal wir stromabwärts fahren. Der Tanz geht wirklich an, und schneller, als ich erwartete, aber laß sie kommen, sie sollen einen warmen Empfang haben."

Sie kehrten jetzt ohne Säumen nach Hause zurück, und theilten in wenigen Worten den Stand der Sachen mit. Die Frauen hörten nur die Bestätigung ihrer Furcht, und ohne Zeit mit nutzlosen Fragen zu verlieren, begann man die Sachen zu packen, und nach einem großen Flachboote zu schaffen, welches Haverland besaß, und auf dem man die Wasserreise unternehmen wollte. Während des Umzuges blieb Seth am Ufer und hielt strenge Wacht, damit ihre Feinde nicht unversehens zurückkommen und sie überrumpeln könnten.

Die Sonne nahte schon dem Horizont, als Alles vollbracht war, und die ganze Gesellschaft sich in's Boot setzte, um die tiefe Dunkelheit der Nacht abzuwarten und dann abzustoßen. Ihre Gedanken waren trüber Natur, und Haverland konnte nicht umhin, denselben Ausdruck zu verleihen. Seine Frau versuchte, ihn zu trösten und sprach die Hoffnung aus, daß sie über kurz oder lang zurückkehren könnten. Mary war die Ruhigste, und flößte Seth durch ihre muthigen Bemerkungen große Achtung ein. Angereizt durch seine Beifallsworte, wollte auch Ina nicht zurückbleiben und sagte keck:

„Ich fürchte mich nicht im Geringsten: ich würde gerne hier bleiben. Ich könnte ganz allein in's dunkle Haus zurückkehren."

„Bleibt doch lieber im Boot," sagte Seth trocken.

„Ich glaube wirklich, Ihr denkt, ich fürchte mich," entgegnete sie, lachend, und sprang mit einem Satze an's Ufer.

„Ina, Ina, was soll das heißen?" fragte Haverland strenge. „Komm' augenblicklich zurück!"

„Ja! — oh Vater, Hülfe! Hülfe!"

„Nehmt das Ruder und stoßt ab!" schrie Seth und sprang in's Wasser, um das Boot abzuschieben.

„Aber, um Himmels Willen, mein Kind!"

„Ihr könnt ihr nicht helfen, die Inschen haben sie. Geschwind nieder, sie schießen."

Zu gleicher Zeit krachten mehrere Büchsen vom Ufer, und das teuflische Geschrei der Wilden schallte durch die Dunkelheit.

Ohne Seth wäre Alles verloren gewesen. Er begriff ihre Lage mit Blitzesschnelle und rettete die Andern.

„Vater! Mutter! die Indianer haben mich!" kam es in herzzerreißenden Tönen vom Ufer.

„Barmherziger Gott! muß ich mein Kind umkommen sehen, ohne ihr Flehen beachten zu können?"

„Sie werden ihr nichts thun," rief Seth, „und wir müssen uns erst selbst helfen, ehe wir ihr helfen können. Bückt Euch, sie können Euch sehen!"

„Vater, willst Du mich verlassen?" kam es wieder, in qualvollen Tönen.

„Sei nur ruhig, Kleine," rief Seth, „verlier den Muth nicht. Ich will Dich schon holen, wenn Du artig bist, so gewiß wie ich Seth Jones heiße!"

Die letzten Worte wurden laut gerufen, da das Boot jetzt anfing, stromabwärts zu gleiten.

Die Mutter hatte Alles gehört, sagte aber nichts. Sie begriff die Sachlage und sank mit einem Seufzer auf ihren Sitz zurück. Mary's Augen funkelten gleich denen einer Tigerin und schossen Blitze des Unwillens auf Seth, weil er das Kind so kaltblütig seinem schrecklichen Schicksale überlassen hatte. Aber auch sie war still, und saß bleich und ruhig, wie eine Bildsäule, während

Seth seine feurigen luchsartigen Augen auf sie heftete. Was ihn selbst endlich anbetrifft, so war er ruhig und unbefangen, als ob nichts vorgefallen wäre und flößte den Uebrigen bald die Ueberzeugung ein, daß er für solche außerordentlichen Fälle geboren sei.

Sie floßen jetzt rasch den Strom hinab; die tiefe Dunkelheit verbarg gänzlich die Ufer, und mit kummervollem Herzen fuhren die Flüchtlinge dahin.

Capitel 4.

Die verlorene Heimath und der gefundene Freund.

Es war am Mittag desselben Tages, dessen Ende wir soeben betrachtet haben, als ein einzelner Reiter durch den Wald ritt. Es war ein junger Mann von 20 — 30 Jahren und sein Zustand, wie der des abgetriebenen Pferdes, deuteten auf eine lange Reise hin. Er war in einen Jägeranzug gekleidet und von einnehmendem Aeußern. Die Nase war von römischem Schnitt, Haare und Auge spielten in's Dunkle, und ein kurzer Schnauzbart verlieh dem Gesichte einen kecken Anstrich. Auf dem Sattelknopfe ruhte die blanke Büchse, bereit, ihre tödtliche Sprache zu sprechen, wenn Gefahr drohte. Das Pferd war, wie gesagt, beschmutzt und mit Staub bedeckt, und als der Tag sich neigte, schaute der Reiter sich sorgfältig um, als ob er ein Merkmal suche, das ihm die rechte Straße anzeigen sollte. Zuletzt lief ein freudiger Ausdruck über sein Gesicht, als wenn er das Gewünschte gefunden hätte, und er beschleunigte den matten Schritt des Pferdes.

„Komm, gutes Thier," sagte er, „das Haus kann nicht ferne sein, und ein gutes Nachtmahl wartet unser."

Kurze Zeit nachher ritt er durch einen kleinen Fluß mit felsigen Ufern und in den Wald, welcher sich bis nach Haverland's Hause erstreckte. Aber er hatte sich sehr in der Entfernung geirrt, denn es dunkelte schon als er denselben kleinen Fluß wieder antraf, und zwar noch mehrere Meilen oberhalb des Platzes, wo die Flüchtlinge sich dem Schooße desselben anvertraut hatten. Um den Weg nicht zu verlieren, verfolgte er jetzt den Lauf des Flusses und brach sich durch Büsche und Schlinggewächse mühsam Bahn bis plötzlich, etwa eine Meile oberhalb der Hütte, ein heller Schimmer zu ihm drang und von Minute zu Minute an Helligkeit gewann.

„Was kann das bedeuten?" fragte sich der Reiter. „Sollte Haverland's Haus in Flammen stehen? Unmöglich! und doch ist's derselbe Punkt."

Angetrieben durch ängstliche Gefühle, trieb Everard Graham (das war der Name des Reiters) sein Pferd nach dem Punkte hin, woher der Schein kam. Zuletzt stieg er ab, band sein Pferd an, und setzte vorsichtig seinen Weg zu Fuße fort.

Endlich kam er an, und ein Blick zeigte ihm Alles. Haverland's Haus, das Haus worin er zu übernachten erwartet hatte, stand gänzlich in Flammen, und rings umher, beleuchtet von geisterhaftem Lichte, tanzten und sprangen dunkle Gestalten, wie höllische Teufel.

Graham stand wie angewurzelt. Er erwartete jeden Augenblick die blutigen Leichname seiner gemordeten Freunde zu sehen, und wandte sein suchendes Auge in allen Richtungen; doch, wie wir wissen, ohne Erfolg, und er kam zuletzt zu der Ueberzeugung, daß die Familie abwesend sei, ob frei oder gefangen—das konnte er natürlich nicht entscheiden.

Nach und nach wurde die Flamme kleiner, und das Geheul der Wilden weniger laut. Zuletzt starb beides dahin, die Indianer verschwanden, und das niedergebrannte Haus glühte nur noch mit seinen rothen Kohlen durch die dunkle Nacht.

Graham wartete eine Stunde und länger; als Alles still blieb, schlich er näher und unterwarf den Schauplatz der Gewaltthat einer sorgfältigen Untersuchung. Scheu umging er das Haus und schaute mit Zagen in die Trümmer, als wenn er noch immer erwarte, die Ueberbleibsel seiner Freunde zu finden. Doch nichts bot sich dar, seine Furcht zu bestätigen und mit einem Seufzer der Erleichterung sagte er endlich, halblaut:

„Ich sehe nichts; sie müssen entkommen sein; und doch, wer könnte sie gewarnt haben? Ach, schrecklich ist das Schicksal der Unbeschützten in solchen Zeiten!"

„Wirklich, das ist so!" sagte eine Stimme. Graham drehte sich um, als wenn ihn eine Kugel getroffen hätte, und sah wenige Schritte von sich die Umrisse eines Mannes, der ihn anschaute.

„Und wer seid Ihr," fragte er, „daß Ihr zu solcher Zeit auf solchem Platze erscheint?"

„Ich bin Seth Jones, von N— H—; und wer seid Ihr, der zu dieser aparten Zeit hier erscheinen thut?"

„Wer ich bin! Everard Graham, ein Freund des Mannes, dessen Haus in Asche liegt, und der, wie ich fürchte, mit seiner ganzen Familie gemordet worden ist."

„Grad so! Aber sprecht leise; Andere könnten hier sein, wißt Ihr, die es nicht zu hören brauchen. Laßt uns eben 'n Bischen in den Schatten treten."

Seth ging, und Graham folgte, anfänglich ein wenig argwöhnisch, aber bald beruhigt durch den Ton und das Benehmen des Fremden. Auf die Frage desselben theilte er mit, daß er Haverland, als alten Freund seines Vaters, habe besuchen wollen, einem längst gegebenen Versprechen zufolge.

„Ihr habt 'ne kitzliche Zeit gewählt," sagte Seth.

„Wohl wahr, aber nun sagt mir, was Ihr von der Familie wißt. Sind sie todt oder gefangen?"

„Keins von Beiden."

„Ist es möglich, daß sie entkommen sind?"

„Grad so, ich half 'n Bischen."

„Dank Himmel! Wo sind sie?"

„Den Fluß hinab in einer der Ansiedlungen."

„Wie weit ist es?"

„Vielleicht 'n Dutzend Meilen; vielleicht mehr, vielleicht weniger."

„Nun, dann laßt uns zu ihnen eilen—mich wenigstens, da nichts mich aufhält."

„Mir recht. Aber ich vergaß zu sagen, daß die Tochter in den Händen der Inschen ist."

Graham fuhr zurück. Ihretwegen gerade war er gekommen; denn aus den Erinnerungen der Kindheit war ihr Bild aufgetaucht und hatte ihn in die Wildniß gelockt. Er hatte gehofft, das liebliche Kind als lieblichere Jungfrau wieder zu finden, und diese Jungfrau sein nennen zu dürfen. Und diese Hoffnungen hatten Seth's Worte mit einem Schlage zertrümmert. Doch bezwang er sich, und frug seinen Begleiter:

„Welcher Stamm nahm Ina gefangen?"

„Die verteufelten Mohawks, glaub ich."

„Wie lang ist es her?"

„Nur einige Stunden, wie Ihr an den Kohlen sehen könnt."

„Wollt Ihr mir erzählen, wie es zuging?"

Seth willfahrte, und erzählte nicht allein die Einzelnheiten des letzten Capitels, sondern fügte auch hinzu, daß die Frauen und Haverland in Sicherheit seien. Er hatte sie selbst nach der nächsten Ansiedlung gebracht, und dann bei seiner Rückkehr Graham getroffen.

„Und was hat Euch zurückgebracht?" fragte Graham.

„Das ist 'ne schöne Frage! Was Euch auch her gebracht hat. Ich bin gekommen, auszufinden, was aus Ina, der hübschen Tochter, geworden ist."

„Verzeiht, Freund! Ich bin sehr erfreut über Eueren Edelmuth, und werde Euch nach Kräften helfen. Wir sollten Freunde werden; wollt Ihr einschlagen?"

„Von Herzen gern, und zu Zweien sollte es uns nicht so schwer werden, das hübsche Kind zu befreien."

Während sie diesen wichtigen Punkt besprechen, wollen wir uns Zeit nehmen zu sagen, daß es wirklich die Mohawks waren, welche Ina geraubt hatten. Sie waren eine der berühmten fünf Nationen, welche sich in dem Kriege auf die Seite der Engländer schlugen, und auf den Grenzen entsetzlichen Schaden anrichteten.

Sie bildeten einen mächtigen Bund, und wenn Seth Jones jetzt den Plan faßte, Ina zu befreien, so begreift man augenblicklich, daß dies nicht durch offene Gewalt, sondern nur durch List geschehen konnte.

Capitel 5.

Auf der Spur, und wie Seth plötzlich abbiegt.

„Also die Mohawks, denkt Ihr, haben sie geraubt?"

„Ja, ich kam gerade an, als sie gingen, und glaube, sie erkannt zu haben. Aber es bleibt sich gleich, eine der fünf Nationen ist so schlecht wie die andere. Sie sind Alle bei der Hand, wenn's darauf ankommt, ein Mädchen zu stehlen."

„Es bleibt sich, wie gesagt, gleich, wer sie hat; aber es frägt sich jetzt, wie wir es anzufangen haben. Die Mohawks sind eine verzweifelt schlaue Nation."

„Das läßt sich nicht bestreiten."

„Dann aber, wenn wir sie überlisten, so sind wir nicht die ersten Bleichgesichter, die dies thun."

„Das läßt sich wieder nicht bestreiten. Jetzt still einen Augenblick, ich muß nachdenken."

Seth dachte tief und lange, endlich rief er aus: „Ich hab's!"

„Was? den Plan der Verfolgung?"

„Ich denke."

„Und wie lautet er?"

„So: wir müssen das Mädchen unter allen Umständen haben."

Trotz ihrer Lage fing Graham an zu lachen; aber Seth unterbrach ihn augenblicklich.

„Nur Geduld; aber was ist das? ein zweites Haus in Flammen?"

„Nein, es ist die Morgendämmerung," sagte Graham, nachdem er aufmerksam hingeschaut hatte.

„Das ist gut," sagte Seth, „denn wir brauchen Licht in der Sache."

Bald erschien die Sonne über dem Horizonte, und Seth und Graham gingen nach dem Flusse. Der Letztere suchte sein Pferd auf, und fand es schlafend auf dem Boden. Da er es auf der Verfolgung nicht brauchen konnte, so nahm er ihm Sattel und Zaum ab, und ließ es weiden, gewiß, daß er es seiner Zeit leicht wieder finden würde. Dann kehrte er zu seinem Gefährten zurück und sagte: „Ich bin bereit, Seth."

Der Angeredete machte kehrtum, und ging, ohne ein Wort zu sagen, in der Richtung der Lichtung fort. Als sie die Trümmer erreicht hatten, sagte Seth ganz lakonisch:

„Sucht die Spur!"

Beide neigten den Kopf gegen den Boden und bewegten sich im Kreise durch die Lichtung. Graham hielt plötzlich an, ging einige Schritte in den Wald, und rief aus:

„Hier ist sie, Seth!"

Seth eilte zu ihm hin, bückte sich, ging rück- und vorwärts, und sagte zuletzt:

„Dies ist die Spur. Sie sind hier nicht sehr vorsichtig gewesen, aber freßt mich, wenn wir nicht unsere Gucker aufzureißen haben, wenn wir im Walde sind."

Jetzt, als die Spur gefunden war, schickten sie sich an, dieselbe zu verfolgen. Seth, als der erfahrene Kundschafter, ging voran, und da seine ganze Aufmerksamkeit auf den Boden gerichtet war, fiel es Graham anheim, ihm in kurzer Entfernung zu folgen und den umliegenden Wald mit möglichster Sorgfalt zu durchspähen, damit sie nicht unverhoffter Weise in einen Hinterhalt der Indianer fielen.

Die Zeichen, denen Seth folgte, waren sehr unbedeutender Art, und für einen gewöhnlichen Beobachter in der That gänzlich unsichtbar. Obgleich die Indianer wenig Ursache hatten, eine Verfolgung zu befürchten, so waren sie doch zu schlau und vorsichtig, Maßregeln zu vernachlässigen, wodurch etwaige Verfolger irre geleitet werden konnten. Sie gingen im Gänsemarsch, der

Hintere in die Fußtapfen des Vorderen tretend, so daß die Spur aussah, als ob nur ein einziger Indianer des Weges gezogen sei. Auch Ina mußte auf diese Weise marschiren, und wenn sie dann und wann einen Fehltritt machte, war ein grausamer Schlag die Folge.

Zuweilen schien selbst der geringste Abdruck auf den Blättern zu fehlen, und erst bei genauer Beobachtung bemerkte man die Umrisse des Mokassins darauf, oder sah ein Blatt verschoben oder ein Reis, welches durch menschlichen Fuß gehoben und noch nicht in seine alte Lage zurückgekehrt war. Diese schwachen Anzeichen genügten Seth, und er machte rasche Fortschritte, als er plötzlich stehen blieb und Graham zurief:

„Wir kommen ihnen näher!"

„Wirklich? das freut mich. Wann werden wir sie wahrscheinlich einholen?"

„Kann's nicht genau sagen, für's Erste nicht. Sie nehmen ziemliche Schritte und rasteten letzte Nacht nur dann und wann, damit Ina sich erholen könnte. Hol' sie der Teufel, Ina wird noch manchmal rasten müssen, ehe sie am Ziele sind."

„Wie hoch schätzt Ihr ihre Zahl?"

„Es sind ungefähr zwanzig der besten Mohawkkrieger. Seid Ihr hungrig?"

„Nein, ich kann es bis Mittag ohne Mühe aushalten."

„Ich auch, also vorwärts."

Wieder warf sich Seth in den Wald, wieder folgte Graham mit wachsamen Augen. Dann und wann kreuzten sie Bäche und kleine Flüsse, und die Sonne stand hoch am Himmel, als Seth wiederum stehen blieb und die Hände erhob.

„Was soll das heißen?" fragte er sich und blickte seitwärts von der Spur ab. Graham trat näher.

„Was giebt's?" fragte er.

„Die Spur theilt sich. Sie müssen sich getrennt haben, obgleich ich den Grund nicht einsehe."

„Sollte es nicht eine List sein, um uns irre zu leiten?"

„Ich glaube. Hier, folgt der Hauptspur, während ich die andere nehme. Wir werden ja bald sehen."

Graham that, wie ihm geheißen war, obgleich mit sichtlicher Mühe. Es war, wie sie gedacht hatten; nach kurzer Zeit liefen die Spuren wieder zusammen.

„Wir müssen uns auf solche Sachen gefaßt machen," sagte Seth. Ich muß den Boden untersuchen und Ihr den Wald, damit wir nicht unversehens in ein Hornißnest fallen."

Wieder ging es weiter, bis sie gegen vier Uhr Nachmittags an einem großen Flusse anhielten. Seth holte trockenes Hirschfleisch hervor, welches er aus der Ansiedlung mitgebracht hatte, und die beiden Gefährten hielten eine kurze, aber reichliche Mahlzeit. Dann erhoben sie sich und setzten ihren Weg fort.

„Seht doch," sagte Seth und zeigte auf einen Stein mitten im Flusse. „Seht Ihr den Abdruck des Mokaffins darauf? Einer von ihnen ist davon abgeglitten, verlaßt Euch drauf."

Er stieg in's Wasser und watete vorsichtig durch den Fluß, gefolgt von Graham. Als sie das jenseitige Ufer betraten, sammelten sich die Abendschatten über dem Walde, und die Vögel gingen zur Ruhe. Aber der Vollmond schien fast mit Tageshelle, und mit seiner Hülfe beschlossen die Gefährten, die Verfolgung die Nacht hindurch fortzusetzen.

Ihr Fortschritt war jetzt natürlich verhältnißmäßig gering, da Seth seines ganzen Scharfsinnes bedurfte, um die Zeichen zu finden. Oft kroch er auf Händen und Füßen, und wäre der Wald nicht sehr offen gewesen, sie hätten es ganz aufgeben müssen. Sie sahen kein Zeichen von einem indianischen Lager und schlossen daraus, daß die Wilden entweder nicht rasten wollten, ehe sie ihren Stamm erreicht hatten, oder daß sie ganz in der Nähe waren. Die letztere Voraussetzung war die wahrscheinliche, und sie verdoppelten deßhalb ihre Wachsamkeit. Plötzlich bemerkte Graham, daß der Wald immer lichter wurde, und ehe er Seth anreden konnte, standen sie an den Ufern eines Flusses, von dessen gegenseitigem Ufer sich eine weite, baumlose Ebene ausdehnte. Die Strömung des Flusses war reißend, aber da er nur von ge=

ringer Breite war, schwammen sie hindurch und erstiegen bald das jenseitige Ufer.

„Müssen wir hinüber?" fragte Graham, auf die offene Ebene deutend.

„Ich sehe keinen Ausweg. Wir können sie nicht umgehen, denn sie scheint sich vier tausend drei hundert Meilen hinzuziehen, während man die gegenüberliegende Gränze sehen kann."

„Wäre es nicht besser, bis morgen zu warten?"

„Warum? bei Tage können wir den Indschen noch besser zur Zielscheibe dienen."

„Nun denn, also vorwärts!" sagte Graham, und die Freunde betraten die offene Ebene. Die Spur lief schnurstracks auf den gegenüberliegenden Wald zu, der etwa fünf Meilen entfernt sein mochte. Es konnte ungefähr Mitternacht sein, als sie den Saum erreichten und vorsichtig in das Dunkel der Bäume traten. Kein Lüftchen regte sich und die herrschende Stille machte ein leises Vordringen doppelt nothwendig. Seth ging wieder voran und Graham folgte, allein sie waren noch keine fünf hundert Schritte gegangen, als sie Stimmen hörten. Vorsichtig und stille stahlen sie sich vorwärts, und sahen bald den Schein eines Feuers in den Kronen der Bäume. Das Feuer selbst war unsichtbar, konnte aber nicht weit entfernt sein. Seth flüsterte Graham zu, sich stille zu verhalten, während er weiter ging. Er erreichte bald einen massiven Erdrücken, den er auf Händen und Füßen hinankroch. Oben angekommen, blickte er hinüber und entdeckte am Fuße des jenseitigen Abhanges das ganze Indianerlager. Ueber zwanzig saßen und lagen auf der Erde umher, die Meisten im Schlafe befangen, während Einige rauchten und gedankenlos in's Feuer schauten. Seth wußte, daß die Letztern Schildwachen waren und daß das geringste Geräusch sie verrathen konnte. Er war daher überrascht und ziemlich ärgerlich, als Graham trotz der erhaltenen Weisung an seiner Seite erschien, und ebenfalls einen Blick in das Indianerlager warf. Allein dies war der Platz nicht, ihm Vorwürfe zu machen und er begnügte sich deßhalb, den jungen Mann durch eine Handbewegung zu erneuter

Vorsicht aufzufordern. So lagen sie Beide eine geraume Zeit im Hinterhalte, bis die Morgendämmerung graute und die Wilden anfingen, Anstalten zu ihrem Morgenmahle zu treffen. Bis jetzt hatten die Freunde keine Spur von Ina entdecken können, und Beide fingen an zu fürchten, sie wäre nicht im Lager. Die Ungeduld, sie zu sehen, trug wieder über Graham's Vorsicht den Sieg davon. Sich auf den Gefährten stützend, schob er den Kopf zu weit vor. Die Gesträuche vor und unter Seth gaben nach, und ehe Graham überlegen konnte, was er angerichtet hatte, rollte der Kundschafter mitten unter seine erstaunten Feinde.

Capitel 6.
Ein Lauf um's Leben.

Als der ebenberichtete Unfall sich zutrug, erkannte Graham sogleich, daß auch er in Gefahr war und daß sein Leben von seinen Anstrengungen abhing. An Widerstand war nicht zu denken, und ohne das Schicksal Seth's abzuwarten, sprang er sogleich den Abhang hinab, in der Richtung der großen Lichtung, und floh dem Gehölz zu, welches den Fluß säumte. Er mochte einige Hundert Schritte zurückgelegt haben, als lautes Geschrei in seinem Rücken ankündigte, daß er entdeckt und ein Flüchtling auf Leben und Tod sei. Er warf einen Blick zurück und erblickte fünf oder sechs Indianer, welche ihn verfolgten. Und jetzt begann ein Wettlauf auf Leben und Tod. Graham war leichtfüßig wie ein Hirsch und dazu im Laufen geübt; aber seine Verfolger waren die schnellsten Läufer der Mohawks, und er fürchtete, zuletzt seinen Meister gefunden zu haben. Indessen war er ebenso schlau, wie sehnig und gewandt, und da er seinen Verfolgern größere Ausdauer zutraute, als sich selbst, so beschloß er, sie zu täuschen und sie wo möglich zur Aufwendung ihrer ganzen Kraft zu bewegen. Zu diesem Zwecke schwang er seine Arme, wie Jemand, der nahezu erschöpft ist und nur noch mit der größten Anstrengung seine Schnelligkeit beibehalten kann. Seine List gelang; die Indianer stießen ein Triumpfgeschrei aus und stürzten mit größter Eile vorwärts, weil Jeder von Ihnen die Ehre erstrebte, den Flüchtling zu tödten. Als Graham glaubte, daß ihr Athem erschöpft sei, kehrte er zu seinen vorigen gleichmäßigen Bewegungen zurück und gewann bald wieder die frühere Entfernung von seinen Verfolgern. Den größten Theil derselben hatte seine List außer Stand gesetzt, ihm ferner zu schaden; aber zwei derselben zeigten sich ihm völlig gewachsen und behielten die gleiche Entfernung von Graham bei, als die Andern schon längst in der Ferne zurückgeblieben waren. Er sah deßhalb ein, daß seine einzige Aussicht auf Rettung in der Möglichkeit bestand, den Fluß vor seinen Feinden zu erreichen, und zur Erreichung dieses Zweckes richtete er jetzt alle seine Bewegungen ein. Die Entfernung der beiden Wälder von einander betrug, wie schon gesagt, etwa fünf Meilen, und drei derselben hatte er noch vor sich. Er mußte also haushalten mit seinen Kräften, damit sie ihn im Augenblicke der Entscheidung nicht verließen und beobachtete eine mäßige, unveränderte Schnelligkeit, wohl wissend, daß auch seine Verfolger nicht wagen würden, davon abzugehen.

Auf diese Art legten die beiden Parteien Meile nach Meile zurück, und so gleichmäßig waren ihre Bewegungen, daß sie genau dieselbe Distance beibehielten. Einen seltsamen Anblick muß diese Jagd geboten haben, denn gespensterartig war das Aussehen der drei Männer, als sie, anscheinend ohne Bewegung, über die Prärie dahin glitten.

Endlich sah Graham den befreundeten Wald nahe vor sich; die Bäume schienen ihm zu winken, und schnaufend und ächzend stürzte er unter sie, zwischen ihnen durch, bis er am Ufer des großen, reißenden Stromes stand. Dort schaute er sich hastig um und besann sich. Es war keine Zeit zu verlieren und nach zehn Sekunden war er fertig mit dem Plane, der ihm das Leben retten solle. Seine Büchse wegwerfend, watete er brusttief in's Wasser und schwamm eine Strecke von hundert Schritt aufwärts; dort angelangt, schwamm er in schräger Richtung auf's jenseitige Ufer zu, um keinen Grund zu verlieren. Dort angekommen, sprang er hastig an's Ufer und lief einige Schritte stromabwärts, wobei er Sorge trug, die Spur so deutlich wie möglich zu ma= chen. Dann stieg er wieder in's Wasser und schwamm zum zweiten Male stromaufwärts, doch nahe am Lande, um die Strö= mung zu vermeiden. Als er seine Verfolger nahe glaubte, glitt er unter einen der dichten Büsche, welche das Ufer überhingen und wartete dort auf die weitere Entwickelung der Dinge. Fast augenblicklich hinterher erschienen beide Indianer auf dem entge= gengesetzten Ufer und schwammen durch den Fluß, ohne sich zu besinnen. Auf dieser Seite angekommen, begannen sie sogleich ihre Untersuchung und stießen ein Triumpfgeschrei aus, als sie die Spur entdeckten. Allein ein zweites Geschrei anderer Natur folgte, als sie dieselbe plötzlich im Wasser verloren. Sie dach= ten, der Flüchtling habe sich wieder in den Fluß gestürzt und sei dort entweder ertrunken oder habe das jenseitige Ufer erreicht. Sie hatten eine sichere Beute verloren, und mit Gefühlen unbe= friedigter Wuth kehrten sie auf die andere Seite zurück, wo sie die fruchtlose Nachforschung noch eine Stunde lang fortsetzten, und dann ihren Gefährten nacheilten.

Capitel 7.

Seth's Erlebnisse.

"Bei meiner Seele, das ist eine neumodische Manier, sich ein= zuführen!" rief Seth aus, als er unter die Wilden rollte und sich dann erhob.

Die Bestürzung der Indianer läßt sich leicht denken, und es nahm ihre ganze Gedankenschnelligkeit in Anspruch, die wahre Sachlage im Augenblicke auszufinden. Graham's Flucht in=

dessen hatte ihnen gezeigt, daß sie Nichts zu befürchten hatten, und während Einige dem Flüchtlinge nachsetzten, sprangen die Andern mit erhobenen Beilen auf den Eindringling los. Doch schon hatte Seth Zeit gefunden, ihnen zu begegnen.

„Nur ruhig Blut", sagte er, „solche Eile ist gar nicht nöthig. Meinen Skalp könnt Ihr noch immer früh genug kriegen. Das ist so, bei meiner Seele!"

Seine halb ernste, halb komische Weise belustigte seine Gegner. Sie hielten inne und warteten auf einen weitern Ausbruch seiner Laune, während Seth sich damit begnügte, sie mit Blicken der Verachtung anzuschauen. Als sie dies sahen, sprang einer vorwärts, erfaßte seine Haare und zischte ihn an:

„O! Verfluchter Yankee, wir ihn brennen!"

„Wenn Du weißt, was Dir gut ist, alter Bursche, so nimmst Du Deine Hand geschwind aus meinen Haaren. Wenn nicht, so möchtest Du's bereuen."

Der Wilde schien seiner Laune nachgeben zu wollen. Er nahm seine Hand fort, aber auch Seth's Büchse.

„Ich leih' sie Dir schon 'n Weilchen, wenn Du sie heil wieder ablieferst. Nimm sie 'n Wenig in Acht, denn sie kostet 'n Heidengeld."

Der Leser wird längst gesehen haben, daß Seth eine Rolle spielte. Bei seinem unfreiwilligen Erscheinen hatte er sogleich eingesehen, daß das leiseste Zeichen von Furcht, oder selbst Ergebung seinen Tod besiegeln würde. Deßhalb nahm er die trotzige Kühnheit an, welche den Indianern so imponirt und ihre Tomahawks abgewendet hatte. Seth hatte einen Charakter, wie man ihn nicht häufig findet. Selbst offen und gutmüthig, konnte er dennoch die Gedanken Anderer unter der dichtesten Maske erkennen, und wenn es ihm selbst einfiel, seine wahre Natur zu verbergen und eine Rolle zu spielen, so that er dies mit einer Geschicklichkeit, welche eine Entdeckung fast unmöglich machte. Bei den Indianern wollte er für einen schwachsinnigen Tölpel gelten und hatte seinen Zweck vollkommen erreicht.

„Wie Du lieben brennen?" grinste ihn ein Wilder an.

„Kann's nicht sagen, hab's niemals versucht," war die kaltblütige Antwort.

„Ih! Du versuchen, Yankee!"

„Das wüßt' ich doch nicht, darüber sind unsere Ansichten verschieden, mein Lieber. Wenn's geschieht, will ich's glauben."

„Du solch schön Fleisch für Brennen," grins'te ein anderer Wilder und ergriff seinen Arm.

„Laß das Kneifen!" brummte Seth.

Allein der Wilde kniff um so stärker, zuletzt mit aller Macht, um dem Gefangenen einen Laut des Schmerzes zu entlocken; aber vergebens. Ein Anderer nahm seine Hand in derselben Absicht, aber mit demselben Resultat. Er drückte, daß die Knochen wichen, aber Seth verzog keine Miene.

„Gut, Yankee, Du Druck vertragen."

„O, Du hast nicht gedrückt; hast Du?" fragte Seth unschuldig und drückte seinerseits die Hand des Indianers mit solcher furchtbaren Kraft, daß alle Gelenke krachten und der Wilde in ein Schmerzgebrüll ausbrach.

„Oh, hab ich Dir weh gethan?" fragte Seth, mit anscheinend theilnehmendem Tone, als die Hand des Andern wie ein nasser Handschuh aus der seinen glitt.

Unter dem Gelächter seiner Gefährten trat der Gefoppte zurück und machte Andern Platz, welche die Nerven des Gefangenen ebenfalls erproben wollten. Dank seiner Kenntniß der Indianersprache konnte Seth ihre Absicht immer vorher errathen und fand es deßhalb verhältnißmäßig leichter, ihren Versuchen zu trotzen. Aber wenn er auch äußerlich kühl und gleichgiltig blieb, so kochte doch innerlich ingrimmige Wuth, und er gelobte sich furchtbare Rache. Dies war vorzüglich der Fall, als ein Indianer die Haare seiner Schläfe faßte und mit plötzlichem Ruck eine Hand voll nebst der dazu behörigen Haut abriß. Trotz der Höllenpein bewältigte er jedes äußere Zeichen des Schmerzes und prägte sich blos die Züge seines Quälers tief in's Gedächtniß ein.

Zuletzt trat noch ein Krieger an ihn heran und setzte ihn einer

Probe aus, welche zwar an sich nicht schmerzhaft war, der er aber doch ohne seine Vorkenntniß ihrer Absichten vielleicht unterlegen sein möchte. Der Wilde ergriff nämlich sein Haupthaar, zog sein langes Skalpirmesser und beschrieb mit demselben eine blitzschnelle Bewegung um seinen Kopf. Doch blieb seine Haut unverletzt, und als Seth jetzt dem Blicke seiner Feinde mit trotzigem Auge begegnete, entstand unter ihnen ein Gemurmel der Bewunderung und des Beifalls. Sie schienen überzeugt, daß sie den Nerven des Gefangenen Nichts anhaben könnten, und standen von weiteren Prüfungen ab.

Seth aber seinerseits war keineswegs befriedigt und ging aus der Vertheidigung zum Angriff über. Er wandte sich an den Häuptling:

„Kann der weiße Mann jetzt den Muth des rothen erproben?"

Der Häuptling nickte Beifall, und sogleich trat Seth auf die Krieger zu. Er wählte denjenigen aus, welcher ihn so höllisch gepeinigt hatte und fing damit an, seinen Arm mäßig zu drücken. Der Wilde ließ ein Grunzen der Verachtung hören. Jetzt nahm ihm Seth leise den Tomahawk aus dem Gürtel und holte zum Schlage aus. Der Wilde lächelte noch immer verächtlich, denn er war weit entfernt, den furchtbaren Ernst von Seth's Absichten zu ahnen. Der Arm hob sich zur höchsten Höhe, und mit Blitzes Kraft und Schnelligkeit niederfliegend, legte der Tomahawk den Kopf des Wilden in zwei Hälften.

Capitel 8.
Unerwartete Begegnung.

Müde und erschöpft kroch Graham aus dem Wasser und legte sich in's Gras zum Ruhen. Hier, überkommen von der schrecklichen Anstrengung, überraschte ihn der Schlaf, und als er wieder erwachte, war Mittag längst vorüber. Als er den Schlaf völlig abgeschüttelt hatte, fing er an, zu überlegen, was er jetzt beginnen sollte. Er stand allein, mitten in der Wildniß und wußte nicht, ob er Haverland aufsuchen, oder lieber die Verfolgung auf seine eigene Faust fortsetzen sollte.

Noch waren diese Fragen unbeantwortet, als ein Blick stromaufwärts ihn ein kleines Canoe gewahren ließ, in welchem zwei weiße Männer saßen. Der Jüngere handhabte die Ruder, während der Aeltere das Boot steuerte und die Ufer aufmerksam bewachte. Als sie näher kamen, glaubte Graham in dem jüngern Manne auf einmal eine große Aehnlichkeit mit Haverland zu entdecken, den er nun seit mehreren Jahren nicht gesehen hatte. Er wollte das Canoe jedenfalls nicht vorbeilassen, ohne seiner Sache gewiß zu sein, und stieß deßhalb einen halblauten Ruf aus, ohne sich jedoch zu zeigen. Der Ruderer hielt einen Augenblick inne und untersuchte das Ufer mit aufmerksamem Auge; dann auf ein Zeichen seines Gefährten ruderte er weiter.

Graham sah ein, daß er sich zeigen mußte.

Er trat aus dem Walde in's Freie und sagte: „Fürchtet Nichts, es ist ein Freund!"

Die Männer hielten jetzt an.

„Wer seid Ihr, und was thut Ihr hier?" fragte der Aeltere.

„Das könnte ich mit demselben Rechte Euch fragen."

„Wir haben keine Zeit, mit Euch zu streiten: wenn Ihr nicht antworten wollt: weiter, Haverland!"

„Halt! Haverland? Ist er bei Euch?"

„Gesetzt den Fall; was geht's Euch an?"

„Ich suche ihn vor Allen Anderen. Ich heiße Everard Graham, vielleicht gedenkt er meines Namens."

Haverland drehte sich um und betrachtete den Fremden aufmerksam. Eine Minute genügte.

„So wahr ich lebe, Ned, er ist's!"

Mit diesen Worten fuhr er nach dem Lande, sprang an's Ufer und drückte die Hand des Freundes.

Jetzt folgten Erklärungen, und Graham berichtete seine Erlebnisse. Als er geendet hatte, stellte Haverland seinen Freund als einen gewissen Ned Halvidge vor, dessen Geschichte wir in einigen Umrissen zeichnen wollen. Er hatte in seiner Jugend mehrere erfolgreiche Züge gegen lästige Indianerbanden ausgeführt, und dadurch den Haß derselben auf sich geladen. Eines Tages, als er gerade von Hause abwesend war, überfielen die Wilden seine Hütte und stillten, als sie ihn nicht finden konnten, ihre Rache an seiner Familie, welche Halvidge bei seiner Rückkehr ermordet und skalpirt fand. Seit jener schrecklichen Stunde hatte er nur der Rache gelebt und mit eigner Hand alle an dem Ueberfalle betheiligten Indianer getödtet. Damit aber nicht zufrieden, hatte er den Wilden im Allgemeinen nach Kräften geschadet und sich einen gefürchteten Namen bei ihnen erworben. Als er Ina's Schicksal erfuhr, bewogen ihn sein alter Haß und seine rege Theilnahme, Haverland seinen Beistand anzubieten, als dieser erklärte, sich nicht auf Seth's Anstrengungen allein verlassen, sondern selbst an der Befreiung seiner Tochter arbeiten zu wollen. Die Zwei hatten den Weg vermittelst des Canoes rasch zurückgelegt und, wie wir erzählt haben, Graham zur rechten Zeit getroffen.

Nach den nöthigen Erklärungen zwischen den Freunden, erhob sich die Frage, welche Maßregeln sie treffen sollten, um ihren Zweck, die Befreiung Ina's, am sichersten zu erreichen.

„Können wir jetzt, zu Dreien, und mit einem Freunde im feindlichen Lager, Nichts mit Gewalt erreichen?" fragte Graham.

Halvidge schüttelte den Kopf und sagte: „List ist das Einzige, was bei diesen Rothbäuten zum Ziele führt."

„Und der Himmel weiß, ob Das zum Ziele führen wird," sagte Haverland, niedergeschlagen.

Halvidge sprach ihm Muth ein und ermahnte dann zum Aufbruch, da sie Eile hätten. Er schlug vor, den Fluß noch einige Meilen zu verfolgen und dann zu landen, weil man dort den Wilden am besten nahen könnte. Aber als Graham hierauf berichtete, daß die Wilden nicht weit entfernt seien, beschloß man einmüthig, in dem Canoe über den Fluß zu setzen und ihre Spur zu verfolgen. Dieser Beschluß sollte eben in's Werk gesetzt werden, als Graham an der oberen Flußbiegung ein Canoe gewahrte, welches Indianer enthielt und stromabwärts kam. Geschwind zogen sie ihr eigenes Boot an's Land und legten sich in den Büschen auf die Lauer.

Unterdeß war das fremde Canoe näher gekommen und enthielt, außer drei indianischen Kriegern, ein weibliches Wesen, dessen ganze Gestalt in eine wollene Decke gehüllt war.

Haverland und Graham zitterten vor Aufregung bei dem Gedanken, daß es Ina sein könnte. Jetzt bewegte sich die Gestalt, und als die Hülle abfiel, gewahrten die drei Gefährten die kummergebeugte Gestalt und das schmerzensbleiche Gesicht von Ina Haverland.

„Bei'm Himmel! Sie ist's," flüsterte Haverland.

„Ned, laß uns die Schurken auf's Korn nehmen und niederschießen und dann mein Kind auf einmal befreien."

Haverland wollte die That dem Worte folgen lassen, aber Haldidge wehrte ihm.

„Es geht nicht, wir dürfen nicht! denn wir wissen nicht, wie viel noch in der Nähe sind. Laß sie nur gehen, wir werden sie schon kriegen. Die Nacht ist nahe und dann wollen wir sie verfolgen. Ich habe einen Plan, der gelingen muß. Bezwinge Dich nur eine kurze Zeit, und Du wirst Dinge sehen, die Dich so gut überraschen werden, wie sie."

Haverland gehorchte widerstrebend, und die Drei warteten auf die kommende Nacht. Bald legten sich ihre Schatten über Wald und Fluß, und die Freunde schoben das Canoe in's Wasser zur Wettfahrt auf Tod und Leben.

Capitel 9.

Die Jagd.

Das Canoe, worin sie saßen, hatte Ruder für zwei Personen und Graham unterstützte deßhalb seinen Freund Haverland, während Haldidge seinen alten Posten als Steuermann wieder einnahm. Als sie kühn in das Fahrwasser einlenkten, verschwand eben das indianische Canoe um eine Biegung des Flusses.

„Kommt, das geht nicht!" sagte Haverland, und tauchte seine Ruder tief in's Wasser, „wir dürfen sie nicht aus dem Gesichte verlieren."

„Erst laß uns die Ruder umwickeln," sagte Haldidge, und machte sich sogleich an die Arbeit. Sie hatten Lappen zu diesem Zwecke von der Ansiedlung mitgenommen, und in wenigen Minuten war die Sache geschehen. Dann handhabten die Freunde die Ruder mit solcher Kraft und Geschicklichkeit, daß das Boot zu fliegen schien und die Entscheidung unmöglich lange ausbleiben konnte. Unsere Freunde gaben sich deßhalb der frohen Hoffnung hin, die arme Gefangene in baldigster Kürze den Händen ihrer Peiniger entreißen zu können; aber

„Zwischen Lipp' und Kelchesrand
Schwebt der finstern Mächte Hand!"

Plötzlich erhob sich vom Wasser ein dichter, eigenthümlicher Nebel, wie man ihn oft in Sommernächten über Flüssen findet, und ehe fünf Minuten vergangen waren, hatte sich die Finsterniß der Nacht verdoppelt. Wenn dieser Umstand einerseits ihre unbemerkte Annäherung begünstigte, so entzog er ihnen doch auch andererseits die Möglichkeit, das feindliche Canoe vermittelst des Auges zu entdecken, und erleichterte ein Entkommen der Wilden im hohen Grade.

„Der Nebel kann uns anfangs helfen," bemerkte Haldidge,

„aber wir müssen ihnen vorsichtig nahen, denn wenn sie uns zu früh entdecken, so haben wir das Nachsehen. Also vorwärts, stetig, aber leise."

Das leichte Fahrzeug flog dahin; aber so gut kannte Haldidge den Strom, daß er trotz der tiefen Finsterniß jedes Hinderniß vermied, welches sich als Felsen oder Untiefe oder scharfe Biegung in ihren Weg stellte. Sie hatten mehr als eine Meile zurückgelegt, als ein leises „Halt!" aus Haldidge's Munde das Boot zum Stillstand brachte.

„Horch!" fügte er jetzt hinzu, und als sie lauschten, drang ein ferner Laut in ihre Ohren.

„Das sind ihre Ruder," flüsterte Haldidge, „und jetzt ist's Zeit, auszuholen, denn ich fürchte, sie werden bald landen. Ich will am östlichen Ufer entlang steuern, damit wir sie nicht verfehlen. Flink! sage ich, flink!"

Die Aufforderung war nicht vergebens, und die Ruder bogen sich jetzt dergestalt unter den gewaltigen Schlägen, daß sie zu brechen drohten, und das Canoe einen breiten Schaumstreifen hinter sich ließ. Auch blieben die Anstrengungen der Ruderer nicht ohne Erfolg, denn der Laut vor ihnen wurde immer deutlicher. Haverland zitterte vor Ungeduld, und auch Graham konnte sich einer gewissen Aufregung nicht entwehren, bei dem Gedanken, Ina bald von Angesicht zu Angesicht zu sehen. Nur Haldidge blieb kaltblütig und gefaßt.

„Wenn wir nahe genug sind, sie zu unterscheiden," sagte er, „so feuern wir, und ergreifen Ina auf alle Gefahr."

Unsere Freunde fuhren fort, sich den Indianern zu nähern, und nach ihrer besten Berechnung mußten sie dieselben in wenigen Minuten erreichen. Da hörte plötzlich der Laut vor ihnen gänzlich auf, und Haldidge sprach seine Befürchtung aus, daß die Feinde trotz ihrer Wachsamkeit gelandet seien. Noch tauschten die Freunde ihre Ansichten darüber aus, als sie auf einmal einen Feuerschein bemerkten, welcher regelmäßig mit der Strömung vorwärts floß und ihnen für den ersten Augenblick uner=

klärlich erschien. Haldidge's Erfahrung jedoch half ihnen bald auf die Spur.

„Das ist eine brennende Pfeife in dem Canoe, welches wir suchen. Wenn Ihr zielen könnt, schießt! Seid Ihr fertig? Vorwärts!"

Das Canoe schoß voran und auf das andere los, als wenn es dasselbe in Grund bohren wollte; schon zogen Haverland und Graham die Ruder ein, schon ergriffen sie die Büchsen, da erlosch plötzlich die Pfeife, das Canoe schoß in einen leeren Raum, und das feindliche Fahrzeug war verschwunden.

„Das ist einer ihrer Schliche!" rief Haldidge, ärgerlich; „vorwärts Ihr! sie können nicht weit sein, die Schurken."

Seine Freunde ergriffen von Neuem die Ruder; Haldidge steuerte stromaufwärts, stromabwärts, er steuerte kreuz und steuerte quer, aber die Indianer blieben verschwunden. Sie hatten wahrscheinlich die Verfolger gehört, hatten ebenfalls ihre Ruder umwickelt, und sich so leise entfernt, wie sie gekommen waren.

Unschlüssig hielten die Freunde endlich mit Rudern inne, und sogleich traf ein leichtes Geräusch, wie von rieselndem Wasser, ihre Ohren.

„Das sind sie wieder," rief Haldidge aus; „jetzt, da sie uns nahe wissen, hilft nicht länger List, sondern Stärke; wir müssen sehen, wer am besten rudern kann."

Wieder flog das Canoe über die Wellen. Der Mond war jetzt aufgegangen, und hier und dort, wo der Wind den Nebel zerrissen hatte, lagen der Fluß und seine Ufer hell erleuchtet da. Zuweilen schoß das Fahrzeug durch einen solchen Spalt und begrub sich dann wieder in dem folgenden Nebel. Bei einer solchen Gelegenheit erblickten sie plötzlich wieder das feindliche Canoe nahe am entgegengesetzten Ufer. Sie steuerten darauf los, bis sie auf einmal wieder im tiefen Nebel fuhren und die Richtung verloren. Die Spalten jedoch wurden breiter und immer breiter, und plötzlich hob der Wind den ganzen Schleier vom Flusse weg und warf ihn in den Wald. Die Verfolger benutzten diesen Vortheil und schauten sich nach allen Seiten um, in der Erwartung, das feindliche Fahrzeug wenige Schritte von sich zu entdecken. Aber wieder vergebens. Wohin auch ihre Blicke schweiften, kein Canoe zeigte sich ihren erstaunten Augen und sie mußten sich gestehen, daß die Indianer gelandet und wahrscheinlich schon tief in den Wald gedrungen seien.

„Es hilft uns Alles nichts," sagte Haverland, trübsinnig, „sie sind fort und wir können auch nur gehen."

„Es ist ein harter Schlag," seufzte Graham.

„Für mich so gut, wie für Euch," entgegnete Haldidge. „Ich glaubte, heute Abend einen Theil meiner alten Schuld gegen das Gesindel abtragen zu können; aber es sollte nicht sein. Aufgeschoben übrigens ist nicht aufgehoben. Jetzt laßt uns landen, denn ich habe nicht Lust, ihnen hier als Zielscheibe zu dienen. Am Ufer können wir uns ausruhen und die Sache besprechen."

Capitel 10.

Zwei indianische Gefangene.

So plötzlich war Seth's Schlag gefallen, daß eine Minute lang keiner der Indianer eine Sylbe sprach. Seth selbst setzte sich wieder auf seinen Platz, als wäre gar nichts vorgefallen und fing an zu pfeifen.

Endlich athmeten die Wilden tief auf, und die Rachewuth, welche in Allen kochte, wallte auf und drohte, jede Fessel zu sprengen. Zwanzig Fäuste faßten krampfhaft den Tomahawk, zwanzig Augenpaare warteten auf den leisesten Wink des Häuptlings, um den Körper des frechen Weißen in Atome zu zerhauen — aber der Wink blieb aus. Hatte der alte Häuptling eine Neigung für den kühnen Gefangenen gefaßt? wollte er ihn für fürchterliche Martern aufbewahren? Niemand konnte in seiner Seele lesen; aber auf die fragende Geberde seiner Krieger schüt=

telte er das Haupt und sagte, auf seine Stirne deutend: „Rührt ihn nicht an, er ist nicht recht hier."

Die Andern glaubten dasselbe; aber die sonstige Scheu der Indianer vor Geisteskranken hätte Seth ohne die Einmischung des Häuptlings wohl nicht gerettet, denn der Rachedurst glühte zu heiß in den Herzen der Krieger. Der Wille des Häuptlings jedoch war ihnen Gesetz, und langsam und widerstrebend erstarben die drohenen Geberden.

Seth war in der Ausübung seiner Rache nicht so sehr aus seiner Rolle gefallen, wie man wohl denken mag. Er hatte in der That auf die angedeutete Scheu der Wilden vor Geistesschwäche gebaut; aber andererseits hätte ihn selbst die Gewißheit eines plötzlichen Todes oder die Aussicht gewisser schrecklicher Marter nicht von der Ausübung seiner Rache abbringen können. Die Mißhandlungen des Wilden hatten sein Blut bis auf den Siedepunkt erhitzt; der Schlag war, so zu sagen, der elektrische Funken einer überladenen Batterie. Die That einmal geschehen und die Leidenschaften Seth's kehrten unter die Oberherrschaft der Vernunft zurück: er wurde wieder der kaltblütige, wachsame, schlaue Jäger, der er gewesen war.

Ungefähr zehn Minuten nach der schrecklichen That kehrten die andern Wilden von Graham's Verfolgung zurück, und man traf sofortige Anstalten zum Aufbruche. Der Erschlagene wurde in ein flaches Grab gelegt, mit dem Gesicht nach Osten und sammt seinen Waffen begraben. Dann lud man eine ungeheure Last von gedörrtem Hirschfleisch auf Seth's Schultern, und der Marsch begann. Stark, wie der Gefangene war, er wäre fast unter seiner Bürde erlegen, und nur die Gewißheit, daß der Augenblick des Verzagens auch der Augenblick seines Todes gewesen sein würde, gab ihm die Kraft und den Muth des Ausharrens. Doch ließ er sich andererseits nicht aus seinem langsamen Schritte aufstacheln und als seine Last endlich unerträglich wurde, warf er sie zu Boden und bestand auf einer kurzen Rast, welche ihm auch durch Vermittelung des Häuptlings gewährt wurde. Leider war ne r ar kurz, und er würde sie vielleicht durch Kunstgriffe zu verlängern gesucht haben, wenn ihn die Furcht, die Gunst des Häuptlings zu verlieren, nicht abgehalten hätte. Er lud also die Last geduldig wieder auf und folgte seinen Meistern auf diesem mühsamsten Gang seines Lebens.

Spät am Nachmittag ereignete sich ein Umstand, der seinen Plan in etwas versüßte. Die drei Krieger, welche von unseren andern Freunden erfolglos gejagt worden waren, stießen plötzlich mit ihrer Gefangenen wieder zur Haupttruppe und stillten dadurch die Furcht Seth's, daß er ganz vergebens in diese Klemme gerathen sei. Er hatte anfangs gefürchtet, einer falschen Spur gefolgt zu sein, dann aber vermuthet, daß ein kleiner Theil der Bande sich mit Ina von den Uebrigen getrennt habe, und diese Vermuthung wurde jetzt zur Gewißheit.

Ina bemerkte ihren Mitgefangenen sogleich, und schloß daraus zu ihrer Freude, daß ihre Eltern wenigstens gerettet waren. Allein der Gedanke an den wahrscheinlichen schrecklichen Tod Seth's und ihr eigenes schrecklicheres Schicksal ließen die Freude in ihrem Herzen keine tiefen Wurzeln schlagen. Ihre Hoffnung auf irdische Hilfe war jetzt vernichtet, und ihr Blick richtete sich gegen Himmel, als die einzige Quelle, woraus noch Rettung fließen konnte.

Capitel II.

Noch immer auf der Spur.

„Es scheint, der Teufel selbst hilft den Hallunken," brummte Halbidge, als sie landeten.

„Und der Himmel uns, hoff' ich," entgegnete Haverland.

„Der Himmel hilft denen, die sich selbst helfen; d'rum will ich nicht rasten, bis wir aus dieser Klemme sind. Sucht die Spur!"

„Das ist nicht so leicht bei Mondlicht," sagte Graham.

„Wo Leben ist, ist auch Hoffnung. Breitet Euch am Ufer

aus und untersucht jeden Zoll des Bodens. Die Schurken sind gewiß nicht weit. Ich gehe stromaufwärts."

Mit diesen Worten verschwand Haldidge in einer Richtung und Graham und Haverland gingen in der entgegengesetzten. Sie untersuchten den Boden mit der größten Sorgfalt, konnten aber nichts entdecken und wollten ihre Nachforschung eben aufgeben, als ein Pfiff von Haldidge ihre Aufmerksamkeit auf sich zog

„Er hat etwas entdeckt," sagte Haverland, „laßt uns eilen!"

„Hier ist die Spur," sagte Haldidge, als sie ihn erreichten, „so gewiß, wie ich ein Sünder bin, und ich kalkulire, sie sind nicht sehr weit von hier."

„Wollen wir die Verfolgung bis Tagesanbruch aufschieben?"

„Wir werden wohl müssen, da uns die Zeichen bei Nacht entgehen könnten. Der Tag kann nicht fern sein."

„Mehrere Stunden noch."

„Gut, so wollen wir's uns bequem machen."

Hierauf lagerten sich die Drei auf den Rasen und unterhielten sich mit leiser Stimme bis zum Anbruch des Tages. Sobald das erste matte Licht erschien, nahmen sie die Verfolgung wieder auf, und da die Sommernacht nur kurz war, da ferner die schwache Ina keine langen forcirten Märsche aushalten konnte, so durften sie hoffen, den Feind zu überholen, ehe es Abend wurde.

Ihre einzige Befürchtung war die, daß die drei Wilden, ihrer Verfolgung sich bewußt, eilen möchten, die Hauptbande zu erreichen, und dergestalt jede Hoffnung abzuschneiden. Sie konnten nicht viele Meilen von einander sein, und hatten sicherlich Verabredungen in diesem Sinne getroffen.

Haldidge übernahm die Leitung, und folgte der Spur mit Schnelligkeit und Sicherheit, während die beiden Andern die Aufgabe hatten, den Wald zu bewachen. Haverland fürchtete beständig einen Hinterhalt; aber Haldidge kannte die Indianer besser und wußte, daß sie nur gezwungen Halt machen würden.

„Ah, seht hier!" rief Haldidge plötzlich und wies auf einen

Platz, wo angebrannte Holzscheite den Lagerplatz der Wilden verriethen. „Seht, hier sind glühende Kohlen, sie können den Platz noch keine drei Stunden verlassen haben."

„Wirklich!" rief Haverland, „dann müssen wir ihnen nahe sein. Ich fange an, wieder zu hoffen."

„Hier sind noch mehr Zeichen," rief Graham aus, und zeigte auf einen Zeugstreifen, welcher an einem Dornbusche flatterte; „ist das von Ina's Kleide?"

„Ja, ja! hoffentlich haben sie ihr nicht Gewalt angethan."

„Ich denke eher, sie ließ es hier als Andeutung für uns."

„Das ist sehr wahrscheinlich," sagte Haldidge. „Aber wir gewinnen nichts durch Verzögerung, und sollten lieber vorwärts eilen."

So ermahnt, setzten sie die Verfolgung fort, Haldidge voran, wie zuvor. Der Mittag kam, und immer noch wurde kein Halt gemacht. Wissend, daß der Feind jetzt nahe sein mußte, gebrauchten sie die größte Vorsicht. Das Fallen eines Zweiges brachte sie zum Stillstand, und jedes Wort der Unterhaltung wurde im Flüstertone geführt. Haldidge war ein Dutzend Schritte voraus und erhob plötzlich die Hand, um seinen Gefährten ein „Halt!" anzudeuten. Dann fing er an, die Blätter auf dem Boden sorgfältig zu untersuchen und sagte zuletzt:

„Grad, wie ich fürchtete, die zwei Spuren vereinigen sich hier."

„Du irrst Dich wohl," sagte Haverland, als ob er nur ungern die schlimme Nachricht glaube.

„Ich kann nicht irren; statt drei der Indianer haben wir jetzt vierzig vor uns."

„Sollen wir sie verfolgen?"

„Verfolgen? Ei nun, natürlich; es ist die einzige Aussicht, Ina je wieder zu sehen."

„Ich weiß es; aber sie ist verzweifelt. Sie wissen sich verfolgt, und was können wir gegen eine zehnmal größere Zahl unternehmen?"

„O, wer weiß? Nur vorwärts!"

Bei diesen Worten drehte sich der Jäger herum und drang

tiefer in den Wald. Graham und Haverland folgten stillschweigend, und dieselbe Vorsicht bezeichnete alle ihre Bewegungen.

Bis jetzt hatten unsere Freunde noch Nichts genossen, und fingen an, das Nagen des Hungers zu fühlen; allein unter den Umständen dachte Niemand daran, denselben zu stillen.

Es mochte gegen vier Uhr sein, als sie einen zweiten Lagerplatz des Feindes erreichten. Wenn Haverland noch an der Richtigkeit von Haldidge's Aussagen gezweifelt hatte, so mußte jetzt jeder Zweifel schwinden. Es war klar, daß eine große Bande hier gelagert hatte, und es war ebenfalls klar, daß sie keine Sorge getragen, ihre Spuren zu verbergen; ein Beweis, daß sie die wenigen, sie verfolgenden Weißen nicht länger fürchteten, sondern sie vielmehr verachteten. Haldidge war damit wohl zufrieden; Gewalt war außer Frage, und wenn die Indianer seine List verachteten, so hatte er um so bessere Aussicht, durch sie zum Ziele zu kommen. Die Wilden hatten in ihren Berechnungen den wichtigen Umstand außer Acht gelassen, daß sie einen Feind im eigenen Lager hatten.

Die Gefährten entdeckten beträchtliche Ueberreste der Mahlzeit, und stillten mit denselben für's Erste ihre dringendsten Bedürfnisse. Die frühe Stunde belehrte sie, daß sie sich den Wilden bedeutend genähert hatten, und es war ihr dringender Wunsch, sie bei Anbruch der Nacht zu erreichen. Aber diese Hoffnung sollte wieder fehlschlagen; denn nach wenigen Stunden erreichten sie eine Stelle, wo die Spur sich von Neuem theilte. Selbst der Jäger konnte sich diesen Umstand nicht erklären, und einige Minuten lang standen unsere Freunde rathlos da.

„Das ist doch starker Taback!" rief Graham aus, „was ist jetzt zu thun?"

„Es ist sicher was im Werke," sagte Haldidge, „und wir müssen es ausfinden, ehe wir weiter gehen. Die Spitzbuben müssen uns doch mehr fürchten, als ich dachte, sonst hätten sie nicht zur List ihre Zuflucht genommen. Jetzt ist es an der Zeit, unsere fünf Sinne zusammenzunehmen."

Während dieses Gespräches untersuchte Haldidge den Boden

mit der größten Sorgfalt und sagte dann: „Die Parteien sind sehr ungleich. Die Hauptbande ist in gerader Richtung weiter gegangen, während die kleinere Abtheilung eine westliche Richtung eingeschlagen hat. Soviel ich urtheilen kann, zählt die letztere nicht mehr als vier oder fünf Mann, und doch haben sie nicht den mindesten Versuch gemacht, die Spur zu verbergen. Entweder haben sie einen tiefen Plan gelegt, oder sie fragen den Teufel nach uns. Was schlagt Ihr vor? Sprecht!"

„Ich meinerseits bin für die Verfolgung der kleineren Abtheilung," sagte Graham.

„Warum?" fragte Haverland.

„Einen Grund habe ich nicht, aber mein Gefühl sagt mir, daß Ina bei der kleinern Abtheilung ist."

„Ich bin derselben Ansicht," sagte Haldidge, „so unvernünftig dieselbe scheint. Mein Grund ist dieser: die Indianer wollen uns zu dem Glauben veranlassen, Ina sei bei der Hauptbande; deßhalb schicken sie dieselbe mit der kleinen Abtheilung fort, und legen ihre Hauptmacht in einen Hinterhalt, dem wir schwerlich entrinnen würden."

Haverland fing an, sich zu derselben Ansicht zu neigen, als Graham auf dem Pfade der größern Abtheilung einen zweiten Streifen von Ina's Kleide entdeckte.

„Ihr hattet doch Unrecht, wie Ihr seht," sagte er.

„Unrecht? warum?" entgegnete Haldidge und untersuchte genau den Busch, woran der Fetzen hing. „Jetzt bin ich erst recht überzeugt, daß ich Recht hatte. Die Wilden haben den Lappen dahin gehängt, um uns irre zu führen. Wir müssen Ina bei den Andern suchen."

Haverland schüttelte seinen Kopf und sagte: „Ned, ich hege große Achtung vor Deiner Erfahrung; aber diesmal scheinst Du mir eigensinnig gegen die Vernunft zu sprechen."

„So möge der Zufall entscheiden," sagte Haldidge, „bist Du's zufrieden?" Und als Haverland nickte, nahm er sein Jagdmesser und warf es rückwärts über seinen Kopf. Die Spitze zeigte in der Richtung der kleinern Abtheilung.

„Wie ich dachte!" sagte der Jäger, lächelnd, und da die Sache jetzt entschieden war, so brachen die Freunde ohne weitere Zögerung in westlicher Richtung auf.

An welchen dünnen Fäden hängen oft die größten Ereignisse! Die Messerspitze entschied das Schicksal aller Personen dieser Erzählung. Hätte sie nördlich gezeigt, so wären die Freunde in weniger als einer Stunde in einen Hinterhalt gefallen. Halbidge hatte Recht: Ina war bei der kleinern Abtheilung.

Capitel 12.

Schriftzeichen am Wege.

Haverland hatte zwar immer noch seine Zweifel, indem er sich nicht denken konnte, daß die Indianer thöricht genug sein könnten, im Angesicht der Verfolgung ihre Gefangene einer so kleinen Mannschaft anzuvertrauen; aber die Messerspitze hatte entschieden, und trüben Sinnes folgte er seinem Freunde.

Der Abend war jetzt nahe, und die Wilden konnten nicht fern sein. Die Spur war deutlich, da man keinen Versuch gemacht hatte, sie zu verbergen; aber Halbidge bemühte sich vergebens, die geringste Spur von Ina's zartem Fuße zu entdecken, und fing selbst an, einen leisen Zweifel an der Richtigkeit seiner Ansichten zu hegen. Auch fand er bei näherer Untersuchung, daß die Abtheilung nicht aus drei oder vier bestand, wie er anfangs gedacht hatte, sondern aus wenigstens sechs bis acht Kriegern. Allein die Sache ließ sich jetzt nicht mehr ändern, und entschlossen drang er vorwärts. Plötzlich jedoch hielt er wieder an und rief aus: „Schon wieder Zeichen!"

„Was für welche?" fragten die Andern, eifrig.

„Seht diesen Busch, und sagt, was Ihr davon denkt."

Die Zwei folgten seiner Weisung und sahen einen jungen

Schößling, welcher auf der Erde abgebrochen war, und in der Richtung der Spur lag.

„Das rührt von Ina her!" rief Haverland freudig aus.

„Wohl kaum," entgegnete Haldidge, „der Schößling ist zu dick für ihre Kräfte. Ich denke eher, der weiße Mann hat es gethan, von dem Ihr spracht."

„Was, Seth? Sollten die Indianer wirklich beide Gefangene zwei oder drei Kriegern anvertraut haben?"

„Was zwei oder drei betrifft, so kann ich Dich versichern, daß wenigstens sechs Mohawks diese Spur gemacht haben. Dein Einwand verliert also seine Kraft."

„Aber wir haben noch keine Spur von Ina gefunden; sollte sie nicht möglicher Weise bei den Andern sein?"

„Ich glaube es nicht. Ina ist wahrscheinlich vorangegangen, und der große Mokassin eines Mannes konnte ihre Fußtapfen leicht verlöschen."

„Gott gebe, daß Du Recht hast," seufzte Haverland.

„Der Erfolg wird's lehren; darum vorwärts!"

Die Zeichen wurden jetzt immer frischer, und Haldidge sah deutlich, daß sie in der Nähe der Wilden waren. Gerade, als die Sonne unterging, erreichten sie einen schmalen Fluß, welcher über Felsen schäumte und sprudelte, und die Spur rechtwinklich abschnitt. Sie löschten ihren Durst, und Haldidge wollte wieder weiter eilen, als Graham ihn zurückrief und auf einen großen platten Stein wies, auf dessen weiche Oberfläche die folgenden Worte gekritzelt waren:

„Beeilt Euch! Es sind sechs Indianer, und sie haben Ina „bei sich. Sie beargwöhnen keine Verfolgung und eilen nach „ihrem Dorfe. Ich denke, sie werden zwei bis drei Meilen „von hier lagern. Ahmt den Ton des Wipporwills nach, „wenn Ihr zum Werke schreitet, und ich werde begreifen.

„Der Eurige, achtungsvoll:
„Seth Jones."

„Wenn ich nicht fürchtete, die Canaillen könnten mich hören, so würde ich ihm drei Hurrah's ausbringen. Ein Hauptkerl, dieser Jones!"

„Darauf könnt Ihr Gift nehmen!" versicherte Graham.

„Laßt sehen," fuhr der Jäger fort, „sie werden zwei bis drei Meilen von hier lagern. Die Sonne ist unter, aber wir werden noch Licht genug haben, uns zu leiten. Laßt uns gehen, denn wir haben keine Zeit zu verlieren. Ich werde die Spur verfolgen, und Ihr sperrt Eure Augen ein Bischen auf, damit wir nicht in ein Wespennest gerathen. Seth Jones wird uns gewiß bald wieder ein Zeichen geben."

Jeder verstand jetzt seine Pflicht, und langsam ging es wieder vorwärts, bis Haldidge auf einmal seinen Schatten auf der Erde sah, und zu seinem Bedauern den Vollmond am Himmel gewahrte. Obgleich sein Licht das Auffinden der Spur erleichterte, so machte es zu gleicher Zeit eine Annäherung an's indianische Lager ohne Entdeckung fast unmöglich.

„Pst!" sagte plötzlich Graham, und deutete auf einen zweiten Stein voller Schriftzeichen. Nur mit großer Mühe las er bei'm Mondlicht das Folgende:

„Seid s e h r vorsichtig; die Kobolde fangen an, Argwohn „zu schöpfen. Sie bewachen das Mädchen sorgfältig; denkt „an das Signal, wenn Ihr kommt.

„In Eile, aber mit Achtung, der Eure:

„Seth Jones, Wohlgeboren."

Es war klar, daß die Wilden in unmittelbarster Nähe waren. Nach kurzer Berathung wurde deßhalb beschlossen, daß Haldidge in größerer Entfernung vorangehen, und die Entdeckung des Lagers sogleich mittheilen sollte.

Wieder ging es vorwärts, und nach Verlauf einer halben Stunde legte Graham seine Hand auf Haverland's Schulter und deutete mit der andern auf einen rothen Wiederschein in den Baumgipfeln. Im nächsten Augenblicke stand der Jäger an ihrer Seite:

„Wir haben sie endlich," flüsterte er, „seht nach Euren Pfannen und macht Euch auf heiße Arbeit gefaßt!"

Dies war schon geschehen, und sie brannten vor Begierde, den Kampf zu beginnen. Ihre Herzen schlugen laut, und selbst des Jägers Athem ging kürzer als gewöhnlich. Ohne Zögern, aber vorsichtig, schlichen sie vorwärts.

Capitel 13.

Erklarungen.

Das Dorf der Mohawks war eine beträchtliche Strecke von Haverland's Niederlassung, und da sie ihre Beute mit sich schleppten, so war ihr Fortschritt kein sehr rascher. Anfangs hatten sie keine Verfolgung gefürchtet; aber als Seth in ihr Lager stürzte, als Graham entkam, als die drei Indianer ihrerseits von weitern Verfolgern Kunde brachten, fing der alte Häuptling an, seine Lage für weniger sicher zu halten, und zur List seine Zuflucht zu nehmen. Zu diesem Zwecke sandte er sechs seiner besten Krieger mit den Gefangenen in westlicher Richtung ab und gebot ihnen, so schnell wie möglich nach dem Dorfe der Mohawks zu eilen. Er selbst legte seine Bande in einen Hinterhalt und erwartete mit Zuversicht, daß etwaige Verfolger hinein fallen würden. Die kleinere Abtheilung setzte unterdessen ihre westliche Reise mit möglichster Eile fort, und rastete nur, wenn die Erschöpfung von Ina's Kräften dies unumgänglich nothwendig machte. Der Häuptling hatte ihnen befohlen, die Gefangene so viel wie möglich zu schonen, und sie durften es nicht wagen, diesen Befehl zu mißachten. Sie waren um so bereitwilliger, Ina die nöthige Erholung zu gewähren, da sie keine Verfolgung befürchteten. Zwei der Krieger hatten zu verschiedenen Malen den Rückweg eingeschlagen, und waren jedesmal ohne die geringste Entdeckung zurückgekehrt.

Bei Gelegenheit einer solchen Ruhestunde hatte Seth Muße gefunden, seinen ersten Brief mit einem scharfkantigen Kiesel in den Stein zu schreiben. Zwar hatten die Wilden es entdeckt und die Schrift mit Wasser verlöscht, aber Seth wußte wohl, daß der Kiesel eingeschnitten hatte und daß mit der Trockenheit auch die Schriftzeichen wiederkehren würden.

Bei einer späteren Rast, die gegen Abend gehalten wurde, hatte Seth sein Experiment wiederholt, und dadurch den Argwohn der Indianer wachgerufen, aber auch die Gewißheit erlangt, daß er und Ina gerettet seien, wenn seine Schriftzeichen den Freunden zu Gesichte kämen.

Gern hätten die Wilden die Flucht während der Nacht fortgesetzt, aber Ina's Zustand stellte dies außer Frage, und gerne oder ungerne sahen sie sich endlich gezwungen, Anstalten zum Nachtlager zu treffen. An jeder Seite von Ina setzte sich ein Krieger, bis an die Zähne bewaffnet; Seth's Füße wurden mit starken Stricken gebunden, und in seiner Nähe lagerten sich die übrigen Wilden, mit Ausnahme eines Wachtpostens, welcher sich etwa hundert Schritte rückwärts vom Lager auf den Boden legte, um auf diese Weise die Ankunft des Feindes zu erwarten.

Capitel IV.

Im feindlichen Lager.

Obgleich die Wilden anfangs ein Feuer angezündet hatten, ließen sie es doch bald wieder zusammensinken und ausgehen, damit es ihren Feinden nicht als Signal dienen könnte. Dies war ein günstiger Umstand für die Weißen; denn obgleich das Feuer ihnen anfangs behülflich gewesen, Ina's und Seth's Lage zu erspähen, wäre es ihnen später bei'm Angriff nur im Wege gewesen.

Ehe der Jäger das verabredete Signal gab, hielt er für das Beste, den Aufenthaltsort des fehlenden Indianers auszufinden. Zu diesem Zwecke ließ er seine Büchse in Haverland's Händen zurück, und nachdem er ihn und Graham ersucht hatte, sich nicht von der Stelle zu rühren, begann er sein gefährliches Unternehmen. Wie eine Schlange kroch er auf dem Boden dahin, und so leise und vorsichtig waren seine Bewegungen, daß die Schildwache nicht das Mindeste bemerkte. Einmal erhob sie allerdings den Kopf, in der Meinung, eine leise Bewegung vor sich gehört zu haben; aber nach einem scharfen Blicke sank der Kopf wieder in seine frühere Lage zurück. Der Schatten, den die Bäume und Büsche auf den Boden warfen, war so dicht, daß die zwei sich hätten berühren können, ohne sich zu sehen. Aber der Jäger hatte den erhobenen Kopf des Wilden bemerkt, welcher gegen das erlöschende Feuer abstach, und dies gab ihm einen entschiedenen Vortheil, den er sogleich zu benutzen beschloß.

Ohne das mindeste Geräusch zu machen, glitt er vorwärts, bis er fast den Athem des Indianers hörte; dann gab er absichtlich einen schwachen Laut von sich. Der Indianer erhob erst seinen Kopf und dann langsam seinen ganzen Körper, als plötzlich der Jäger wie ein schwarzer Ball vorwärts schoß, ihn bei der Kehle ergriff und niederriß, und sein Jagdmesser mehrmals bis an's Heft in sein Herz stieß. Erst als der letzte Lebensfunke aus seinem Opfer entflohen war, ließ er die Kehle los und schlich sich zurück zu seinen Gefährten, denen er das Geschehene mittheilte. Die Wilden waren augenscheinlich so sehr auf ihrer Hut, daß die größte Geschicklichkeit nöthig war, ihren Plan in's Werk zu setzen.

Plötzlich fiel Graham ein vortrefflicher Plan ein. Er wollte sich in die Kleider des gefallenen Indianers hüllen, kühn in ihr Lager gehen und dort so verfahren, wie die Umstände gebieten würden. Nach kurzer Berathung willigten die Freunde ein; Haldidge holte die Kleider und Graham warf sie über. Es wurde beschlossen, daß er langsamen Schrittes in's Lager gehen, und daß die Andern ihm in kurzer Entfernung folgen sollten, um im Falle der Noth bei der Hand zu sein. Im Falle einer Entdeckung sollte er Ina ergreifen und mit ihr entfliehen, während die Freunde ihrerseits die Wilden angriffen und im Schach hielten.

Das Feuer war jetzt so schwach, daß Graham kaum eine Entdeckung zu fürchten hatte, ausgenommen im Falle einer Unterredung. Die Wilden fuhren auf, als er in ihrer Mitte erschien, sagten aber glücklicher Weise kein einziges Wort, da sie ihn für ihren Gefährten hielten. Graham ging langsam auf das Feuer zu und setzte sich an Seth's Seite. Die Wilden fuhren fort, ihre Pfeifen zu rauchen.

„Ugh!" grunzte Graham, und starrte Seth in's Gesicht. Der Letztere fuhr ein wenig auf, erwiderte den Blick und verstand Alles. Er zeigte auf seine Füße und Graham nickte.

„Komm, Du!" sagte Seth laut, „Du hast meine Füße zu fest gebunden; mach hier ein Bischen loser, und ich will Dich zu meinem Erben einsetzen."

Graham murmelte etwas und während er anscheinend that, wie ihm geheißen war, schnitt er behendig den Riemen entzwei.

„Schönen Dank! das ist genug; brauchst Dich nicht weiter zu bemühen, alter, beschmierter Heide, Du!"

Während Graham nun darüber nachdachte, wie er Ina einen Wink geben konnte, kam plötzlich ein Wilder auf ihn zu und redete ihn an. Schon wollte Graham die Sache zu Ende bringen und das Zeichen zum Kampfe geben, als Seth auf einmal mit verstellter Stimme und im indischen Dialekte statt seiner antwortete. So gut war die Verstellung, daß der Wilde nicht das Geringste merkte und eine zweite Frage stellte. Seth wollte auch diese eben beantworten, als auf einmal das Geschrei des Whippoorwill erschallte und sämmtliche Indianer auf ihre Füße brachte. Einer hob den Tomahawk über Ina, um sie beim ersten Zeichen eines Ueberfalls zu morden. Aber Graham kam ihm zuvor; ein Hieb seines Beiles sandte den Wilden zu Boden. Ein anderer Indianer, der mit ähnlichen Absichten auf Seth losgesprungen war, hatte keinen bessern Erfolg. Zu seinem Erstaunen erhob sich der gebundene Mann und versetzte ihm einen Schlag, der ihn besinnungslos zur Erde sandte. Unterdessen hatte Graham Ina schon erfaßt und war mit ihr in's Gebüsch geeilt, während Haverland und Haldidge ihrerseits auf dem Schauplatze erschienen und in Verbindung mit Seth einen solch' wüthenden Angriff auf die Indianer machten, daß dieselben nach allen Richtungen entflohen.

Die Schlacht war gewonnen, aber die Gefahr war keineswegs vorüber, denn es ließ sich annehmen, daß die entkommenen Indianer nach der Hauptbande eilen und Hülfe holen würden; Haldidge gab dies den Andern zu verstehen und ermahnte sie, ohne Säumen den Rückweg anzutreten. Ina war die ersten Minuten nach ihrer Befreiung so verwirrt, daß sie den wahren Stand der Dinge kaum fassen könnte. Erst nach einer Weile begriff sie, daß sie in den Händen ihrer Freunde sei.

„Bin ich sicher? Wo ist Vater?" fragte sie.

„Hier, mein theuerstes Kind," antwortete Haverland, und preßte sie in seine Arme.

„Sind Mutter und Mary gerettet?"

„Ja, ja! Alle sind jetzt gerettet, denk ich."

„Und wer sind Deine Gefährten?"

„Dies hier ist Haldidge, ein lieber Freund von mir, dem wir, nächst Gott, Deine Rettung verdanken, und —"

„Halt," unterbrach Haldidge, „das ist schon mehr als genug!"

„Natürlich, ich wollte auch Seth's gedenken, und —"

„Das hoff ich auch, vorzüglich, wenn Du bedenkst, wie nett ich mich fangen ließ," lachte Seth.

„Und wer ist der Dritte?" fragte Ina.

„O, das ist 'n gewisser Graham," antwortete Seth, in neckendem Tone, „expreß hiehergekommen, Dich zu heirathen. Hast Du nicht von ihm gehört?"

Ina trat vor und firirte den Fremden.

„Erinnerst Du Dich meiner nicht?" fragte Graham.

„O, bist Du es! Ich bin so froh, Dich zu sehen!" sagte Ina, und legte beide Hände in die des Freundes.

„Heda!" sagte Seth jetzt, ernsthaft, „ich protestire gegen dies."

„Warum?"

„Wir haben keine Zeit zum Poussiren. Ich rathe Euch das auf eine gelegenere Zeit zu verschieben."

Die Freunde lachten, aber Haldidge sagte:
„Es ist jetzt keine Zeit zum Scherzen, der Weg ist noch weit und ehe wir ihn zurückgelegt haben, dürfen wir uns nicht sicher dünken."

„Das ist wahr," erwiderte Seth, „deßhalb vorwärts!"
Unsere Freunde beschleunigten ihre Schritte und waren entschlossen, nicht eher anzuhalten, als bis Ina's gänzliche Ermüdung dieses nothwendig machen würde. Sie wußten sehr wohl, daß die Mohawks ihre Gefangenen nicht aufgeben würden, so lange sie Aussicht hatten, dieselben wieder zu fangen. Sie fürchteten, daß die Wilden ihnen nachsetzen und sie einholen möchten, und die Folge wird lehren, daß sie nicht so ganz Unrecht hatten.

Capitel 15.

Pläne und Manöver.

Mit Ausnahme eines gelegentlichen Aufenthaltes von wenigen Minuten setzten die Flüchtlinge—denn dieses waren sie nun ihrerseits geworden,—ihren Marsch die ganze Nacht hindurch fort. Als der Tag anbrach, hielten sie in einem kleinen Thale, durch welches ein kleiner Bach plätscherte, während dunkle Waldbäume und dichtes Unterholz es von allen Seiten einschlossen.

Im Augenblicke der Lagerung verschwand Seth in dem nahen Walde und, als er nach einer halben Stunde zurückkehrte, brachte er einen wilden Truthahn mit, welcher der Gesellschaft eine langentbehrte, kräftige Mahlzeit lieferte. Alle fühlten sich durch den Genuß derselben beträchtlich gestärkt, und nach kurzer Berathung wurde beschlossen, eine Stunde zu rasten, damit Ina einen kurzen Schlaf genießen und die folgenden Strapazen um so viel besser aushalten könnte. Ein Lager von wollenen Decken war bald bereitet und ehe fünf Minuten vergangen waren, versank das müde Mädchen in den ersten ruhigen Schlummer, den sie seit Langem genossen hatte. Die Freunde hatten aus mehreren Gründen beschlossen, die Heimreise zu Lande zu machen. Einmal war der Weg bedeutend kürzer und dann auch nicht halb so gefährlich, und dies war kein kleiner Umstand bei einer schon an sich so gefährlichen Reise.

„Auf Ehre," bemerkte Seth, als Ina eingeschlafen war, „ich fühle, Jungens, als ob wir in eine garstige Klemme gerathen würden; das thu' ich, auf Ehre!"

„Ich fühl' auch so was," sagte Haldidge, und kratzte sich hinter den Ohren; „aber ich will Euch was sagen, wir haben ein Bischen Ursache. Wenn die Mohawks die geringste Gelegenheit haben, Wurst wider Wurst zu spielen, so werden sie es thun, verlaßt Euch d'rauf."

„Denkst Du, sie haben Gelegenheit?" fragte Haverland.

„Jedenfalls. Sie kennen die Richtung, welche wir einschlagen, und was hindert sie, vorauszueilen und uns in einen netten Hinterhalt zu locken?"

„Gar nichts, das ist so! Wir müssen merkwürdig schlau sein. Seth, denkt Ihr nicht, Einer von uns sollte Kundschafter spielen?"

„Ich denke es nicht, ich weiß es, und nicht Einen, sondern Zwei. So bald wir aufbrechen, werde ich vorausspazieren und Steuermann spielen; Ihr dagegen müßt zurückfallen und etwaigen Besuch anmelden. Nur auf diese Weise können wir mit der nöthigen Würde umherziehen."

„Was haltet Ihr von den Absichten der Wilden?" fragte Graham.

„Ich glaube, sie sind nicht in der Nachbarschaft, obgleich es verdammt schwer ist, das mit Bestimmtheit zu sagen. Ihr könnt Euch aber d'rauf verlassen, daß sie sich zeigen werden, ehe wir viel weiter sind. Sie kriechen in den Wäldern umher, bis sie uns gefunden haben und dann werden sie versuchen, uns in einen Hinterhalt zu locken. Ich sage Euch, klügere Leute, als wir, sind schon mitten unter sie gelaufen."

Als Ina eine Stunde später erwachte, waren schon alle Vorbereitungen zum Aufbruch getroffen. Sie fühlte sich bedeutend erfrischt und ihre erhöhte Munterkeit übte einen belebenden Einfluß auf die ganze Gesellschaft.

Die Last und Verantwortlichkeit der Reise ruhten natürlich auf Seth und Haldidge. Haverland war zwar ein guter Jäger und Schütze, aber da er wenig mit Indianern in Berührung gekommen war, fehlte ihm die argwöhnische Wachsamkeit, ohne welche sich kein Kundschafter Erfolg versprechen durfte. Graham seiner Seits war wohl argwöhnisch, aber ihm fehlte jegliche Erfahrung, diese erste Lehrmeisterin in allen Lagen des Lebens. Haldidge nahm, verabredetermaßen, seinen Posten einige hundert Schritte hinter dem Zuge ein, während Seth Vorpostendienste that, mit dem Bewußtsein, daß auf seiner Vorsicht und Wachsamkeit die Sicherheit Aller beruhte. Haverland und Graham gingen meistens Seite an Seite, zwischen ihnen Ina. Auch sie beobachteten unaufhörliche Wachsamkeit, als ob ihr Schicksal auf ihren Anstrengungen allein beruhte. Ihre Unterhaltung bestand blos in wenigen unvermeidlichen Fragen und Bemerkungen.

Da Seth überzeugt war, daß die Hauptgefahr in seinem Departement drohe, so wollen wir seinen Bewegungen zunächst unsere Aufmerksamkeit schenken.

Als die Weißen das oberwähnte Thal verlassen hatten, führte ihr Weg eine Weile durch ununterbrochenen Wald; die Gegend war ziemlich eben und dicht mit Unterholz besetzt. Hätte Jemand zufällig den Pfad Seth's gekreuzt, so würden das gelegentliche Knacken eines Reises, das Schlüpfen eines Schattens von Baum zu Baum und die schrillen Signale die einzigen Merkmale menschlicher Gegenwart gewesen sein.

Den Morgen hindurch ereignete sich nichts, das seinen Argwohn wachgerufen hätte, aber gegen Mittag erreichte er einen Punkt, welcher ihn mit lebhafter Unruhe erfüllte. Der Platz bot solche Vortheile für einen indianischen Hinterhalt, daß er das Signal zum Halt gab und die Gegend gründlich zu recognosciren beschloß, ehe er an eine Fortsetzung der Reise dachte. Die erwähnte Stelle sah aus, als ob sie vor Zeiten das Bett eines großen Sees gewesen sei, der später einer dichten üppigen Vegetation Platz gemacht hatte. Kein Baum erschien in der Senkung, welche etwa eine halbe Meile breit und einige Meilen lang sein mochte. Während Seth sein Auge prüfend über das Thal gleiten ließ, entdeckte er zuletzt einen dünnen Faden Rauch, der ihn stutzen machte. Er brannte vor Begierde, die Ursache auszufinden, indem vielleicht die Sicherheit der Gesellschaft von dieser Kunde abhängen mochte, und nachdem er Haverland und Graham von seinem Vorhaben in Kenntniß gesetzt hatte, trat er den gefährlichen Gang an. Auf dem Punkte angelangt, wo er zuerst den Rauch entdeckte, hielt er inne, um einen nochmaligen Blick danach zu thun; aber so leicht war der Rauch, daß selbst sein geübtes Auge geraume Zeit suchen mußte, bis er ihn wieder entdeckte. Dann glitt er in das Dickicht, und machte einen Umweg nach rechts, um den Pfad zu vermeiden, den ein argloser Wanderer wahrscheinlich eingeschlagen haben würde. Von Zeit zu Zeit blieb er stehen und lauschte mit der größten Aufmerksamkeit. Er legte sein Ohr an den Boden und blieb minutenlang in dieser Stellung, konnte aber immer noch nichts Verdächtiges hören. Endlich meinte er in der Nähe des Feuers angelangt zu sein und wirklich, ein knisternder Laut verrieth die Richtigkeit seiner Vermuthung und diente ihm zugleich als Wegweiser. Nach wenigen Minuten fiel sein Auge auf ein Schauspiel, welches ihn mit dem maßlosesten Entsetzen erfüllte. Ein unglückseliges menschliches Wesen war an einen Pfahl gebunden und zu Tode gebrannt worden. Es war schwarz, wie der Tod, bemalt; sein scalpirter Kopf hing vorwärts, so daß Seth von seinem Standpunkte keine Züge unterscheiden konnte. Aber er sah genug, um vor dem schrecklichen Schicksale zurückzuschaudern, dem er selbst mit genauer Noth entgangen war. Jede Spur von Fleisch war bis an die Kniee verschwunden und die weißen Knochen baumelten von den obern verkohlten Gliedern herab. Die hinten gefesselten Hände waren unversehrt geblieben, aber jeder andere Theil des Körpers war buchstäblich gebraten. Der Rauch, den Seth bemerkt hatte, ging von dem Leichnam aus und der Geruch, welcher ihm schon von Weitem aufgefallen war, war in der Nähe fast unerträglich.

„Himmel und Erde!" murmelte er vor sich hin. „Dieses ist das erste Mal, daß ich einen am Marterpfahl verbrannten Menschen sehe, und Gott gebe, daß es das letzte Mal sei. Kann es ein weißer Mann sein?"

Nach einigen vorsichtigen Bewegungen gewann er einen Punkt, von dem er das Gesicht sehen konnte. Zu seiner großen Beruhigung fand er, daß es einer Rothhaut angehörte. Es war wahrscheinlich ein unglückliches Glied eines feindlichen Stammes, das die Mohawks gefangen und ihrer Rachewuth geopfert hatten. Allein was Seth seltsam schien, war der Umstand, daß kein anderer Indianer in Sicht war. Es war nicht die Gewohnheit der Indianer, einen Gefangenen dergestalt zu verlassen, und dieser Umstand machte Seth doppelt argwöhnisch und vorsichtig.

Noch stand er vertieft in die Betrachtung der schrecklichen Scene vor sich, als er durch den Knall von Haldidge's Büchse aufgeschreckt wurde. Er hatte den Ton derselben am vergangenen Abend zu genau gemerkt, um sich zu irren und zerbrach sich jetzt den Kopf über die Ursache, welche Haldidge zum Gebrauch seiner Waffe bewogen haben konnte. Zuletzt beschloß er umzukehren, nachdem er sein eigenes Terrain vorher noch einmal sorgfältig recognoscirt hatte. Auf Händen und Füßen kriechend, gewann er die entgegengesetzte Seite des Feuers und bog von Neuem sein Ohr zum Boden. Ein leises Zittern wurde fühlbar; er hob den Kopf, und hörte, wie die Büsche sich auseinander bogen und Jemanden durchließen. Im nächsten Augenblicke traten fünf Mohawkkrieger in der ganzen Häßlichkeit ihrer Kriegsmalerei auf den offenen Platz, wo ihr Opfer geendet hatte.

Der Knall der Büchse schien der Gegenstand ihrer augenscheinlichen Befürchtung zu sein. Sie sprachen Anfangs in leisem Tone mit heftigem Geberdenspiel und Seth gewahrte bald, daß sie seine Nähe nicht ahnten, denn ihr Gespräch wurde allmählich lauter, bis er Alles verstehen konnte, was sie sagten. Sie wußten, daß der Büchsenknall nicht von ihren Gefährten herrührte und fürchteten, daß ihre Anwesenheit entdeckt sei. Seth erfuhr ferner, daß weitere sechs Indianer in der Nähe waren, deren gemeinsamer Entzweck die Vernichtung der Weißen war. Entweder hatte er diese Sechs in seiner Recognoscirung übersehen, oder sie waren im Rücken und von Haldidge entdeckt worden. Der Schuß sprach für die Richtigkeit der letzteren Annahme und ein Zusammenstoß zwischen dem Jäger und seinen Feinden hatte ohne Zweifel stattgefunden. Seth fühlte, daß seine Gegenwart nöthig war und lenkte seine Schritte rückwärts.

Er hatte sich nicht geirrt; seine Gegenwart war allerdings nöthig, denn Gefahr, dunkel und drohend, nahte dem kleinen Häuflein.

Capitel 16.

Stellt die Nerven des Jägers auf die Probe.

Während Seth den Vortrab führte, fiel es, wie schon gesagt, Haldidge zu, den Zug als Nachhut zu schließen. Obgleich er ebenso wenig, wie Seth, die Gefahr im Rücken erwartete, war er doch ein zu guter Hinterwäldler, seine gewöhnliche Sorgfalt und Wachsamkeit zu vernachlässigen. Zuweilen ging er auf seinen eigenen Spuren zurück und wanderte rechts und links. Dadurch hielt er beständig Wache und machte, im Falle einer Verfolgung, so viele widerstreitende Spuren, daß die Feinde nothwendiger Weise stutzen und aufgehalten werden mußten.

Gegen Mittag, genau um die Zeit, als Seth die thalartige Senkung argwöhnisch betrachtete, gewahrte Haldidge plötzlich drei Indianer vor sich. Sie saßen stumm auf der Erde und schienen auf Jemanden zu warten. Haldidge stutzte: Wußten sie von seiner Nähe und war dies eine Falle, ihn zu fangen? Darüber mußte er sich vor Allem Gewißheit verschaffen. Er hatte übrigens einer Schwierigkeit zu kämpfen: Der Wald war an diese

Stelle offen und faſt entblößt von dem bergenden Unterholze, ſo
daß es ihm unmöglich war, ſich den Wilden zu nähern, ohne ſelbſt
entdeckt zu werden. Endlich bemerkte er, etwa zehn Schritte hin=
ter ihnen, einen dicken abgeſtorbenen, auf der Erde liegenden
Baumſtamm, von welchem er hoffen durfte, jedes Wort der In=
dianer zu hören, im Falle es ihm gelingen ſollte, denſelben unge=
ſehen zu erreichen. Der Plan war faſt tollkühn, aber nicht ſobald
hatte er ihn gefaßt, als er auch beſchloß, ihn auszuführen. Sich
flach auf die Erde legend, kroch er langſam und mit der größten
Behutſamkeit auf den Baumſtamm zu. So langſam waren ſeine
Bewegungen, daß zwanzig Minuten vergingen, ehe er die kurze
Strecke zurückgelegt hatte. Als er den Baumſtamm erreichte, be=
merkte er zu ſeinem Vergnügen, daß er hohl war. Er verlor deßhalb
keine Zeit, hinein zu kriechen, und ſich auf einen möglichſt kleinen
Raum zuſammen zu ziehen. Zu ſeinem Vergnügen bemerkte er
jetzt, daß der Stamm eine enge Spalte hatte, durch welche er die
drei Indianer deutlich erkennen konnte. So begünſtigt durch den
Zufall, nahm er alle ſeine Sinne zur Beobachtung zuſammen.

Die Indianer ſaßen ſtumm wie die Bildſäulen und ſprachen
kein Wort zuſammen. Nach wenigen Minuten jedoch hörte er
Fußtritte; die drei Wilden erhoben ſich, um die Ankommenden zu
empfangen und plötzlich ſetzten ſich ſechs Indianer auf denſelben
Baumſtamm, welcher unſern Freund verbarg. Sie fingen ſogleich
an, ſich in tiefen Kehltönen zu unterhalten und Haldidge horchte
hoch auf, als er erfuhr, daß das Geſpräch ſich um ihn und die
drei Flüchtlinge handelte. Von Seth ſchienen ſie nichts zu wiſ=
ſen. Die Wilden hatten einen Hinterhalt gelegt, um Haverland,
Graham und Ina abzufangen und beriethen ſich jetzt, wie ſie
Haldidge abfertigen wollten. Sie wußten, daß er als Kund=
ſchafter diene und fürchteten, er möge ihren Hinterhalt entdecken,
oder wenigſtens allein entkommen.

In dieſem Augenblicke beugte ſich einer der Indianer, wahr=
ſcheinlich in Folge einer plötzlichen Laune, nieder und ſchaute in
den Baumſtamm. Haldidge merkte es an der plötzlichen Dunkel=
heit und wagte einige Augenblicke lang kaum zu athmen. Allein

da der Baumstamm nur an einer Stelle offen war, verhinderte die darin herrschende Finsterniß den Indianer das Erkennen und die Crisis ging glücklich vorüber. Der Wilde nahm seinen Sitz wieder ein, und Halbidge schickte sich von Neuem an, zu lauschen, als auf einmal eine neue Gefahr drohte, zwar in einer anderen Richtung, aber noch viel furchtbarer als die vorübergegangene. Bei einer leichten Bewegung nämlich, welche Halbidge machte, um besser lauschen zu können, erschallte plötzlich dicht neben ihm ein leichtes Rasseln, das Warnungszeichen der töbt= lichen Klapperschlange! Der obenerwähnte Spalt im Baumstamme erhellte den Raum zwischen Halbidge und dem Ende der Höhlung genügend, um dem Jäger eine mächtige Klap= perschlange zu zeigen, wie sie aufgerollt da lag und den Kopf zum tödtlichen Bisse zurückbog.

Es ist unmöglich, sich eine schrecklichere Lage zu denken, als diejenige, in welcher Halbidge sich befand. Er war buchstäblich vom Tode umringt; derselbe war über ihm und unter ihm, vor ihm und hinter ihm und nirgends eine Aussicht des Entrinnens. Draußen erwartete ihn augenblicklicher Tod von der Hand der Wilden, drinnen nahm er die noch schrecklichere Gestalt der Klap= perschlange an. Und doch beschloß Halbidge zu bleiben und seinem furchtbaren Feinde zu trotzen. Mit einem festen Blicke heftete er sein Auge auf die kleinen glühenden Augen, welche ihm aus dem Halbdunkel entgegenblitzten; aber nach wenigen Augenblicken schon überkam ihn ein seltsames Gefühl: **Die Schlange fing an, ihn zu bezaubern.** Ihre kleinen Augen glänzten wie Sterne und entsandten magnetische Strahlen, dünn, scharf und fühlbar, welche bis in sein Gehirn drangen. Jetzt schienen die hellen glühenden Lichtpunkte zurückzuweichen, jetzt zu wachsen und zu nahen, und jetzt endlich wieder zu zittern und zu tanzen. Halbidge wünschte diesen Einfluß abzuschütteln, welcher ihn in Fesseln hielt, und doch wieder scheute er sich, die Anstrengung zu machen. Das Gefühl war ähnlich dem, welches wir empfinden, wenn wir uns von den starken Wirkungen eines starken Opiats zu erholen beginnen. Er hatte das dunkle Bewußtsein der Au=

ßenwelt, die Gewißheit, daß er Macht besaß, die Bande zu brechen, und doch wieder die seltsame Gleichgültigkeit gegen Anstellung des Versuchs.

Haldidge athmete schwach und langsam und ergab sich mehr und mehr dem verhängnißvollen, tödtlichen Einflusse. Er wußte sich bezaubert, konnte aber nicht widerstehen. Er konnte den Alp von seiner Brust nicht abschütteln; die Außenwelt war, so zu sagen, zurückgewichen und er bewegte sich in einer neuen, unbekannten. Er schien zu schweben, zu sinken, zu steigen, sich auf Wellen von Feuer zu bewegen. Der Zauber war vollkommen. Die sonderbare Kraft, welche der Instinkt über die Vernunft ausübt, die wunderfame Ueberlegenheit, welche die Schlange zuweilen über den Menschen besitzt, zeigte sich jetzt in vollem Maße bei dem Jäger.

In diesem Augenblick schlug einer der Indianer mit dem Tomahawk heftig auf den Baumstamm. Haldidge hörte es; er holte tief Athem, schloß die Augen und kehrte zum Bewußtsein seiner Lage zurück.

Der Zauber war gebrochen; der Jäger hatte die gefährliche Fessel abgeschüttelt. Um nicht von Neuem in die Gefahr zu fallen, senkte er die Stirn auf seine Hände und erwartete mit todesähnlicher Unbeweglichkeit den Biß der Schlange. Allein der Biß blieb aus; die Schlange schien die Nachahmung des Todes für den Tod selbst zu halten; sie wickelte sich mehrere Male auf und ab und kroch endlich über den Nacken des Jägers aus der Höhlung des Baumstammes heraus. Dort angekommen, wurde sie augenblicklich von den Indianern getödtet.

Mittlerweile hatte Haldidge seine Selbstbeherrschung wieder gewonnen und sich zum Handeln fertig gemacht. Die Indianer waren aufgestanden und ihre Stimmen wurden immer schwächer. Endlich konnte er nichts mehr hören und nachdem er noch eine halbe Stunde gewartet hatte, konnte er es nicht mehr in seinem Versteck aushalten. Langsam und vorsichtig kroch er in's Freie und schaute sich nach allen Seiten um. Die Wilden waren verschwunden und, voll der peinlichsten Besorgnisse um seine Freunde, eilte er nach dem Platze, wo er sie vermuthete. Seine Bewegungen waren jedoch vorsichtig, wie immer, und als er sie in Sicht bekam, bemerkte er den Kopf eines Indianers, welcher sich langsam über die Büsche erhob, um einen Blick auf die ahnungslosen Weißen zu werfen. Dieser Blick war sein letzter. Haldidge hob seine Büchse, zielte mit nie fehlender Sicherheit, und als der Schuß krachte, sank die Rothhaut lautlos in die Büsche.

„Deckt Euch!" rief Haldidge jetzt den Freunden zu, zeigte sich einen Augenblick und verbarg sich dann selbst in dem Gesträuche.

Capitel 17.

Gefahr auf allen Seiten.

Haverland begriff die Warnung des Freundes augenblicklich. Ina in die Arme zu nehmen und hinter einen Baum zu springen, war das Werk einer Sekunde.

„Was giebt's, Vater?" fragte Ina leise, da sie seine Bewegungen nicht gleich verstand.

„Sei ruhig, Tochter, und sitze still."

Sie fragte nicht weiter, sondern kauerte still zu seinen Füßen, im frohen Glauben, sein starker Arm könne sie gegen alle Gefahren schützen.

Graham war im Augenblicke der Warnung auf Haldidge zugesprungen, und hatte sich in der Nähe desselben verborgen. Anfangs sprachen die Beiden kein Wort; als aber Minute nach Minute verging, ohne daß der Feind sich sehen ließ, wagte Graham, endlich zu fragen:

„Was mögen sie vorhaben, Haldidge?"

„Sie hecken Teufelspläne aus, denk' ich."

„Es nimmt sie jedenfalls lange."

„Werdet nicht ungeduldig; kommen schon früh genug."
„Wie viel mögen's sein?"
„Ich sah sechs umher kriechen."
„Einer ist's jetzt weniger."
„Das ist so; aber es sind ihrer noch immer genug, um uns zu necken. Wo sind Alfred und das Mädchen?"
„Da drüben. Aber wo mag Seth sein?"
„Hier, zu dienen!" antwortete Seth selbst, als er zur größten Verwunderung der Beiden sich dicht bei ihnen vom Boden erhob.
„Wo kommt Ihr her?" fragte Graham.
„Ich habe Euch bewacht. Ein bischen Verlegenheit, he?"
„Wir haben Nachbarn bekommen."
„Nicht sehr nahe Nachbarn."
„Wie so?"
„Es ist Niemand hier, eine Viertel Meile im Umkreise."
Die Andern sahen ihn voller Erstaunen an.
„Ja, so ist's," wiederholte Seth, „hallo, Haverland! kommt nur heraus; Ihr braucht Euch nicht zu fürchten."

Seth zeigte sich jetzt ganz offen, und obgleich Haverland anfangs etwas zögerte, seiner Aufforderung Folge zu leisten, verschwand doch bald Aller Argwohn, da sie wohl wußten, daß Seth nicht der Mann war, sie unnützer Weise blos zu stellen.

„Nun, was wißt Ihr über die Hallunken?" fragte Haldidge, ungeduldig.

Statt ihm zu antworten, fragte Seth Ina: „Kannst Du 'ne Flinte abschießen?"

„So gut, wie Einer!" sagte sie, lächelnd.

„Um so besser!" sagte Seth, holte die Büchse des erschossenen Indianers und händigte ihr dieselbe nebst Zubehör ein.

„Jetzt sind wir unsere fünf, wohlbewaffnet," fuhr er fort, „und wenn uns die Rothhäute jetzt noch was anhaben, so verdienen wir's nicht besser. Ihrer zwölf haben uns einen Hinterhalt gelegt; wenn wir den Hinterhalt glücklich passiren, sind wir in Sicherheit. Vorwärts! diese Nacht muß es geschehen."

Capitel 18.

Aus der Wildniß.

Die Nacht sank dunkel und trübe auf den Wald herab. Man hörte nichts, als das dumpfe Rauschen des Windes in den Gipfeln der Bäume und das gelegentliche Geheul eines Wolfes oder Panthers. Schwere, dichte Wolkenmassen rollten sich über den Himmel, und machten die Nacht so dunkel, daß sie wie ein undurchdringlicher Schleier auf der offenen Senkung lag.

Nach und nach hörte man das ferne Rollen des Donners und dann zitterte ein feuriger Zickzack einen Augenblick lang am Saume der dunklen Wolke. Dieselbe wurde mit jeder Minute dunkler und riesenhafter und umfaßte zuletzt den ganzen westlichen Himmel, wie ein Schloß mit Thürmen und Zinnen. Der Donner wurde schwerer, bis er wie das Rollen von schweren Kriegswagen klang, welche über das Himmelsgewölbe gezogen wurden, und die Blitze flossen wie Lichtströme an den Zinnen des Wolkenschlosses herab. Dann und wann flammten alle die Blitze in einen Brennpunkt zusammen und der Donnerschlag entlud sich bei solchen Gelegenheiten unmittelbar über den Häuptern der Flüchtlinge.

„Haltet Euch zu mir," sagte Seth, „und tretet leise auf, denn diese Blitze sind verteufelt hell, sag ich Euch."

Er hatte die Lichtung sorgfältig untersucht und einen Pfad entdeckt, entstanden durch die Hufe wilder Thiere. Hier hatten die Indianer Hinterhalt gelegt, bis plötzlich der Tod eines allzukühnen Kriegers die Andern überzeugt zu haben schien, daß ihre Absichten entdeckt seien. Diesen Pfad suchte Seth zu vermeiden und führte die Freunde länger als zwei Stunde hin und her. Allein seine Bemühungen waren vergebens; schon glaubte er gewonnen zu haben, als er plötzlich beim Lichte eines hellen Blitzes denselben Pfad vor sich erblickte, den er so sorgfältig zu vermeiden bemüht gewesen war. Er erschrack nicht wenig über diese Entdeckung und verließ den Pfad so schnell wie möglich.

„St! Nieder mit Euch!" flüsterte er plötzlich, und ging den Andern mit seinem Beispiele voran.

Der Platz, wo sie waren, mochte zehn Schritte von dem Pfade entfernt sein und sie hörten plötzliche deutlich Fußtritte. Die Dunkelheit war so groß, daß man nicht das Geringste entdecken konnte, aber so nahe waren ihnen die Feinde, daß ihre ausgestreckten Hände dieselben berührt haben würden.

Ihre Lage war jetzt ausnehmend gefährlich. Die Mohawks gingen nicht auf dem Pfade, sondern waren augenscheinlich selbst bemüht, ihn zu finden. Seth und Haldidge wußten sich zwar noch unentdeckt, sahen aber nicht ein, wie sich ein Zusammenstoß vermeiden ließ. Der Erstere erhob sich deßhalb und flüsterte Haverland in's Ohr:

„Fort mit dem Mädchen, so schnell wie möglich; sie können uns jede Minute entdecken."

Haverland folgte der Mahnung, nahm Ina in die Arme und schlug sich durch die Büsche. Dieß ließ sich natürlich nicht ohne Geräusch thun und die Wilden drangen vorsichtig vorwärts, in der Meinung, daß die Weißen sich alle zurückgezogen hätten. Da geschah es, daß ein Krieger unvermutheter Weise auf Seth stieß, dem diese Begegnung ebenfalls unerwartet kam. Wie zwei Gummibälle fuhren die Gegner zurück und Seth rief aus:

„Bitte tausendmal um Verzeihung, 's war nicht gern geschehen. Verflucht!" fügte er flüsternd hinzu, wenn ich Dich nur 'ne Minute lang sehen könnte."

Seth, Haldidge und Graham manövrirten jetzt gegen fünf oder sechs Indianer und hätte ein plötzlicher Blitz ihnen ihre eigenen Stellungen verrathen, sie würden wahrscheinlich laut darüber gelacht haben. Als die Indianer fanden, wie nahe ihnen ihre tödtlichsten Feinde waren, sprangen sie einige Schritte zurück u' d die Weißen thaten dasselbe. Es würde zu weit führen, wol" t wir alle die Kunstgriffe und Kriegslisten berichten, welche die Gegner bei dieser Gelegenheit anwendeten. Simon Kenton und Daniel Boone erreichten einmal die entgegengesetzten Seiten des Ohio zu gleicher Zeit und manövrirten vierundzwanzig Stunden hindurch, ehe sie sich erkannten. Auf ähnliche Weise suchten und vermieden sich die Indianer und Weißen bei dieser Gelegenheit zwei Stunden lang. Endlich, als Seth Haverland und Ina in Sicherheit glaubte, entschlüpfte er leise und unbemerkt und ließ seinen Gegner im Glauben seiner fortdauernden Anwesenheit. Zehn Minuten später entschlüpften auch Haldidge und Graham und alle drei Freunde erreichten den Saum der Lichtung wenige Schritte von einander. Sie erkannten sich bald und verfolgten den Rand des Thales, in der Erwartung Haverland ebenfalls in der Nähe anzutreffen. Auch hatten sie sich nicht geirrt. Gegen Morgen überholten sie ihn und setzten nun zusammen ihre Reise fort. Kein Halt wurde gemacht, um ein Frühstück zu genießen, denn Alle brannten zu sehr vor Ungeduld, das Ende ihrer Wanderung zu erreichen. Nach Verlauf einer Stunde erreichten sie eine Art Pfad, der von wilden Thieren gemacht war, und dessen hartgetretener Boden einerseits besser zu begehen war und andererseits ihre Spur vortrefflich verbarg.

Noch war die Gefahr nicht vorüber und Seth und Haldidge beobachteten beständig die gleiche Vorsicht. Sie nahmen ihre früheren Posten wieder ein und gelangten gegen Mittag an einen breiten Strom, den sie nothwendigerweise überschreiten mußten und von dessen Ufern ihre Heimath noch zwei Tagereisen entfernt war.

„Meiner Treu!" rief Seth aus, „den Fluß hatte ich ganz vergessen. Ob das Mädchen wohl schwimmen kann? Nicht? Nun, dann müssen wir ein Floß bauen."

Die Freunde erkannten wirklich die Nothwendigkeit dieser Maßregel und machten sich ungesäumt an's Werk. Allein sie fanden unerwartete Schwierigkeiten. Umgefallene passende Baustämme waren nicht zu finden, und ihre Jagdmesser keineswegs geeignet, welche zu fällen. Sie nahmen deßhalb alle trockenen Zweige, welche sie finden konnten, und als der Vorrath der unmittelbaren Umgegend erschöpft war, suchten sie in weiterer Ferne. Bei dieser Gelegenheit waren Seth und Graham stromabwärts gegangen, und als der letztere einen großen angeschwemmten Baumstamm bemerkte, machte er sich daran, ihn flott zu machen. Seth schickte sich eben an, ihm zu helfen, als er sich plötzlich wieder erhob und sagte:

„Graham, ich werde den Baumstamm nicht nehmen; er paßt nicht."

„Paßt nicht! Warum, in aller Welt, paßt er nicht?"

„Laßt den Block zufrieden, sag' ich! Versteht Ihr mich?" Graham blickte auf. Er sah solch schrecklichen Blick in Seth's Augen, daß er beschloß, nachzugeben.

„Kommt mit mir!" befahl Seth, mit heiserer, leidenschaftlicher Stimme.

Graham zögerte nicht, und folgte. Als er nach einer Weile merkte, daß der giftige Blick aus den Augen seines Gefährten verschwunden war, wagte er zu fragen:

„Was soll dies Alles bedeuten?"

„Bedeuten! Habt Ihr nicht gemerkt, daß der Baumstamm hohl war?"

„Ich glaube wohl, obgleich ich ihn nicht sorgfältig untersuchte."

„Well, wenn Ihr ihn untersucht hättet, so würdet Ihr ausgefunden haben, daß ein mächtig großer Mohawk d'rin steckt."

„Ist es möglich? Woher wißt Ihr das?"

„So, wie ich bemerkte, daß der Stamm hohl war, hatte ich gleich meine Gedanken. Als ich dann ferner sah, daß der Stamm am Ende verkratzt war, wußte ich so ziemlich, was die Glocke geschlagen hatte. Endlich bemerkte ich einen Mokassin nicht weit vom Eingang, und nun war die Sache richtig. Wo ein Insch ist, sind ihrer mehrere, dacht ich, und beschloß zu retiriren. Meiner Seel! wenn ich nicht ausgeschaut hätte, als wollt ich Euch fressen, Ihr wäret so bald nicht gegangen, eh?"

„Nein; aber Ihr setztet mich nicht wenig in Erstaunen. Was soll jetzt geschehen?"

„Die feigen Hunde schleichen im Walde umher, um uns eine neue Falle zu stellen. Sie bilden sich nicht ein, daß ich Lunte gerochen habe, und sie sind zu feige, sich zu zeigen, bis sie müssen."

„Soll ich Haverland etwas davon sagen?"

„Nein; aber Haldidge kommt, laßt uns gehen."

„Als sie Haverland und Ina erreichten, brachte Haldidge eben eine Last Holz angeschleppt. Aber es war noch nicht genug, und der Jäger machte sich zum zweiten Male auf den Weg; dieses Mal in Begleitung Seth's. Als sie außer Sicht waren, stieß ihn Seth bedeutungsvoll an und fragte:

„Versteht Ihr?"

„Was?" fragte der erstaunte Jäger.

„Da drüben!"

„Rothhäute?"

„Ich sollt's meinen."

„Hab ich sie doch gerochen! Geht lieber zurück und gebt auf Alfred acht; ich kann schon allein Holz genug kriegen."

„Gefahr?"

„Nein, sie hecken wieder was aus. Wir müssen aufpassen."

Damit kehrte Seth zu den Andern zurück. Graham schnitt Weidenruthen, während Haverland und Ina aufmerksam den Fluß hinaufblickten.

„Ist das nicht ein Baumstamm?" fragte Ina Seth.

Seth sah hin und erblickte zu seiner Verwunderung denselben Baumstamm, über den er sich vor Kurzem mit Graham gestritten hatte. Seine Furcht wurde jetzt rege und er gab Haldidge durch Signale zu verstehen, herbei zu kommen.

„Was giebt's dies Mal?" fragte der Jäger, als er nahte.

Seth deutete mit dem Kopfe nach dem Flusse und sagte:

„Laßt sie nicht merken, daß wir sie beobachten, sie möchten sonst erschrecken."

„Nichtsdestoweniger," drehte sich Haldidge herum und that einen langen Blick.

„Diese Mohawks sind die größten Narren, die mir je vorge=

kommen sind," sagte er, verächtlich, „als ob sie uns mit solchen Schlichen beikommen könnten."

„Was meinst Du denn?" fragte Haverland.

„Nun, siehst Du nicht jenen Baumstamm im Wasser? Dahinter stecken vier oder fünf Mohawks."

„Vielleicht ist's nur ein Baumstamm, der das Wasser hinabfließt?"

„So!" spottete der Jäger, „seit wann fließen denn die Baumstämme stromaufwärts?"

„Wirklich, er kommt näher!" sagte Graham.

„Nicht sehr schnell," antwortete Seth. „Ich verstehe jetzt, was die Schurken beabsichtigen. Sie wollen so nahe kommen, wie sie können, und wenn wir im Wasser sind, wollen sie unversehens über uns herfallen und uns verschlingen. So ist's, so wahr ich lebe."

„Nun," sagte Haldidge, „den Spaß wollen wir ihnen schon verderben. Alfred, bleib Du hier mit Ina und verwende kein Auge von dem Baumstamm. Wir wollen unterdeß den Strom hinabgehen, bis wir hinter die Coulissen gucken können. Aber einzeln, sag' ich Euch, damit die Hallunken den Braten nicht riechen."

Die drei betraten den Wald auf verschiedenen Seiten und erst als sie außer Sicht waren, stießen sie wieder zusammen. Sie gingen nun stromabwärts, bis sie dachten, unterhalb des Baumstammes angelangt zu sein, und schlugen dann die Richtung nach dem Strome ein. Glücklicher Weise war das Ufer dicht mit Binsen bewachsen, so daß sie sich ungesehen hinanschleichen konnten. Seth war der vorderste, und es kam Graham vor, als ob er sich mit der Leichtigkeit der Schlange durch die Binsen wände. Am Ufer angelangt, erhoben sie langsam den Kopf und blickten durch die Binsen nach dem Baumstamme. Richtig, dort war er, aber kein Indianer ließ sich blicken. Nichtsdestoweniger widerstand der Baum der Strömung.

„Es muß etwas dort sein," flüsterte Graham.

„St! Wartet nur und paßt auf; Ihr werdet schon sehen!" ermahnte Seth.

Im nächsten Augenblick veränderte der Baumstamm ein wenig seine Lage. Dabei sah Seth etwas Glänzendes darauf liegen, welches sein geübtes Auge sogleich als Büchsenläufe erkannte. Während er sich noch wunderte, wo in aller Welt der Eigenthümer dieser Büchsen stecken mochten, theilte sich plötzlich das Wasser und das Kupfergesicht eines Indianers kam zum Vorschein. Es stieg höher und höher, bis die Schultern aus dem Wasser waren und warf dann einen vorsichtigen Blick auf Haverland. Anscheinend zufriedengestellt, sank der Kopf zurück, aber nicht ganz in's Wasser; er legte sich vielmehr so dicht an den Baumstamm, daß selbst das schärfste Auge ihn leicht für einen natürlichen Auswuchs hätte halten können. Jetzt, da Graham's Aufmerksamkeit erregt war, bemerkte er noch zwei fernere Auswüchse und kam auf diese Weise zu der Ueberzeugung, daß drei völlig bewaffnete Mohawks sich im Flusse versteckt hatten und ihr Möglichstes thaten, sich den Flüchtlingen unbemerkt zu nähern.

„Für Jeden Einer, so wahr ich lebe!" rief Seth triumphirend. „Macht Euch fertig für Euren Mann. Graham nimmt den auf seiner Seite, Haldidge den mittleren, und ich werde den dritten bedienen. Macht Euch schnell fertig, sonst schrei ich wahrhaftig Hurrah! vor der Zeit."

Die drei Büchsen hoben sich gegen die ahnungslosen Wilden. Jeder zielte lange und sicher.

„Jetzt zusammen: Feuer!"

Das Pulver in den drei Pfannen blitzte zu gleicher Zeit; aber nur zwei sandte die tödtlichen Boten; Seth's Gewehr versagte, und der Wilde, dem seine Kugel gegolten hatte, säumte nicht, die gegebene Frist zu benutzen. Während seine beiden Gefährten ohne Weiteres untersanken, schwamm er mit Schnelligkeit dem entgegengesetzten Ufer zu.

„Blitz und Hagel!" schrie Seth, und sprang zu seinen Füßen. „Reicht mir Eure Büchse, Graham; meiner fehlt was, und der Schurke entkömmt am Ende. Geschwind, sag' ich!"

Er nahm die Büchse und lud sie so schnell wie möglich, während er kein Auge von dem schwimmenden Wilden ließ.

„Ist Eure Büchse geladen, Haldidge?" fragte er.

„Nein; ich habe Euch zugesehen und darüber das Laden vergessen."

„Ladet nur, sag' ich Euch, sonst wenn diese Waffe auch versagt, entkömmt der Kerl, so gewiß wie zwei mal zwei vier ist. Seht, dort landet er schon."

Der Indianer hob sich langsam aus dem Wasser, als ob er die Gefahr verachte, und schritt ebenso langsam dem Walde zu.

„So, mein Theurer, jetzt sieh' mal zu, wie das schmeckt," sagte Seth, und zielte von Neuem, aber zum zweiten Male versagte ihm das Gewehr und zu seinem großen Kummer mußte er sehen, wie der Indianer zwischen den Büschen verschwand. Noch schalt er über sein „P e ch," wie er es nannte, als plötzlich drüben ein Schuß fiel und eine Kugel sein Haupt streifte. Eine Locke fiel zu Boden und als Seth dieselbe vom Boden aufhob, sagte er, ganz kühl:

„Gar nicht übel, das ist so!"

„Um Himmelswillen, deckt Euch!" rief Graham und versuchte ihn bei seinem Rocke nieder zu ziehen.

„Well, ich glaube wirklich, das wird wohl das Beste sein," sagte Seth, und sank auf seine Knie, „da drüben scheint ein ganzes Nest voll zu sein."

Sie zogen sich jetzt in den Wald zurück und suchten Haverland auf, welcher sich ebenfalls gedeckt hatte. An's Uebersetzen war jetzt nicht länger zu denken, wenigstens nicht an dieser Stelle und da der Abend schon dunkelte, so beschloß man, den Lauf des Flusses während der Nacht zu verfolgen und den fehlgeschlagenen Versuch bei der ersten günstigen Gelegenheit zu erneuern. Als sie aufbrachen, zeigten sich wieder die Vorboten eines Sturmes; aber der Donner war noch fern und das Blitzen so schwach, daß es ihnen weder nützte noch schadete. Dicke Regentropfen kamen nieder und da Keiner den Grund und Boden kannte, so kann man sich leicht vorstellen, daß der Marsch nicht zu den angenehmsten gehörte. Alle waren still, außer Seth, dessen frohen Muth so leicht keine

Verhältnisse dämpfen konnten. Er prahlte eben damit, daß er vortrefflich sehen könne und den Weg ganz passabel finde, als er auf einmal in einen mit Schmutz und Wasser gefüllte Vertiefung fiel und die Gefährten mit einem wahren Schmutzregen bedachte. Noch lachten sie auf eine heitere, aber geräuschlose Weise, als Seth schon wieder auf den Beinen war.

„Was lacht Ihr denn, Ihr Mondkälber?" rief er, ärgerlich. „Denkt wohl gar, ich wäre gefallen? Da seid Ihr schief gewickelt, Ich wollte nur eine Entdeckung machen, das ist Alles."

„Und welche denn, wenn man fragen darf?" entgegnete Graham.

„Da! seht Ihr wohl? Lachen können sie, aber unwissend sind sie, wie die Heiden. Was ich entdeckt habe? Nun, ganz einfach ein Boot!"

Und so war es. Seth's Fall hatte allerdings zur Entdeckung eines großen Canoes geführt und der Entdecker trieb jetzt seine Gefährten an, hineinzusteigen, um ohne Verzug auf die andere Seite des Flusses überzusetzen. Als Alle darin waren, schob er es in den Fluß und folgte dann selbst nach. Aber, ach! unsere Freunde waren zu voreilig gewesen, denn bei näherer Besichtigung fand es sich, daß kein einziges Ruder im Canoe war. Sie mußten sich also ganz einfach vom Strome treiben lassen und jeden Augenblick gewärtigen, entweder an Felsen zu stoßen und umzuschlagen, oder auf irgend eine andere Weise Schiffbruch zu leiden. Als Seth sah, daß sich die Sache nicht ändern ließ, ergab es sich mit seinem unzerstörbaren Frohsinne in die Verhältnisse, und stieg über seine Freunde hinweg, um in dem hintern Ende des Canoes ein bequemes Plätzchen zu finden. Statt jedoch beim Niederlassen den Boden zu erreichen, setzte er sich vielmehr auf eine weiche Masse, welche plötzlich ein Grunzen vernehmen ließ.

„Was ist das?" fragte Haldidge.

„Hol mich der Teufel!" sagte Seth, „wenn es nicht ein fetter Mohawk ist. Nun, das bietet doch Alles. Uebrigens ein famoser Sitz, das ist 'mal sicher."

„Ihr werdet doch den Hallunken nicht leben lassen?"

„Warum nicht? Ich fertige das Gewürm nur ab, wenn es

mir im Wege ist. Dieser da ist ganz harmlos und giebt überdieß einen herrlichen Sitz ab."

„Nun," sagte Halbidge, lachend, „ich dürfte nicht an seiner Stelle sein, sonst würdet Ihr schlecht fahren."

Bisher hatte der erschreckte Wilde sich nicht gerührt; ob er nun aber seine Geistesgegenwart wieder gewann, oder ob er Halbidge's Worte verstand und den gegebenen Wink benutzte — genug, daß Seth auf einmal hastig in die Luft flog, Halbidge umwarf und sammt demselben auf dem Boden des Canoes umherzappelte. Als sich Beide wieder aufrichteten, war der Wilde verschwunden und man hörte eben noch das Rauschen des Wassers, welches er schwimmend durchschnitt.

Seth kratzte sich hinter den Ohren:

„Die undankbare Kröte!" sagte er. „Da spreche Einer von Erkenntlichkeit. Wahrhaftig, man sollte gar Niemanden mehr eine Gefälligkeit erweisen."

Capitel 19.

Entwicklung.

Seth würde am Ende noch lange fortphilosophirt haben, wenn der Lauf des Canoes nicht Aller Aufmerksamkeit in Anspruch genommen hätte. Langsam trieb es dahin und die Lage der Flüchtlinge wurde mit jedem Augenblicke unerträglicher. Die beständige Erwartung eines Unfalls strengte ihre Nerven mehr an, als die wirkliche Gefahr dies gethan haben würde. Allein was war zu thun? Sie mußten geduldig ausharren und Stunde auf Stunde verrann, ohne ihre Erwartungen zu verwirklichen. Endlich streifte der Kiel des Bootes einen harten Gegenstand und fing an, einen Kreis zu beschreiben.

„Geschwind, steigt aus!" rief Seth; „das Canoe füllt sich!"

Alle folgten seiner Weisung und fanden das Wasser glücklicher

Weise von geringer Tiefe. Das erleichterte Canoe richtete sich wieder auf, entglitt ihren Händen und war bald in der Dunkelheit verschwunden.

„Jetzt bewegt Euch nicht, bis ich sondirt habe," sagte Seth und ging ohne Verzug an's Werk. Die Strömung untersuchend, durchschnitt er sie dergestalt, daß er das gewünschte Ufer erreichen mußte. Es war näher, als er gehofft hatte, denn bald merkte er an umstehenden Bäumen, daß er schon darauf stand und daß der angeschwollene Strom aus seinem Bette getreten sei.

„Hierher!" rief er den Freunden zu, als er eine höher gelegene trockene Stelle erreicht hatte, und bald sah er sich von den Andern umringt. Sie fühlten sich Alle zu müde, um an eine sofortige Wiederaufnahme der Reise zu denken. Der Regen hatte ganz nachgelassen und da die unteren Blätterschichten trocken geblieben waren, gelang es den Anstrengungen der Männer bald, ein Feuer anzuzünden. Dieß war zwar nicht ohne Gefahr, aber die erlittenen Strapazen hatten sie zu sehr abgestumpft, um sich viel an die möglichen Folgen zu kehren und bald lagerte sich die müde Gesellschaft, um die wohlthuende Glut mit einem Gefühle des Wohlbehagens, das sie selten oder nie vorher gehabt hatten. Ina vor Allen bedurfte der Wärme, wie der Ruhe, im höchsten Grade und war bald in einen tiefen Schlaf versunken. Auch die Männer legten sich zur Ruhe nieder und nur Einer hielt abwechselnd Wache, um die bösen Folgen einer Ueberraschung zu verhindern.

Am nächsten Morgen erwachte die Gesellschaft neu gestärkt. Haldidge war gerade abwesend, kehrte aber nach Verlauf einer halben Stunde zurück mit einem Rehbock auf der Schulter, dessen feiste Schulter ohne Säumen zu einem saftigen Braten zugerichtet wurde. In das frische Fell gewickelt, damit der köstliche Saft nicht verloren ginge, briet die Keule zu einem schmackhaften Braun und empfing dann von den Händen ihrer Verehrer die ihr gebührende Achtung.

Als Alle ihren Hunger gestillt hatten und eben aufbrechen wollten, sagte Haldidge:

„Ehe Ihr geht, müßt Ihr mir auf jenen Hügel folgen und die herrliche Aussicht genießen, welche er gewährt.

Allein der Vorschlag fand wenig Beifall und Alle schützten den Mangel an Zeit und ihre große Ungeduld als Entschuldigung vor. Haldidge jedoch wollte sich nicht abweisen lassen und drang so lange in die Gefährten, bis sie endlich seinen Wünschen nachgaben. Sie folgten ihrem Führer mit gespannter Erwartung, indem seine Beharrlichkeit allerdings auf etwas Besonderes schließen ließ. Jetzt war der Hügel erstiegen und die Aussicht lag vor ihnen. Sieh da! kaum eine halbe Meile entfernt lag die friedliche Ansiedlung, das Ziel ihrer Reise.

„Nun, wie gefällt Euch die Aussicht?" fragte Haldidge, lächelnd; aber er brauchte keine langen Worte, um ihre Antwort zu deuten. Die Ausbrüche frohen Erstaunens von Aller Lippen sprachen zu deutlich, um mißverstanden zu werden. Die schönsten Alpenthäler würden ihnen in diesem Augenblicke nicht halb so gut gefallen haben, wie das kleine Waldthal zu ihren Füßen. Da lagen die Hütten so friedlich im Sonnenschein und entsandten den bläulichen Rauch in die klare heitere Luft, da war auch das kleine Fort, mit der messingenen Kanone auf dem flachen Dache, deren Lauf im Sonnenlichte blitzte. Nie war ihnen der Platz halb so schön erschienen, und doch dürfen wir glauben, daß sie sich nicht zu lange über dem bloßen Beschauen aufhielten. Im Gegentheil, sie setzten sich schon nach wenigen Minuten wieder in Bewegung, aber jetzt im Angesichte des Dorfes kam auf einmal eine seltsame Bewegung und Veränderung über Seth Jones. Er seufzte mehrmals tief und der komische Jänkee-Ausdruck war ganz aus seinem Gesichte verschwunden. Seine Beine verloren den schlendernden Gang, seine Gestalt hob sich und Seth Jones sah auf einmal wie ein stattliches Menschenkind aus. So auffällig war der Wechsel, daß seine Gefährten sich erstaunt ansahen und unwillkührlich fragten: Ist das Seth Jones?

Nicht sobald jedoch bemerkte Seth die forschenden Blicke, als er auf einmal wieder in seinen alten Charakter zurück fiel. Der Körper sank, die Beine schlenderten, das Gesicht spitzte sich und aus den Augen blitzte die halb schlaue, halb neckende Laune, welche ihn als Yankee bezeichnet hatte.

Die Schildwachen im Fort hatten die Flüchtlinge entdeckt und als sie bei der Pallisade anlangten, welche das Dorf umgab, fanden sie die ganze Bevölkerung bereit, sie zu empfangen.

„Ich werde Euch wiedersehen," sagte Haverland, und sich von ihnen trennend, schlug er die Richtung zu seiner Hütte ein.

Haverland wartete einige Minuten, um die Neugier der Menge zu befriedigen, und zeigte dann den Weg zu der Hütte, wo er Weib und Schwester geborgen wußte. Hier angekommen, fand er, daß ihm die guten Ansiedler während seiner Abwesenheit ein eigenes Haus errichtet hatten. Leise ging er auf die Thüre zu, um die Lieben zu überraschen. Aber an der Thür trat ihm seine Frau entgegen, und sank ihm, aus sie ihn erblickte, mit einem Ausrufe des Entzückens in die Arme. Im nächsten Augenblicke hielten sich Mutter und Tochter eng umschlungen.

„Dank dir, Himmel! Dank dir! O mein theueres Kind, Du schon verloren geglaubtes!"

Graham und Seth traten ehrfurchtsvoll zur Seite, bis die ersten Empfindungen vorüber waren. Seth wischte sich mehrere Male die Augen mit seinem Aermel auf eine sehr verdächtige Weise. Als Mrs. Haverland ihre Fassung wiedergewann, erkannte sie Graham und begrüßte ihn auf's Wärmste.

„Und auch Ihr, sagte sie, Seth's Hand ergreifend, seid mehr als Freund für uns gewesen. Möge der Himmel Euch lohnen! wir können es nicht."

„O, hört auf! ich bitt' Euch; huh! huh! ich glaube wahrhaftig, ich habe mich in der Nachtluft erkältet!"

Allein Verstellung half nichts, die Thränen kamen unwiderstehlich zum Vorschein, und eine Minute lang weinte Seth wie ein Kind. Doch schienen die Thränen nicht zu schmerzen, denn ein Lächeln schaute hindurch.

Sie gingen Alle in's Haus und sagten ein inniges Dankgebet. Als sie sich von ihren Knieen erhoben, trat Mary, Haverland's Schwester, in's Gemach und es kam Graham vor, als ob Seth bei ihrem Anblick zugleich erbleichte und erröthete. Allein Seth bezwang sich und lauschte ihren Worten, als sie ihm wieder und wieder ihren Dank ausdrückte. Doch schien sein Wesen gezwungen und abwesend, und sein Blick strebte den ihren zu vermeiden. Sie bemerkte seine Verlegenheit und wußte dieselbe anfangs nicht zu deuten, bis ihr plötzlich die Möglichkeit einer Neigung seinerseits einfiel. Sie erblaßte nun ebenfalls und wurde einsilbig. Der Gedanke schien eine trübende Wirkung auf sie zu haben; vielleicht hatte er alte Wunden aufgerissen.

Haverland's Haus wurde den ganzen Tag von Besuchern nicht leer, und bis spät in die Nacht lauschten theilnehmende Nachbarn ihren Abenteuern.

Acht Tage waren vergangen und Seth und Graham weilten noch immer im Hause Haverland's. Graham war der glückliche Verlobte Ina's geworden und sollte sie am nächsten Tage heimführen. Ueber Seth war eine seltsame Rastlosigkeit gekommen, und er konnte es keine fünf Minuten an demselben Platze aushalten. Am allerrastlosesten war er aber in Mary's Gegenwart. Zwar wich sein Auge selten von ihrer Gestalt; aber seine Beine schienen beständig in Versuchung des Ausreißens zu kommen, wenn sie ihm nahte. Und doch war er augenscheinlich eifersüchtig auf jeden Andern, der es wagte, ihre holde Nähe aufzusuchen.

„Alfred!" fragte er eines Tages, „was hat der große rothhaarige Schlingel hier so viel zu schaffen?"

„Ja, da mußt Du Mary fragen," lachte Haverland.

„O, ich verstehe, es sollen morgen Abend zwei Hochzeiten gemacht werden. Nicht wahr, Mary?"

„Nicht, daß ich wüßte; ich denke nicht daran, irgend Jemand zu heirathen."

„Nicht, warum denn nicht? wenn man fragen darf."

„Ich fürchte, Mary wird sich niemals verheirathen," sagte Haverland, „sie hat die besten Anträge ausgeschlagen."

„Seltsam! hat man je so was gehört?"

„Ihre Liebe liegt lange begraben," flüsterte Haverland Seth in's Ohr. Aber Seth hörte ihn nicht. Er neigte sich gegen das Mädchen und flüsterte bedeutungsvoll: „Mary!"

Dieses eine Wort schien eine merkwürdige Wirkung auf sie zu üben. Ihre Augen strahlten Feuer, als sie ihn anblickte; dann wurde sie blaß wie der Tod und würde umgesunken sein, wenn Seth sie nicht aufgefangen hätte.

„Sie ist die Meine!" rief Seth jubelnd und in einem Tone, der jede Spur des Näselns verloren hatte.

„Gerechter Himmel!" rief Haverland, aufspringend, „ist das nicht Eugen Morton?"

„Grad so!" erfolgte die Antwort durch die Nase.

„Bist Du von den Todten erstanden?"

„Ich bin zu neuem Leben erwacht, war aber nicht gerade bei den Todten."

Diese Antwort wurde in demselben reichen, wohlklingenden Basse gegeben, welcher Mary so aufgeregt hatte. Er rief sie auch jetzt in's Leben zurück; sie wollte aufstehen, aber er, der sie hielt, wollte sie nicht lassen, und drückte sie mit Inbrunst an seine Brust. In diesem Augenblicke traten Graham und Haldidge in's Zimmer und fragten nach Seth, ohne sich um den Fremden zu bekümmern, den sie nicht vorher gesehen zu haben glaubten.

Seth fing an zu lachen und ergötzte sich über ihr maßloses Erstaunen, als sie ihn endlich erkannten.

„Wenige Worte" sagte Morton (so wollen wir ihn jetzt nennen), „werden Euch Alles klar machen. Seth Jones ist eine Fabel, mein wirklicher Name ist Eugen Morton. Vor zehn Jahren verlobte ich mich mit Mary Haverland, und unsere Hochzeit stand nahe bevor, als auf einmal der Befreiungskrieg losbrach. Ich ergriff die Waffen und focht die Schlacht bei Bunkerhill mit. Dort wurde ich gefährlich verwundet, und blieb bei einem benachbarten Farmer, bis ich wieder genesen war. Ich benachrichtigte Mary von meiner Lage, aber die Botschaft gelangte nie zu ihr. Wohl aber eine andere, falsche. In unserer Compagnie war ein Mann, der sie auch liebte. Dieser Mann desertirte und theilte ihr mit, ich sei gefallen. Als ich von seinem Weglaufen hörte, schöpfte ich Argwohn und kehrte in die Heimath zurück. Dort angekommen, erfuhr ich, Haverland sei mit jenem Deserteur nach dem Westen ausgewandert, und der Letztere werde Mary heirathen. Es fiel mir nicht ein, diese Nachricht zu bezweifeln; im Gegentheil, ich nahm Alles für baare Münze und wünschte mir den Tod.

Zur Armee zurückgekehrt, focht ich alle blutigen Schlachten mit; aber der Tod, den ich suchte, mied mich. Endlich stieg der Gedanke in mir auf, Mary möge am Ende doch noch ledig sein, und wollte mich seitdem nicht wieder verlassen. Als der Krieg aus war, beschloß ich, genauere Nachforschungen anzustellen, konnte aber nichts Näheres erfahren. Entschlossen, der Sache auf den Grund zu kommen, suchte ich selbst diese Gegenden auf, und würde mich längst zu erkennen gegeben haben, wenn ich nicht zu solch' verhängnißvoller Stunde gekommen wäre und gefürchtet hätte, die große Aufregung der Frauen noch zu steigern. Ich hatte lange genug unter den grünen Jägern von Vermont gedient, ihren Dialekt täuschend nachzuahmen, und daher rührt der Charakter, der Euch so lange belustigt hat. Zuweilen ließ ich Euch absichtlich einen Blick unter die Maske thun, und erreichte dadurch meinen Zweck, Euch zu mystifiziren und stutzig zu machen. Jetzt habe ich ausgespielt und den Preis gewonnen. Graham, ich darf Euch zu dem Eurigen gratuliren; Ihr führt ihn morgen Abend heim. Mary, willst Du zu gleicher Zeit die Meine werden?"

„Ja!" antwortete das glückliche Mädchen, strahlend vor Freude, und legte ihre Hand in die seinige. „Mein Herz hast Du während allen diesen kummervollen Jahren besessen."

Morton küßte sie auf die Stirne und sagte: „Jetzt gratulirt mir."

Alle drängten sich um ihn, und solch' glückliche Gesichter, wie diese Gesellschaft bot, sind selten zu finden.

Am nächsten Morgen begannen die Vorbereitungen. Alle Nachbarn, nah und fern, wurden eingeladen, und stellten sich mit der Dämmerung pünktlich ein. Das Haus Haverland's konnte die Versammlung kaum fassen, als die beiden Brautpaare jetzt vor den Prediger der Ansiedlung traten. Die Bräute strahlten im vollen Schmucke jugendlicher Schönheit, und zahlreich wie herzhaft war der Beifall, den der männliche Theil der Gesellschaft ihnen zollte. Selbst die Weiber stimmten ein; ein unwiderleglicher Beweis, daß die Bräute die Engel übertroffen haben müssen.

Unter den Zuschauern befand sich unter Andern ein junger, wettergebräunter, breitschulteriger Mann, den seine blühende Nachbarin mit dem Namen „Josias" anredete. Der reizende Anblick schien ihn so tief von der Glückseligkeit des Ehelebens zu überzeugen, daß er ohne Säumen in seine Nachbarin drang, ihm zu gleicher Seligkeit zu verhelfen. Anfangs erschreckt durch die Plötzlichkeit und Heftigkeit der Attacke, verrieth die jungfräuliche Festung doch so viele schwache Punkte, daß der junge Freier einen zweiten kühnern Angriff wagte und den Platz richtig mit Sturm einnahm. In diesem Augenblicke hatte der Geistliche seine Arbeit am andern Ende des Zimmers eben vollendet, und der Hinterwäldler nahm seinen Vortheil wahr.

„He, Mr.!" rief er, „ich meine Euch! Pastor, denke ich, heißen sie Euch. Macht Euch noch nicht unsichtbar, hier giebt's noch mehr zusammenzuschmieden."

Die Umstehenden fingen an zu lachen, und machten dem Geistlichen begreiflich, was man von ihm verlangte. Der gute Mann bezeigte sogleich seine Bereitwilligkeit, und das neue Paar wurde vor ihn geführt. Sally (so hieß die Schöne) eröthete einmal über's andere und konnte sich anfangs gar nicht in die Umstände finden; aber Josias redete so kräftig zu, daß sie sich endlich faßte. Nach fünf Minuten war sie Mrs. Josias und erstickte fast unter den lärmenden und stürmischen Glückwünschen der Gesellschaft.

Der Prediger war nun fertig und der Geiger kam an die Reihe. Es war ein bejahrter Ansiedler, der diese wichtige Rolle übernahm. Eine umgestürzte Kiste war sein Thron, und von dort entlockte er seinem unscheinbaren Instrumente bald solch' lockende Töne, daß nicht allein junge Füße zuckten und zappelten, sondern nach und nach auch die Alten von der Tanzwuth ergriffen wurden, und bis tief in die Nacht ein Menuet nach dem anderen abwickelten. Endlich brach die Gesellschaft auf und schlief den Schlaf der Gerechten nach solch' unerhörten Anstrengungen.

Wir verlassen unsere jungen Paare an der Thüre ihrer Brautgemächer, deren Heiligkeit wir um keinen Preis entweihen möchten. Welche Schicksale ihnen auch noch bevorstehen mögen, laßt uns hoffen, daß ihre dunkelsten Tage hinter ihnen liegen.

Ende.

Stereotypirt von Johnson & Co.,
Philadelphia, Pa.

Werke eigenen Verlags
von
J. M. Hoffmann u. Bruder,
Pittsburg, Pa.

———•———

Abenteuer eines deutschen Soldaten in Virginien. Novellete von Rudolph Leonhart.................. 15 Cts.

Der kleine Tambour des —und zwanzigsten Regiments von Illinois. Erzählung einer höchst sonderbaren Schicksalsfügung. Frei nach dem Englischen bearbeitet.......... 12 Cts.

Die besten Deklamationen. Enthaltend Komische und prosaische Vorträge, Gelegenheitsreden, Toaste und Trinksprüche .... 20 Cts.

Abenteuer unter den Indianern, oder: Ina's Gefangenschaft unter den Wilden und ihre wunderbare Befreiung. Frei nach dem Englischen bearbeitet.......... 20 Cts.

Illustrirtes ABC-Buch für Elementar- und Sonntags-Schulen. Geb., per Dutzend 75 Cts.

Prämien-Büchlein für fleißige Schüler.
Nr. 1. 25 interessante Erzählungen, von Christoph Schmidt, per Hundert $3
Nr. 2. Gespräche für die Jugend, per Hundert $3
Nr. 3. Auszug aus Hebel's Schatzkästlein, per Hundert $3
Alle drei Nummern zusammen, gebunden, per Hundert $6

Im Verlage von Ernst Luft sind erschienen und durch J. M. Hoffmann u. Bruder, Pittsburg, Pa., zu beziehen:

Nieritz, Gustav. Alexander Menzikoff, oder: Die Gefahren des Reichthums. Eine wahre Geschichte zur Unterhaltung in Familienkreisen. Geh. .... 15 Cts.

Nieritz, Gustav. Der junge Trommelschläger, oder: Der gute Sohn. Eine Geschichte aus der letzten Kriegszeit. Geh. ..... 15 Cts.

Mehrere andere interessante Volks- und Jugendschriften werden in Kürze folgen.

Gegen Einsendung des Betrags verschicken wir diese Bücher portofrei nach allen Staaten der Union.

In der Buchhandlung von **J. M. Hoffmann u. Bruder**, No. 51 Fünfte Straße, Pittsburg, Pa., sind immer folgende Bücher vorräthig:

Appleton's ausführliche Englische Grammatik. Gebunden..............................$.100

Der große Amerikanische Dollmetscher. Gebunden...................... 40 Cts.

Ahn's Lehrgang zur leichten Erlernung der Englischen Sprache. 2 Theile........25—30 Cts.

Oehlschläger's Englisch-Deutsches Wörterbuch (Dictionary). Gebunden,..............$.100

Englisch-Deutscher Verein. Staaten Briefsteller. Gebunden $1.00

Stark's Handbuch. Gebunden, mit Schließen....$1.10

Hofacker's Predigtbuch. Gebunden..............$2.50

Schmolken's Himmlisches Vergnügen......$2.00

Zschokke's Novellen $6.00

Schiller's Werke..$2.00

Göthe's Werke $6.00

Lessing's Werke $2.00

Rellstab, 1812. Historischer Roman. Gebunden..$1.75

——, Drei Jahre von Dreißigen............$2.00

Dumas, Der Graf von Monte-Christo. $1.50
Fortsetzung dazu: **Die Todtenhand**........60 Cts.

——, Der Herr der Welt......................$1.00

Stolle, 1813. Historischer Roman..............60 Cts.

Franz Hoffmann's Jugendschriften. 25 Bändchen, jedes......................................15 Cts.

Volks-Bücher: „Käthchen von Heilbronn," „Pfarrerstochter von Taubenheim," „Eulenspiegel," „Dr. Faust," „Geneveva," „Griseldis," „Drei Müllerstöchter," „Emma von Finkenstein," „Heinrich von Eichenfels," „Rosenstock," „Weihnachtsabend u. a. m., per Stück......12 Cts.

Gegen Einsendung des Betrages verschicken wir die Bücher portofrei nach allen Staaten der Union.

J. M. Hoffmann u. Bruder.

WITHDRAWN

**No longer the property of the
Boston Public Library.
Sale of this material benefited the Library.**